THE
Steelhead Trout
Life History — *Early Angling*
Contemporary Steelheading

By Trey Combs

FRANK AMATO PUBLICATIONS
Box 02112
Portland, Oregon 97202
503-653-8108

Update on Wild Steelhead

Bill Bakke was my friend and mentor. When I was stil learning the rudiments of fly casting and line mending, Bill had mastered the finer points of A.H.E. Wood's techniques as described in *Grease Line Fishing for Salmon*. I still remember with delight the first time I went through his fly book and saw flies scarcely more than bare hooks, Bill's version of "Toys" and "Redshanks." He told me about the Portland hitch around that time too, and the first really fine steelhead I ever caught on a fly happened while I was fishing his October Caddis using a hitch. Ten years before waking dry flies became the rage in British Columbia, Bill was using his Dragon Fly to bring fish up on Washington waters. My first dry fly steelhead came on the Wind. I was with Bill that day, and we raised steelhead until his supply of flies ran out. When I decided to put some of the things he had taught me in book form, it was Bill who did the editing. But years after the first publication of *The Steelhead Trout* in 1971, it has not been Bill's precocious talents as an angler that have left the greatest impression on me.

Beyond all other passions, Bill was an advocate of wild steelhead — and an outspoken opponent of steelhead stocking programs. To stock a steelhead stream as a countermeasure for stream neglect was, to Bill, a high crime against common sense. Twenty years ago, his was a voice in the wilderness. No longer.

Today there are thousands of members of the Federaticn of Fly Fishermen, Trout Unlimited, the B.C. Steelhead Society, Cal Trout and Oregon Trout, with Bill Bakke as its Director), who advocate a quality fishery and proper care of habitat. When I read *The Osprey*, I know that Bill's wisdom has now, taken hold. "Wild steelhead," and "catch and release" are on everyone's lips. But the ultimate challenge remains.

There are now many hard core steelheaders, both gear and fly fishermen, who are working to preserve the native strains of steelhead. They feel as I do that hatchery steelhead, regardless of numbers, are a poor replacement as an angling resource. I say this knowing that nearly every steelhead stream south of British Columbia has been 'supported" by stocking programs. On some rivers, such as Washington's Washougal, the native steelhead is now nearly extinct. Wherever it is still possible to do so, these fragile numbers, this irreplacable gene pool, must be preserved.

Trey Combs

Fall, 1988
Port Townsend, Washington

DEDICATION

To Mark and Patty

Second Printing 1988
ISBN: 0-936608-77-3
Cover Photo: Frank W. Amato

Acknowledgments

Grateful thanks are due first to those state, federal and provincial agencies that generously gave assistance in helping me comprehensively develop the steelhead's life history: California Department of Fish and Game, Fish Commission of Oregon, Oregon State Game Commission, Idaho Fish and Game Department, Washington State Department of Game, University of Washington Fisheries Research Institute, Alaska Department of Fish and Game, United States Fish and Wildlife Service, International North Pacific Fisheries Commission, British Columbia Department of Recreation and Conservation, the Fisheries Research Board of Canada and the British Columbia Department of Fisheries. Behind these agency titles are more than three dozen men who patiently answered my questions and introduced me to many important studies.

Of the more than a hundred people who provided advice, flies and facts, a few must be given special mention. Lloyd Silvius sent me many flies and stories of California angling that began my understanding of steelheading history. Dennis Black, Tommy Brayshaw, Wes Drain, Capt. Mark Kerridge, U.S.N. (Ret.), Mike Kennedy, Roderick Haig-Brown, Al Knudson, Ralph Wahl, Ward Cummings and Victor Moore all contributed steelhead fly patterns of significant historical importance. A.W. Agnew and Leon Martuch sent me much needed information on fly line developments. Ed Clark told me fascinating tales of Alaskan rainbow trout while George Eicher worked to educate me on dams and anadromous fish. Myron Gregory made available to me his exhaustive studies on different fly lines. Karl Mausser allowed me to use his story on his world record steelhead. Ken McLeod told me of his early Washington angling; Willie Korf wrote me of his efforts to produce new steelhead lures. Polly Rosborough sent me many letters on the long ago and gave me a starting point for a number of subjects. John Zervas, the Director of Public Information for the American Fishing Tackle Manufacturers Association, kindly answered my many, many queries. The Encyclopaedia Britannica Library Research Service generously supplied data I had otherwise been unable to obtain. Joseph Keen a half-a-world away in Bedfordshire, England, fortified a sometime sagging spirit with encouragement and no end of useful information.

I would also like to thank Bill and Jean Bakke for working to ready the book for publication, and Frank Amato for allowing me to re-use material previously published in *Salmon Trout Steelheader* magazine.

Trey Combs

Port Townsend, Washington

Contents

CHAPTER ONE

Our Anadromous Rivers

That the moisture laden clouds pushed by prevailing winds should condense on the seaward side of our coastal mountains is the happiest of circumstances. For mountains and rain complement each other admirably and no more so than along our western coast. The mountains rise to gather rain in abundance and store it as glacial ice, as snow, or let it slip from their grasp to become a system of rivers beyond compare.

The distance from these mountains to the sea, from the amorphous beginnings of a river high within the clouds to where a river subdued yet still powerful meets with the crashing ocean waves, can be spanned by a sighting from a single vantage point. The intervening lands, whatever their breadth, pass through biotic zones that follow a climatic timetable dependent on their elevation.

It is at the highest elevations of our coastal mountains where under the incessant glare of a hot summer sun the melting of a hundred snows is led by gentle slopes to conceive a trickle, rivulet and creek that cuts a snowfield and cascades off a hillside. These nameless waters that course wildly down the mountains to join others of their kind contain all the undisciplined vigor of sudden ascendency. They run white with glacial silt—frigid, infertile, often with channels not of permanent substance. Yet from such a system are born the rivers of our Pacific Coast.

With the exception of Spanish California, the majority of these waters possess Indian names. No tribes had economies so inextricably intertwined with the river's bounty as those of the far West. Consequently, these people, unlike their plains-dwelling brethren, were of a more sedentary nature and the names of their rivers are today their tribal names: Skagit, Nisqually, Hoh, Queets, Quinault, Snake and Yakima, to list but a few. Other rivers still have names of Indian origin and may, as with the Hamma Hamma or Duckabush, titilate with their nonsensical quality and ease of oral delivery. A few rivers are named for their Anglo-Saxon discoverers. The Fraser and Thompson in British Columbia, the Lewis in Washington, Oregon's McKenzie and California's Smith are such examples. California south of the Klamath had been settled by the Spanish for more than a hundred years before the gold rush. During this period they had time to name just about every prominent landmark. These earliest settlers were first Franciscan then Dominican friars whose purpose was to stamp out the last vestiges of heathenism among the aboriginal tribes originally residing there. The

Garcia, Navarro, San Lorenzo and the Santa Ynez are waters christened during this lengthy occupation.

The timber rich Pacific slope has become the traditional setting for our anadromous rivers and properly so, for they exist from San Francisco to Alaska by the hundreds. Were these our only waters we could consider ourselves blessed as few others. But there are rivers, dozens in fact, that penetrate more aberrant varieties of western terrain and climate. A more comprehensive view will reveal a few determined giants, such as the Columbia, sweeping first through interior lands of arid desolation or the myriad of rivers emanating as serpentine spokes from the immense hub of white crowned Olympic Mountains become, on their short trip to the sea, the only natural opening in a rain forest impasse. But whatever the temporary direction taken, their final resting place will be the Pacific's endless expanse.

Perhaps the most obvious common denominator of these rivers is the anadromous habits of their fish. That is, the salmon and trout that inhabit these waters do so temporarily spending the majority of their lives as ocean residents, returning only to the rivers of their birth to perpetuate their kind. It will never be known when these fish first hatched in rivers to follow currents to the sea, but seek the ocean's abundance they do. Here they wax fat and here they feel the first twinge of sexual maturity that triggers the unerring accuracy of their return. As salmon they die shortly after spawning, but as trout they might live to grow in the ocean again and, if the elements are kind, return to spawn a second time.

The first to arrive are the chinook salmon. Leaving the ocean they time their entrance into estuary water with the tide and begin passing upstream in summer's peak abundance. Possibly it is the coolness of an August evening or a September morning that announces with intangible delicacy that changes are imminent and a tired summer need not be viewed much longer. As the river current beckons, elusive iridescence and smart suits of bronze-blue and white are lost to a series of dull browns, blacks and greys. Moving upstream, the fish are huge and dark, occasionally rolling as they pursue their destination. This migration of chinook salmon that began sporadically, changes to one of massive proportions with the first heavy rains of fall. As autumn advances the diminutive cutthroat trout, the spirited silver and commercially important dog, pink, and sockeye salmon run to the rivers.

It is paradoxical that the rains bringing up life in such numbers have the opposite effect on the alpine regions. Here the transition from summer to winter is not a slow one. Rain in the valley may fall as snow on crag and highland meadow. When this land is covered, the creeks that have been so diligently feeding our rivers are stilled, locked in winter's permanence. Should an Indian summer now descend to kiss the land and hold in abeyance the flooding rains of late fall, the rivers will drop to their lowest levels. Water will be seen flowing against dry, dusty banks and eddying about pebbles and boulders that but a month before passed unnoticed as part of the river bottom topography. No glacial silt or mud mars the water's clarity and the salmon, moving furtively if at all, are trapped by the exposure. The deepest pools in the main channel now mark their station and only there are they still pleasing to the eye.

Nature's miracle of change is at once macabre and beautifully functional. A salmon's head becomes a huge cruel jaw, studded with fierce canine teeth. Symmetrical elegance too is lost, for they become more and more hydrodynamically inept as body form is distorted. But the life span of the salmon is set; strength and size increase to bring them back to their beginnings. In the scheme of that life spawning is not compatible with growth and one terminates when the other begins. Finally arriving at their destination, reproduction is the only desire. Changes in body chemistry will permit the greatest possible spawning at the expense of all else: color, form, life itself.

Beyond the rivers, the conifers that range in continuous flow have made visual room for their deciduous neighbors. The big leaf maples' splashes of orange glow like embers on the distant hills. The streamside alder traces a river's course by winding a ribbon of pastel yellow through the greens of fir and hemlock. Brightest of all is the vine maple that stood for months unnoticed, an understory nonentity, that now commands our attention by bathing itself in near fluorescent cerise. Time has brought these changes but to the first frost befalls the task of final tempering, demanding a temporary recession of life. We feel the finality of impending dormancy, see the readiness in those annually burnished colors, and are touched by the exuberance of expecting change that is fall.

The rains that terminate Indian summers are cold and introduce our rivers to winter. They strip the trees and silence the land. Summer that but a week before held out against the encroachment of frost and thunderstorms suddenly disappears. These are not the rains carrying the transient violence of spring or fall; their strength lies in their continuity. Drizzling skies blanket the mountains and look down on rising waters that will accompany the salmon's final act. Though others have

A spent coho salmon with patches of **saproleginia** well developed over the body. The "kype" or hook to the upper jaw is seen more in the Pacific salmon than in the steelhead which predominately form a kype on the lower jaw.

preceded them to the spawning grounds, the rains promise a unanimity of movement so that the single drama of spawning and death is multiplied. The culmination of life's processes is now seen on a grand scale. Into a series of freshly dug shallow holes the eggs are deposited and fertilized. Their spawning completed and purpose for being ended, the dying salmon drift in limbo with a river current once a comforting guide. Bodies engaged in the most feeble movements are cast ashore on gravel bars and, when high water crests the bank, within the branches of nearby trees. Here they are eaten by mink, otter, bear and a variety of gulls. Death is now a natural parting, for the tenuous hold the salmon have on life is contained in the eggs deposited. The rains continue, the rivers rise, and the land submits to the changing season.

The steelhead have moved from the ocean's vastness to enter the confines of the tidal estuary. They are in sharp contrast to the spawning salmon. Their form denotes speed and strength typifying a pelagic predator. Scales shine flecks of bright silver and cover colors of formal beauty—a back of gray spotted black from head to broad tail, a belly intensely white and the two separated by the faintest hint of opalescent pink. The head is glass smooth and would appear to be semi-transparent. Contour is that of a trout. This is the rainbow trout nature has endowed with the inclination to migrate to the sea. Their sojourn through the North Pacific takes several months to four years. Such a period is fraught with dangers and takes a heavy toll; of a hundred born to the river, only a few survive to return.

Acclimation to fresh water has taken place at the mouth of the river but the fish are indecisive. On the rising tide, water that rushed headlong to meet the sea is stopped and backed up. The fish move with it. The route is clear, instincts that brought the steelhead to their spawning river will move them along a course marked by the inherent traits of the species. At high tide the lagoon assumes the characteristics of a lake. The flotsam of trees battered into chips of bark and wood now bob about, pushed by the wind and ensuing wave action. Here they mix with kelp torn loose from far away depths. But this power that stills a river is temporary and ebb tide again reveals a river channel. Debris litters the mud banks and the smells of the sea pounding in the distance grow pungent with the drop in water level. For the steelhead the last vestige of their ocean life is carried out to sea. They are part of the river when the current is felt. They head into it and begin to pursue its source. The last segment of their migration has started.

Such is the ebb and flow of life and land. There are variations to this; indeed, to describe the sum total of all the rivers is necessarily done at the expense of the one. The pattern, however, is accurate. On nearly all rivers the steelhead will follow the salmon, but on many of these same waters they will precede the salmon as summer-run or accompany the salmon as fall-run fish. Actually it can be said of these anadromous trout that on some river in their range they are ascending fresh from the sea every week of the year.

Our early western angler spent much of his time interpreting the gradually less confusing movements of these migratory fish. First he applied what he knew to his discoveries and continued to look still further for answers. After previous knowledge became altered by new conceptions, the angler began to develop the seasonal expectations that now keynote our anadromous fishing. New ideas at the expense of the old and tackle accordingly designed with new techniques in mind were to coalesce on unexplored rivers and give us regional traditions that today flow as part of our steelheading heritage.

This is the story of that heritage. Like the angler of bygone days, we must understand the habits of the steelhead before telling tales of their capture.

CHAPTER TWO

The Steelhead's Return

The steelhead are a paradox and only their return is viewed with absolute certainty. They are composed of exceptions—every "fact" about their upstream migration will almost always contain an opposite number somewhere else.

A steelhead's habits depend on the nature and life history of that river race of steelhead, the character behavior of individual fish, and the infinite changes in environment that produce corresponding behavioral changes in the ascending steelhead. Indeed, the very realization that there is no stereotyping the steelhead may well mark the beginning of the steelheader's education.

The steelhead live their life in individual effort. They roam the sea as single fish and at no time purposely congregate, thus the river mouth may force the first gathering since pre-migrant days. Rviers with substantial seasonal fluctuations often present the steelhead with insufficient flow. Their numbers swell until a heavy rain, erasing these conditions, allows their free passage. It is of particular importance that in California the fish are often introduced to the river in this manner. If the main river does not present this problem to the steelhead, the many tributaries often will. Sometimes steelhead can be found at the mouth of feeder streams awaiting rains to inspire their continued migration.

Groups of steelhead also form while actually ascending the main river. This comes as the result of the one word that best describes what is required of a river to activate its steelhead: change. A change in weather produces a corresponding change in the river and directly affects migrating steelhead. Fish in a river that is consistently low and clear or high and muddy lengthens their ascending time by forcing them to hold a single station. A "station" is broadly defined to include any part of the river steelhead find suitable for resting. It can be slots of calm water behind fallen trees and boulders, or the larger pools and deep runs referred to as "drifts," "riffles" and "holes." If deep stretches still maintain speed and turbulance, the steelhead rest just to the side of it, escaping its tiring force.

A river changing from one extreme to another, from either high and muddy to clear, or from clear to discolored, tends to release steelhead from their holding places. Let us assume for a moment a river is rising from continual rain, the steelhead are active and moving freely upstream. Several pools are passed but eventually they stop and rest.

Those fish following continue their migration until the same pool is reached. In this manner a variety of temporary stations will contribute to a single large pool holding many steelhead. They have, in steelheading parlance, "stacked-up." Here they tend to remain until the river again begins to clear. Most will then leave this sanctuary and continue their migration. The same tendency can again prevail; the steelhead will begin to "hole-up" when the river drops and clears. Of the two extremes, low, clear water has the greater propensity for forcing fish into the safety of deep resting places.

If a river "goes out" for weeks, steelhead cannot be expected to call a halt to all upstream migration. Because of the fish's greatly reduced visibility, the angler is at a disadvantage—his lure will likely pass unnoticed. During these times the plunker—those who still fish by placing a well anchored lure or bait in the path of ascending steelhead—really come into their own. The drift fishermen also turn to bait to take advantage of the steelhead's olfactory senses, while fly anglers change to the large fluorescent patterns.

Faced with long periods of clear water, steelhead will still move, but are more likely to progress with gray dawns and the fading light of evening.

Most steelheaders fishing the river near tidewater favor an ebb tide. A rapidly rising stream will bring fish in from the ocean while moving those already in the stream. The lack of complete water clarity conceals both fish and fishermen. The next most favorable condition is a river falling and clearing.

With some reservations, we can say that steelhead migrate at night. Some years ago the Washington Department of Game captured nine steelhead at the Bonneville Dam fish ladders. Using a rubber band, they attached a small transmitter behind the head of each fish which permitted them to track the steelhead's movements. Migration did take place at night but this cannot be described as typical of the species for all rivers; the Columbia River in this area is almost an inland sea in dimensions. One of the nine steelhead waited for three days before moving at all. Then on the third night it traveled almost 25 miles.

It is felt that steelhead migrate at night and especially do so on the lower, open and easy flowing sections of river. Fish taken in Indian nets reaffirm this belief. When rapids are reached, migration is probably best held to daylight. Despite an advanced sensory system acute to changes in pressure and vibration, steelhead would still prefer to ascend perilous water during periods of light.

How steelhead with such incredible accuracy and perfect timing make their way back to their home rivers is not known. Ultrasonic tagging devices have shown that Pacific salmon (and certainly anadromous trout) need not follow any undersea trail but are quite capable of homing in on a distant river. Several theories are offered as contributing to this amazing capability. The steelhead may have a sextant-like ability to interpret the sun's position for directional aid. This seems reasonable; however, movements toward rivers remain undiminished at night or when the sun is hidden behind a cloud blanket. If the sun's position does guide steelhead, its application must be limited. Another possible explanation relates to the faint voltage emitted by ocean currents as salt water passes through the earth's magnetic field. Perhaps steelhead are sensitive enough to "receive" this and use it as a guide.

There is one homing ability proven without question. Steelhead and salmon have extremely advanced olfactory powers. It has been demonstrated that dissolved mineral matter in a stream makes that water distinct from any other. How far at sea steelhead can identify this "smell" is not clear but it may be considerable. Not only can steelhead identify the proper watershed at the river mouth from their ocean position, but they can follow the river to their correct nursery tributary. Two experiments with anadromous fish graphically illustrate this ability. Sockeye salmon on two Alaskan tributaries were transported downstream to the main river. Before releasing them a color coded balloon was attached to each fish. The ascending sockeye, visible by the floating balloon, accurately followed the river to their previous tributary.

A reverse of this experiment was carried out by a University of Wisconsin research team on Washington's Issaquah Creek. Trapped silver salmon from two branches of the creek were carried downstream. Some of the fish were released in a natural condition while others were released only after they had their nostrils plugged with cotton balls soaked in petroleum jelly. All the salmon resumed migration but those with their sense of smell impaired ascended the correct tributary with no more than chance odds.

1. SUMMER-RUN AND WINTER-RUN STEELHEAD

These two terms describe the time of year steelhead choose to ascend our rivers. Broadly speaking, summer-run steelhead will ascend in the spring, summer and fall, while the winter-run come during the late fall, winter and early spring. We can also say that on most rivers the two groups will spawn at the same time: late winter and early spring. And finally, because summer-run steelhead must reside in fresh water for such a long period before spawning, they enter from the ocean in a "green" condition; the winter-runs migrate "ripe" and more nearly ready to spawn.

Chance entry at various times of the year does not place the steelhead in one or the other category. Winter-run and summer-run fish are distinct races that maintain a racial integrity in selecting their time for fresh water residency and spawning. There is no mingling of the races, though summer-run and winter-run can and do enter at the same time though rarely on the same river.

A hypothetical river will show how this might work. I will give it the name Calorwash for aspects of this river can be found in California, Oregon and Washington. So that we may easily visualize the situation, let us say that the river receives a total of 144 steelhead a year at the rate of exactly 12 per month. Let us also assume that whatever race the steelhead are, they will spawn from February to June. "W" stands for winter-run and "S" for summer-run steelhead in the following month-by-month tabulation:

January 12W	July 12S
February 12W	August 12S
March . . . . 9W and 3S	September 12S
April . . . . 6W and 6S	October 12S
May 12S	November . . . . . . 3S and 9W
June 12S	December 12W

I might give some apoplexy with this remark, but it is made in the most general sense. The larger steelhead tend to show toward the end of their migratory season; conversely, the smallest tend to precede their particular migratory season. Examining November first, I will not try to specifically break these 12 steelhead down into age groups for it would only lend confusion to the example. (Chapter 5 discusses the age and size of steelhead throughout their range.) As shown, 3 summer-run and 9 winter-run steelhead will ascend in November. What is the difference if both races spawn sometime during the next several months? The summer-run fish may well be among the largest of that race seen during their migratory year. The tendency to produce larger steelhead toward the end of the run is more prevalent in winter than summer, but the informed angler will also choose to fish the summer-run in the fall months in hopes of getting one of the 12 to 18 pounders.

A fresh-run maiden steelhead. Note sea lice near the anal fin.

The "grilse," or "half-pounder," will be the dominating member of the November winter-run steelhead. They will average 10-24 inches long and weigh up to three pounds or more. These fish have spent from a few months to just over a year in salt water. They are males that sexually matured at an early date and will now await the main run to assure a sufficient sexual balance.

But is it not possible for two seven-pound female steelhead to enter the Calorwash River in November? Yes. Then how does one tell whether they are late summer-run or early winter-run fish. It is not possible at least not at a glance. November provides us with the only overlapping of the races. Such an overlap, however, is unusual. I have created this problem because October traditionally ends the summer-run season while November sees the first winter-run arrivals. The fishermen may note that these months mark the racial separation, but the summer-run that does not follow this neat bit of categorizing is unable to make the metamorphosis to winter-run despite the month. They certainly do overlap and provide the two disparate groups described. But, again, what of the two female steelhead? We must go back to our original series of generalizations for an answer. Size and time being equal, the difference may be found in the extent of their individual sexual maturity. The late summer-run will not immediately spawn and will hold in the river for a month or two before making the last leg of her journey to the spawning area. The winter-run will continue her migration with no major interruption until the spawning area is reached. Also, the winter female will soon be in the company of grilse as she ascends. while the summer-run will join earlier arriving members of her race and await final developments. The reader may be dissatisfied with this final discrimination between the two races as not being positive enough. I would agree, for it is within the realm of possibility that both females would spawn at the same time and in the same vicinity. However, the steelhead themselves provide the final proof. The summer-run will spawn with a male of her race that has preceded her by months and clearly is a summer-run fish.*

The three winter months pose no problem. They show only winter-run steelhead. Now we can pass beyond this period to March, the next month showing a racial overlap. Now the difference between the two races is marked; there can be no confusion in making a distinction. The three summer-run steelhead, called "springers,"** are· the least sexually mature and strongest—in terms of their own weight—that the Calorwash will receive. These fish won't spawn for nearly a year.

The nine winter-run steelhead that ascended in March and the six ascending in April are in every way different from the springers. Though they are less in number than their earlier arriving relatives, they will probably average more in weight and the trophy 20 pound fish will show as a greater percentage of the monthly whole. The winter-run are ripe fish and will waste little time in seeking out their spawning beds; more of them are inclined toward spawning in the lower river.

We have mentioned the November grilse. The summer-run steelhead contains his counterpart, entering the Calorwash in August and September and straggling in from May to October. Less than a single summer in salt water will bring back some grilse hardly larger than when they left.

*I. L. Withler, in his study, Variability in Life History Characteristics of Steelhead Trout (Salmo gairdneri) Along the Pacific Coast of North America—1965, has found that summer and winter runs of steelhead are separated by obstacles in the river. Waterfalls or narrows that concentrate the river's flow during periods of high water effectively separate the spawning adults of both races. The Oregon State Game Commission, in its Ecological and Fish Cultural Study of summer steelhead, found that summer steelhead spawned in smaller streams and at an earlier time (almost 60 days earlier) than did the winter race; therefore, the summer steelhead were reproductively separated in space and time from the winter steelhead.
*A word long applied to Irish and Scottish Atlantic salmon choosing this season for upstream migration.

Releasing the Calorwash from the contormity of our imagination, the steelhead population would more likely ascend in assorted peaks and valleys.

November	6	May	0
December	25	June	2
January	37	July	3
February	18	August	20
March	9	September	14
April	5	October	5

Provided with a 12 month, 365 days a year fishing season, the angler would want to be fishing during the five months containing the winter-run and summer-run peaks. That period shows 114 steelhead of the 144 total or 79 per cent of the annual run. All steelhead rivers, from Alaska to California, will show similar peaks of ascending steelhead populations.

Beginning in 1961, the Washington Department of Game required steelheaders to carry an all season steelhead "punch card." This card has 30 punch holes (the annual limit for steelhead) whereby the angler who kills a steelhead 20 inches or more in length must punch out a hole and record the date and river. I have graphed five river profiles using figures supplied by the compilation from these punch cards. The year is really unimportant, but it happens to be 1964. The five rivers selected are the Kalama, Chehalis, Klickitat, Satsop and Hoh. They are without any geographic consideration, but were chosen for the way they typify the seasonal peaks I wish to demonstrate.

2. PHYSIOLOGICAL CHANGES

The fresh water changes a steelhead undergoes are more than simple ones of coloration. Most anglers who have seen steelhead notice that some are extremely "bright" with silver grey-green and white colors. Other are "dark," having reverted to the typical rainbow hues of the species.

It is presumed that the transition from bright to dark is the direct result of time spent in fresh water—the bright fish are the most recent arrivals from salt water. In a sense this supposition is true, for no doubt fresh water dims the steelhead's silver sheen. However, it is not water as such but is instead sexual maturation in combination with this change in environment that transforms a fish from bright to dark. The lake held Kamloop rainbow is a case in point. Here rainbows spend their entire life in fresh water yet rival the bright steelhead in coloration and certainly are cleaner than spawning steelhead unless they too are spawning.

Preparation for spawning requires changes in body chemistry, and those changes in dress are but a single manifestation of impending reproduction. The male's head, already more elongated than the female's, becomes even more so with the lengthening of his jaw. The

19

lower maxillary develops a "kype"* or knobbing at the tip. This is typical of most male salmonids and chars. Rarely does the kype on steelhead hook to the degree seen on Atlantic salmon and brown trout. Recognizing that the marked difference in jaw and head separated the two sexes, early hatchery workers applied "buck" and "doe" to the male and female steelhead. Doe is not in popular usage, but most anglers do refer to the male steelhead as a buck; the female has become a "hen."

Pacific salmon also develop a kype on the lower jaw as a pre-spawning change. This fits into the extremely hooked upper jaw. A down hooking snout is more often found among Pacific salmon with nearly the opposite true for steelhead.

The male steelhead's jaw grows extra large teeth as spawning approaches. These are not as fully developed as those in some species of Pacific salmon. The male develops a ridging of the back that increases its total body depth and gives it a chunkier, less streamlined appearance than the female. The scales of both sexes are quite loose in salt water. As they make their way to the spawning grounds, the scales become firmly imbedded. Once again, this characteristic is more severe in males. It seems reasonable that this helps protect fish during their protracted fast and when they are preparing to deposit eggs, and when they are courting.

Steelhead of either sex develop a pink to red lateral line extending to include the gill covers (opercles). The male's back proceeds towards more motley hues of somber colors and from a distance can appear almost black. All of these changes become more pronounced as the fish continue to ripen.

The correlation of spawning to physical change is positive but is not 100 per cent. Just as the occasional silver salmon spawns and dies while still bright, so steelhead can be found that ascend, spawn and scarcely worse for the experience, carry to the sea a clean suit of silver barely tarnished by the fresh water stay. Invariably it is the winter-run female that is able to fit this description.

A steelhead's "gestation period" will meet the demands of the river ascended. Some steelhead migrating to short, small coastal streams may enter already "dark" and spawn only a mile or two from the tidal estuary. If winter-run fish, they can cover this distance in an hour and shortly begin selecting a "redd" site. Others, such as summer-run steelhead ascending the Columbia River, travel hundreds of miles over a period of several weeks before reaching their spawning beds. Each river's steelhead will arrive at their destination in a similar condition, having their respective sexual maturities equally advanced.

---

*The origin of kype is not clear. The Scots refer to anything upturned as "kiped" or "kippered," and their "kipper" refers to spawned-out Atlantic salmon and sea trout. According to William Markham Morton, The Taxonomic Significance of the Kype in American Salmonids, 1965; Francis Day, British and Irish Salmonidae, 1887, introduced "kype" in reference to the hooked jaw of Atlantic salmon and did so as a misspelling of "kipe."

A ten-pound buck and seven-pound hen clearly illustrate how differently maturation in preparation for spawning affect the two sexes. The buck was taken a dozen miles from tidewater, the hen but a few hundred yards. But this difference alone is hardly responsible for the difference in coloration. The buck is more the "rainbow" with gill and lateral line areas highly colored. Its back is ridging — deepening — while a distinct kype is beginning to develop. Scales are also adhering more tightly. The hen with a smaller jaw presents a far more streamlined appearance and her bright coloration will hold longer during spawning. The two fish also suggest how early anglers thought of such buck-colored steelhead as "rainbows" and such hen-colored steelhead as "steelhead."

3. SPAWNING

For the purpose of spawning, steelhead will select a stream bottom containing a layer of gravel size rock with swift water traveling over and through it. Sites most favored will be at the head of a riffle just below where the water, six inches to several feet deep, breaks from the pool. The female chooses the spawning or redd site. Several potential spots may be tentatively tried and found lacking the necessary ingredients before final selection is made.

A sexually ripe 15-pound female steelhead that is beginning to darken.

As many as four generations of males will be sufficiently attracted to the female's labors of upstream migration to follow her about while fighting among themselves for her favor. One dominant male will evolve that is usually the largest and most aggressive of the group. However, an especially pugnacious smaller male by sheer persistence can achieve the same status. Once the dominant male has established himself, some order is restored though the "accessory" males will not leave until the spawning is completed. They seem to acknowledge the hard won rights of the dominant male but are not above forgetting themselves. When one of the scorned suitors can no longer resist the female's manifest attractions, he draws dangerously close. The dominant male will then reassert himself and viciously attack the intruder.

If the spawning male and female are average two-year-stream, two-year-ocean fish, each will weigh in the neighborhood of seven pounds. Working from this assumption, the potential age composition of the accessory males might be as follows: one or more males of comparable age and size, males with one complete year of ocean life behind them and weighing two to three pounds, males of ten to fifteen inches that have only summered in salt water, and some stream pre-migrants six to seven inches long with dreams of grandeur. This last ditch group (referred to as "egg eaters" by anglers) are apparently capable of fertilizing eggs in the event no other males are available.

Having selected the redd site, the female digs a depression by turning on her side and disturbing the stream bottom with powerful lateral arching of her body. The gravel suddenly held in suspension drifts away with the current. The process is repeated again and again until a hole is formed large enough to accommodate the pair. This will be about a foot to eighteen inches in diameter and a few inches to a foot deep. She may fit herself into this nest testing it for size several times between diggings before fully satisfied. These efforts will require from one to three hours. When all is ready, the female moves parallel with the male over the depression. Side by side and vents parallel, they arch their backs and force their bodies down. Heads with mouths open are pointed up as the eggs and milt are simultaneously discharged. It takes but a few seconds. The depth of the hole creates an eddy so the eggs settle to the bottom undisturbed by the current. Few eggs are lost. Filling the nest, like its digging, is done without the male's assistance. The female will move just above and to each side of the nest, slapping bottom gravel which is carried into the hole.

Such strenuous efforts only account for 10-20 per cent of the total eggs carried. Several feet directly upstream the whole process is repeated. The gravel dug here is carried downstream and further secures the safety of the recently deposited eggs. A completed redd will contain half a dozen nests and measure about twelve by five feet.

The female is usually unable to deposit all the eggs carried. Probably no more than 20 will remain. They cause no trouble and are eventually reabsorbed. It is interesting to note that when steelhead are artificially stripped of their eggs for hatchery use, fully 10 per cent of the eggs will remain. When these fish are released back in the stream, they will continue on to spawn in a normal manner.

Biologists have worked out a rather complex formula for determining the average egg production of steelhead. Taking this formula, a 24 inch steelhead would produce about 5,000 eggs with a potential spread of 3,800 to 7,800. A 20 inch fish will contain roughly 3,500 eggs, a 28 inch fish some 8,000 eggs and a 32 inch steelhead 10,000-12,000 eggs. A five to ten pound steelhead, generally will contain as many eggs as it has pounds multiplied by a thousand.

4. DO STEELHEAD FEED IN FRESH WATER?

Throw that question out to a group of steelheaders and you will get a variety of answers. The varied responses are partially the result of what we mean by "feed." Does it refer to steelhead actively feeding and digesting in a normal manner the stream life indigenous to their river? Or does a steelhead's Pavlovian reaction to a floating insect constitute feeding? Would you call the taking of salmon and steelhead spawn feeding? And if steelhead do not feed in fresh water, why then do they strike insect and minnow imitating baits? Or if they do feed, why are their stomachs almost always found empty?

It is up to the individual to decide what he means by "feeding" and then determine whether steelhead under that definition do or do not feed.

THE STEELHEAD TROUT

Two statements of fact can be made that will help answer the above questions. First, all members of the *Salmo genus* will eat the eggs of their own and those of closely related species. Secondly, it is not necessary for mature steelhead to feed in rivers to sustain life. If it is felt the taking and swallowing of spawn constitutes feeding then without question steelhead do feed. Personally, I would discount the taking of eggs as actively feeding. The pre-migrants are known to take eggs even more readily than the ascending adult, yet in neither group do eggs account for more than a fraction of their diet. Free floating eggs are simply a rarity in rivers even though stream gravel may contain them by the millions. The only place where they form a substantial part of the trout's diet is in lakes or in streams where eggs are commonly used for bait. Some anglers are going to shriek that pre-migrants, cutthroat trout and steelhead see ripe salmon as swimming lunch wagons. They do and there is no doubt eggs are taken at such a time. This food is still a very small part of the annual total. The juveniles that have never eaten salmon or steelhead spawn before migrating to sea. eventually return to their home river and there are hooked while grabbing a gob of eggs they in no way need. It is, of course, impossible to say why the eggs were taken. We think of anything solid put into the mouth and swallowed as eating. But among lower animals including fish this need not be the case. It is probable that when steelhead swallow eggs, the act is is no way related to hunger. For our purposes, though, we can say only that all steelhead will eat trout and salmon eggs if given the chance.

If steelhead actively feed, they must first depend on reflex actions followed by continued pursuit. It is possible out of recalled juvenile habit and inherent instinct for the fish to become sufficiently attracted to a passing insect to swing up and take it with real decisiveness. But will this lead to continued feeding or is it, as the psychologists say, a "Freudian slip"? We can say "yes" on both counts depending on the steelhead's age, range and time of year ascending.

Several factors come into play when deciding on a rationale for what the steelhead's fresh water eating habits are. Steelhead are more likely to feed actively the farther south we go in the river range, the younger the ascending steelhead, the shorter the amount of time that has elapsed since the fish's pre-migrant days and if the steelhead are summer rather than winter-run fish. If all these aspects are combined, we arrive at steelhead that have migrated to sea in the spring, returned to a California or Oregon river in the fall, and are then but a foot or so long. In nearly the same category are the one year older half-pounders that feed only a bit less eagerly. The Rogue, Klamath and Trinity are rivers that come to mind containing these steelhead in great numbers.

The older steelhead of either sex with two, three or four uninterrupted ocean years behind them not only discontinue feeding, but have digestive systems so atrophied as a result of fasting it's doubtful what little food is taken could be adequately digested. Still, it is known that very large steelhead, over ten pounds, have risen to large insects or floating flies. I think they have done this out of a remembered reflex harkening back to times when their survival depend on this ability.

Steelhead lures can be divided into three types: those simulating eggs, insects, and a variety of food seen in the ocean such as shrimp, forage fish, and perhaps squid and eels. The attraction for eggs has been described so the fluorescent lure or fly probably fascinates for the same reason. Certainly some of the pregnant hackle flies made of large diameter fluorescent chenille is nothing more than a frank imitation of spawn. Those flies suggesting stream insects are more popular on southern rivers where, as pointed out, steelhead can be frequently encountered taking such food in the course of their river migration.

The pursuit of food is the prime motivational force of the ocean dwelling steelhead. It would seem that despite a drastic change in environment and purpose, the steelhead (to our everlasting benefit) is unable to divorce himself from these past habits. They usually pick up eggs most gingerly, simply stop the downstream drifting bobber and fluorescent fly, and slam with abandon the spoon, spinner and flashing fly.

5. THE DESCENDING STEELHEAD

Spawned out steelhead referred to as "kelts"—a name for Atlantic salmon at the same stage—"downstreamers," "spawners," and in direct reference to their condition, "spent," lose much of their dark but distinct color following reproduction. Females particularly tend toward an all grey "washed out" appearance. Physically, both sexes are in good shape after an initial spawning whether summer-run or winter-run fish.

There is no set standard for post-spawning behavior. Many presume all steelhead immediately begin their emigration to the sea when spawning is completed. All do not, and the longer odds against a repeat spawning among males must be due in a large measure to their longer than necessary stay in fresh water. I say, "longer than necessary," which is an all too human opinion. Their desires to actively feed, their physical regeneration, indeed, their very salvation, is realized only when salt water is reached. Let us go back and examine our original group of spawning female, dominant male and accessory males and imagine their progress following the successful spawning.

The inability of the accessory males to participate in this mating drives them on to seek other females. No investigator to this writer's knowledge has been able to determine exactly how long they maintain this pursuit if failure is repeated. It is supposed that they are no different from successfully mated males for both are polygamous, courting and serving as many females as they are physically able. A single female can spawn only once. Spawning completed, she slowly makes her way downstream, pausing in pools for hours, even days. However slowly, the direction is positive. Not so for our many "love" stricken males. While the last feeling of domesticity has been lost on the descending female, the males will still be tearing around the shallows in a preposterous tempting of fates. Time will not necessarily run out for them here, but a longer stay reduces their chances of ever returning to the ocean. Even as the male begins his downstream migration, he lingers, casting long glances over his shoulder while aimlessly making his way.

We have seen that steelhead are able to withstand the rigors of a fast that may be up to a year long, and how the physical changes are due to the steelhead's sexual maturation that culminates in their spawning. Now, when spawning is complete, any delay in returning to the ocean leads to a rapid physical deterioration and a corresponding lack of purpose. Frequently the emaciated battle-scarred male, veteran of the nuptial wars, is unable to resume life even when salt water is reached.

So despite the female's enormous physical effort in spawning, and the easier time the male has for the single spawning, it is the male in the final analysis that pays the highest price for reproducing his own. But because he does stay longer in the river, all females are assured a male with which to spawn.

The eggs deposited hatch to give an even balance of the sexes. However, sexual maturity descends on the two in an unlike manner. At the end of one year in the ocean, a far greater percentage of males than females will return to their parental rivers. As a consequence, a single generation of females is further assured of a successful spawning.

We may see this as a check and balance. Admittedly, the male's chances of returning to spawn again are slight. But they would be slight even if the male's ardor did not restrain him from his salt water environment. The survival of the species is dependent on the successful fertilization and hatching of the eggs, not on the ability of either sex to make repeated spawnings. Actually, few females return to spawn a second time. So we must consider the steelhead as a single generation fish potentially capable of surviving to spawn a second, third or fourth time.

A kelt steelhead being returned to the river. These spawned-out fish are encountered by fishermen primarily in the months of March and April. Many streams are closed entirely, or in most of their upper reaches, at the end of February to protect spent and spawning steelhead. This spring closure is a necessary conservation practice that benefits the wild steelhead directly. Note the sunken belly of the fish in the photograph. The line running the length of the belly is a sure identification of a kelt.

CHAPTER THREE

A New Generation Is Born

The time required for steelhead eggs to hatch varies with the water temperature. A commonly used rule of thumb is 50 days at 50 degrees F. Three days are added for every drop of one degree or subtracted for every degree the water temperature is raised. Thus at 60 degrees F., the eggs would hatch in about 20 days, or at 40 degrees F., 80 days would be needed. A river's water temperature is not going to remain absolutely constant, so this "formula" will be subject to some error.

For convenience, the development of steelhead eggs may be divided into three steps. First is the pre-eyed stage. Lasting but a short time, it is the period from egg fertilization to the time when the dark developing eyes of the fish can be seen through the egg's opaque surface. The eggs are now said to be "eyed." The last stage that will directly lead to the free swimming fry is the hatched alevin. They are then a shade under ¾ of an inch; 270 will weigh an ounce. These quivering bulbous-eyed bits of life are imprisoned by the gravel bed of their environment and the yolk sac that nourishes their stationary life. Two to three weeks will be required for the fish to absorb the yolk sac and move toward the surface. Though the distance to be traveled is only a matter of inches, the trip will require an additional two weeks.

Under optimal conditions more than 80 per cent of the eggs deposited will successfully pre-eyed hatch. The principal reason for an egg loss in the pre-eyed stage, is the degree of silting which reduces osmosis and percolation (passage of oxygenated water in the gravel). Heavy silting from eroding hills and waste dumpage can drastically reduce hatchability or even prevent survival by cementing alevins into the gravel.

Those nest eggs not fertilized often develop a fungus infection, *Saproleginia* that in time will spread to the developing eyed eggs. *Saproleginia* and silting account for the 20 per cent egg loss in the hatching state. Once the fish are hatched, their losses in gravel drop to one per cent or less.

When the yolk sac and fish have consolidated, the thin sliver of silver is about an inch long and will weigh 1/180 of an ounce. Now their lives no longer depend on the protecting fates; the terrible attrition that is the steelhead's life begins immediately. Like all the children of life, that first flight from the uterine safety of their origins is wobbly and disoriented. The water that rushed overhead like a never ending storm is

27

The eyes of the developing alevin can be seen through the opaque cell membrane in the "eyed-egg" stage.

The young steelhead does not hatch but develops beyond the confines of the egg membrane. (This alevin is at the yolk sac stage.)

Egg and fish as one; the nucleus (dark spot in yolk sac) is clearly visible.

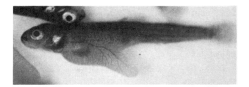

The alevin begins to absorb the yolk sac while the nucleus moves toward the body cavity.

The yolk sac is now almost completely absorbed and the parr marks (vertical bars) will begin to appear.

When the yolk sac is completely absorbed and the parr marks have appeared, the fish is said to be a "parr" — or in the parr stage of development. The parr now feeds actively in the stream.

tested when the stream bottom is left. Fry are cast with its mood and turbulence in a helpless escape to reality. Relief is found in the calm and shallow water along shore. Others join them as the gravel continues to release its new generation of steelhead. It is a bright world of plenty for these arrivals. Competition for food is encountered for the first time; minuscule plant and animal life is abundant and growth is rapid.

The fish by common circumstance "school," but it is a school of individuals isolated by the demands of survival. This halfway house of calm water and food aplenty carries a staggering mortality rate, the highest the future steelhead will ever know. Predators abound where fry are concentrated; let a new life falter, commit an indiscretion, and it becomes one of those weeded out by nature's ultimate balance.

Ironically, one of the enemies the emerging steelhead will encounter comes from his own fraternal camp. The upper class that survived their beginnings a year ago have learned their lessons well. The same plant and animal life eagerly seized by the freshman crop whets the yearling's taste buds too—nothing quite like fry to satisfy this perked up appetite! When older rainbows are not stalking these fry, other trout and the young of salmon are. The fry are likely to become history when they cross paths with silver salmon pre-migrants. The sea-run cutthroat's more sporadic wanderings bring them in contact with young steelhead while Dolly Varden char, whether anadromous and coming from salt water or leaving a lake in the river system, view these fry with equal delight.

The great blue heron will walk his haunt in river shallows and stop to stand in frozen preparation. His strong "S" neck drives a long dagger bill in the midst of the stampeding fry. He swallows his catch and moves on in Ichabod grace. The happy dipper is a buzzing bee of feathered energy by comparison. Feet and shape would not seem to mark this stream inhabitant for underwater work. But powerful wings make him an efficient hunter of small steelhead. As if to boast of his fishing prowess, the dipper will sometimes lay his catch out on streamside rocks to perhaps eat later when hunger demands. The kingfisher combines some of the tactics practiced by the dipper and heron. Perching on an overhanging branch, he views his watery domain in unmoving silence. When a fish of the proper size is spied, he becomes a projectile of no mean accuracy. A voluble defender of his fishing rights, the angler sees him raucously cursing intruders with a mule skinner's abandon.

There are many additional birds that sometimes count young steelhead as part of their diet. Sea ducks like the exquisite harlequin, several species of loon and the "fish duck"—mergansers—are all skilled fishers. Their predations on steelhead fry are not as numerous as those by other species (considering only our rivers) and generally represent a culling minority.

Those streams beyond civilization's doorstep harbor a few mammals such as mink and otter that can pursue young steelhead with appreciable success. Other mammals may dine on trout but are limited to those members dying or dead and easily secured with a flip of their paw. Raccoons especially are fond of fish and trout mortally wounded by predators are likely to become twilight dinners for them.

Giant water bugs of the family *Belostomatidae* may account for a few fry, particularly when they are just emerging from the gravel. Crayfish too will capture the occasional fish though it seems doubtful a young steelhead with all his faculties would come to this demise.

Two to three months after emergence, probably a combination of size, warming weather, and in some cases a drop in stream level, move the pre-migrant steelhead (parr) from the shallows to deeper water. The move carries with it a maturity and new sense of individuality. A fish now establishes a small territory amid the invisible currents. It will be defended and sustained for months and carry the rainbow into winter. Within the territory is a station where the fish feels most comfortable; it darts from here to a passing insect but returns to position itself as before.

It is impossible to exactly assay proportionally the type of insect life consumed by the pre-migrant for it will vary from one watershed to another. Indicative of this variety are the Shapavalov and Taft studies on steelhead life histories in Waddell Creek, California. They list the stomach contents of 55 pre-migrants examined by Shepherd in 1926-27. Caddisflies *(Trichoptera)*, almost entirely in the larvae and pupae stages formed 75.6 per cent of the insect life consumed. True flies *(Diptera)* accounted for an additional 18.4 per cent. The isopods (pillbugs) at 28 per cent and amphipods at 11.4 per cent made up the bulk of the non-insect organisms. The four groups totaled more than 90 per cent of the steelhead's diet. The remainder consisted of bugs *(Hemiptera)*, leafhoppers *(Homoptera)*, beetles *(Coleoptera)*, stone flies *(Plecoptera)*, mayflies *(Ephemeroptera)*, dragonflies *(Odonata)*, bees, ants and wasps *(Hymenoptera)*, psocids *(Corrodentia)*, water mites *(Arachnida)*, and roundworms—possibly parasitic *(Nemathelminthes)*. Among the 55 fish examined, 35 salmon eggs were found as opposed to 3,703 other forms of life.

1. THE DOWNSTREAM MIGRANT

The downstream migrant (smolt) may be of any age from nearly day one to four years. What promotes their decision to leave for the ocean is not fully understood. That they will at some time leave their stream is an inherent trait, but environmental changes and no small measure of whim seem to be factors as deciding as any devoutly followed genetic timetable.

Most pre-migrants are "programmed" to descend during the spring. Within this time their movements are partially controlled by water conditions. Rains and rising water coinciding with the right migration time will increase emigration while low water will noticeably slow descending movement. Southern streams subject to extreme seasonal flow may push their young steelhead out by sheer inhospitality. Lack of water and insufficient oxygen, alone or in combination with pollution, are also factors.

Possibly the abundance of food under the most optimum conditions fails to satisfy appetites.

Whether there is a direct correlation between the time adults spent in the river during their pre-migrant days and the time their progeny will spend has not been determined. It is likely that there is little or none, for the percentage of downstream migrants for a given age will vary considerably from year to year.

Individual trout will show migratory inconsistencies, but as a group there are consistencies as to when they choose to descend. To examine these, it is necessary to divide the trout into four age groups. Those steelhead migrating to sea from the time of emergence to one year later will be referred to as "+" fish. Those leaving after one year are "1" and so on until the oldest "4" fish are reached. The "+" fish make their greatest downstream migratory effort in June and to a lesser degree in July, August and September. Most "1" juveniles descend in May, the "2" pre-migrants in April, while the "3" pre-migrants choose March. The "4" group apparently leaves any month; fish of this age are' quite rare in most areas.

Taking steelhead over their whole range, those spending two years in fresh water dominate. Nevertheless, this preference can vary enormously. In the Waddell Creek study, downstream migrants were trapped and scales removed for age analysis. It was determined (1933-34) that += 19 per cent, 1 = 24 per cent, 2 = 53 per cent, 3 = 4 per cent and 4 = less than 1 per cent. This was not the result of some long range trend; the intervening period shows no such pattern. For example, the "+" trout in 1938-39 comprised a high of 64 per cent while the previous year they accounted for only 11 per cent of the whole. We only know with assurance that environmental factors played an important role in deciding the duration of these periods of river residency.

2. THE TIDEWATER TROUT

For many rainbow migrating to sea for the first time, the lower tidewater offers more than a quickly passed piece of marine geography. Yet this is the least understood, most neglected part of the steelhead's life history. We do know that tidewater is a place where adjustment can be made to the chemical differences in salt water and changed variety of food. We know, too, that some migrants will pass from the brackish lagoon to the ocean and back, ascend the river for a distance, and return to their new base of operations that for a time is the best of two worlds. How many young steelhead adjust in this manner and for how long? That is the rub, for no one really knows. Many an angler fishing near the tidal estuary has hooked a rainbow decidedly salt water in its dress. The fish did not populate any run and apparently was the single odd representative. I am aware that the migrant is given to a variety of silver colors. It is not to these variations I refer, but to those trout whose initial periods of salt water residency vary almost with the tides.

Tidewater is at the end of the predatory gantlet's first third and harbors the final resident test in the promise for ocean maturity. Between river and sea is the juvenile's Grendel—the sculpin *(Cottus sp.)*, an evil looking mouth and appetite. And for all its toady appearance, *Cottus* is fast enough on the dash to slice through migrant convoys with dreadful efficiency. Fortunately, it is largest at six to seven inches and must limit depredations to trout and salmon a year or less old.

The Sculpin (Cottus Sp.)

It would be impossible to confine a river's trout to the comparatively small tidal estuary, for even a fraction of them would glut this part of the river. Then too, many rivers have an area only remotely resembling a "tidal estuary." The river undramatically meets the sea at low tide and the sea meets the river at high. The length of river channel in conflict with both will depend on the river's volume and gradient; it can be measured by the mile or foot. To the degree that descending rainbow adapts to this water must be contingent on the estuary's ability to support a temporary residency and how favorable it is to periodic re-entry by indecisive trout-steelhead.

However the time is spent here, there comes a day when the world of falling water that has umbilically depressed the seaward migration is disavowed and severed. The familiar haunts that guided movements and contained secrets can now only nurture their return. They are replaced by the freedom of fathomless depths. River and land fade to a dim memory as the waiting sea is joined.

CHAPTER FOUR

Oceanic Odyssey

Just as the developing patterns of a migratory habit permitted Ahab to find and strike Moby Dick, so high seas biologists have gradually discovered and compiled and pushed back the unknown frontiers of the steelhead's oceanic movements.

CANADA

The deep hull of the **G. B. Reed** rode the ocean swells with confidence and stability. She represented the Fisheries Research Board of Canada and had her home port at the Biological Station in Nanaimo, British Columbia. For more than two miles astern ran a long-line made up of 30 "skates." Dangling at eight foot intervals from each 400 foot skate were one meter lines called "ganglions" that terminated with a hook baited with salted anchovy. For many hours the currents had brushed the nearly 1500 baits passing in review.

From a position just off the north Oregon coast, the ship had for a week been keeping to a western course. She passed beyond the continental shelf and was now 300 miles from the mouth of the Columbia River. The crew scurried about in readiness as the power winch began bringing in the long-line. As the thrashing fish came aboard, they were removed and kept for examination or tagged and returned unharmed. The pertinent data was recorded in the ship's log. Date: April 13, 1963. Position: 46 degrees 8 minutes N. latitude, 140 degrees W. longitude. Surface temperature: 46.22 degrees F. Catch: 14 pink salmon, 3 chum salmon, 1 silver salmon and 41 steelhead

UNITED STATES

In 1956 the **Paragon** was one of five vessels employed by the U.S. Fish and Wildlife Service with headquarters in Seattle, Washington. From May until October, she would sweep the Gulf of Alaska waters in hopes of determining the oceanic movements of Pacific salmon. Sister ships would travel north, east, south, and west of the **Paragon.** Together, two million square miles, from the Washington and Oregon coast west to 175 degrees W. longitude and north to 60 degrees N. latitude—the Bering Sea area—would be covered.

The **Paragon** was at 90 feet the longest ship in this little fleet. A 165 horse power engine pushed her 58 ton bulk along at an 8½ knot cruising speed. Like the other research ships, she contained a large freezer and sophisticated array of navigational equipment that included loran, radar, radio direction finder, fathometer, and automatic pilot. All the ships used gill nets instead of long-lines during the cruise.

A gill net "set" consisted of 18 "shackles" where each shackle was 50 fathoms of net 20 feet wide. A "cork line" holding cedar or spongex floats kept the net's edge floating while a "lead line" kept the sinking edge deep. Several 18 inch fabricated and glass floats supplemented the cork line floats. To the boat end of the net was a 40 foot triangular "shock net" that joined the end of the cork line at a flagpole marker. To the flagpole point was a drift cable that attached to the heavy sisal rope mooring line running to the ship. The mooring line and drift cable totaled 250 fathoms, so the net started 1500 feet astern of the **Paragon**.

While the ship drifted downwind at four knots the 850 fathom gill net would slip off her stern. After the last shackle had left, the **Paragon** then executed a 180 degree turn. Simultaneously the heavy mooring line attached to a bow cleat. The whole operation took from 15 to 20 minutes. Nets were fished from five in the evening until six the following morning.

On the morning of September third, the **Paragon** was about 100 miles east of the Unalaska Island, one of many Aleutian Islands. The nets set the past evening were hauled over a roller on the starboard side by a power gurdy. Two crewmen from the ship's complement of seven picked salmon from the net and placed them in deck bins coded to the assorted net mesh sizes. An oceanographer from the University of Washington and a Fish and Wildlife biologist recorded the species, their apparent direction of movement and their depth in the net. To the left gill cover of each fish was attached a numbered, colored strap tag for later identification. Some blood samples were taken by cutting through the caudal peduncle, then letting the blood drop in a sterile jar. After the fork length of each fish was taken, they were placed in the ship's freezer for future laboratory examination. The night's catch: 14 sockeye, 17 chum, 2 silver, 1 chinook, and 2 pink salmon; the incidental catch included 7 steelhead trout.

JAPAN

The **Etsu-zan-maru** is a research vessel operated in the Aleutian mothership fishing industry by the Fisheries Agency of Japan. She is nearly three times as heavy and twice as powerful as the **Paragon**. On May 16, 1960, the **Etsu-zan-maru** left Hokkaido's largest port of Hokodato and followed a northeast course. Twelve days later her gill nets were set for the first time 200 miles south of the Islands of the Four Mountains, a tiny series of storm-s-swept peaks east of Amuka Pass in Alaska's Aleutians. From this point, using both gill nets and long-lines, the ship followed the 50-degree N. latitude line east of Attu Island. After steaming several hundred miles north, the **Etsu-zan-maru** traveled east, working the Bering Sea waters.

The purpose of this voyage was to make a comprehensive age determination of net caught salmon and study migratory habits by tagging and releasing those caught on long-lines. Large salmon were marked with a red and white celluloid disc 14mm. in diameter that attached to a 65mm. long wire to be inserted in the fish. Immature salmon were tagged with a fine diameter tube bearing the identification legend. A total of 3,157 salmon were disc tagged, 3,249 received the tube tag.

No Bering Sea steelhead were caught, though sister ship **Takuro-maru** did account for one. The fish was taken so far east—43-45 degrees N. latitude, 153-160 degrees E. longitude—it was perhaps destined for Kamchatka Peninsula waters.

Representatives from the governments of Canada, United States, and Japan met on June 12, 1953, at the International Convention for the High Seas Fisheries of the North Pacific Ocean. Their task was to promote scientific study through joint cooperation and make conservation recommendations that would give the maximum sustained yield of Pacific salmon for those countries attending. They also hoped to determine to what extent eastern and western salmon races intermingle on the high seas. A treaty in 1952 had set a provisional abstention line of 175 degrees W. longitude, east of which Japan would not take salmon.

The convention established the International North Pacific Fisheries Commission with headquarters in Vancouver, British Columbia. Information gathered by each country has been made available to this organization for final compilation and mutual enlightenment. While salmon is the principle concern, steelhead caught on the high seas are made part of their records. Much of what we presently understand about the steelhead's ocean migration has come as a result of these joint efforts.

When steelhead join with the sea, they are driven by a wanderlust pursuit that can carry them thousands of miles from their native shores. The ocean is their land and the sun-warmed waters their summer. Swimming below the surface swells, they work toward longer days. The exacting price of survival is forgotten for the change in environment makes a hunter of the hunted.

When summer climaxes its efforts, our steelhead will be patrolling the Gulf of Alaska, changing currents and misty distant lands with indifference. The beads of rock horizons that are the Aleutians become their guideline and they swing with its sweeping direction. Few will get farther than 180 degrees W. longitude before fall's cooling waters turn them south.

Ideally, pre-migrants have chosen spring to begin ocean migration. Coastal waters are then warm with an ideal 48-52 degree F.* range;

*All temperatures listed are those for the upper 30 feet of water — the depth layer preferred by ocean steelhead.

time divided here will inure them to ocean living. From British Columbia to Northern California this continental shelf Pacific represents part of the winter range of already established steelhead. It is a winter distribution that can be likened to a giant cornucopia resting on the 40 degree N. latitude line with its narrow end extending to about 180 degrees W. longitude. The top of the distribution line begins at 41-42 degrees N. latitude and gradually rises to meet the 50 degree N. latitude line a hundred miles off the north tip of Vancouver Island. The open end of the cornucopia spreads like a blunderbuss muzzle up the coast of British Columbia and down the coast of California. Within this distribution, the greatest steelhead concentration will be along the 45 degree N. latitude line from the coast to 145 degrees W. longitude. While the total steelhead winter range holds a temperature spread of 43-53 degrees F., the described concentration rests in the optimum 48-52 degree F. range.

Steelhead distribution and ocean temperatures remain little changed in March. Warmer weather first reaches to the ocean and its steelhead in April. An example will show how this trend proceeds and how it affects north-west traveling steelhead. We can begin by taking two specific points — 130 and 145 degrees W. longitude—on the 50 degree N. latitude line. The first point is in our cornucopia and has a winter temperature of 46-47 degrees F. The second point is just as far north but farther out to sea; it holds a temperature range of 40-42 degrees F. The close coastal waters do have steelhead while the area beyond is outside the preferred temperature range and is barren. May, and the temperature there has increased to 43 degrees F. and will progress to 44-46 degrees F. by the month's end. We would expect steelhead to seek this advantage and they do.

The steelhead's ocean movements result from surface temperatures simultaneously rising from two directions. As spring progresses, temperatures increase from south to north and the steelhead move north. As coastal waters warm to a greater degree, the steelhead are pushed west.

Summer distribution is quite broad and its full extent is not fully understood. It does cover the Gulf of Alaska west of the coastal areas and along the southern part of the Aleutians to at least 180 degree W. longitude. They show the greatest concentration from 150-180 degrees W. longitude above 50 degrees N. latitude—water just south of the Aleutians having an August temperature range of 48-52 degrees F.

We have come a long way towards unraveling the steelhead's oceanic movements. Like all early discoveries, it glaringly points out those areas where we are still very much in the dark. Long-line and ocean gill net catches have shown that steelhead most often travel in the upper 30 to 40 feet of water. But how consistently is this layer held and how deep will they go for food?

A good idea of what governs the steelhead's movements is

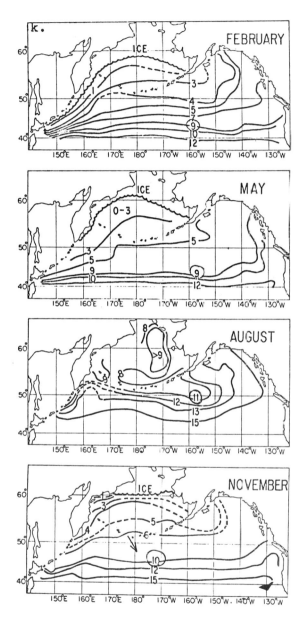

*Distribution of sea surface isotherms in the North Pacific and Bering Sea during February, May, August and November. Temperature is given in centigrade. 10°C. = 50°F. The 9°-11°C. sea surface isotherm line will carry the ocean steelhead as it moves from south to north and back known, so with some degree of accuracy we can predict where their main numbers will be at a given time of the year. This is at best a general reference. We do not yet know how steelhead from different rivers intermingle on the high seas. Tagging operations have been carried out from research vessels such as those described. The total steelhead tagged and few river recoveries made have not offered conclusive evidence but there is probably a general migratory consistency whether the fish are Oregon or Alaska stock. If a race of steelhead does not follow the oceanic routes described, they are likely to be those from California that see the ocean for but a few months at a time.

The little investigation into the dietary habits of the ocean traveling steelhead shows that food is probably taken as it is available. If, for example, squid comprises the greatest percentage of preferred fare in a given ocean area, squid will likely dominate in the diet of those steelhead. The three main classes of food most frequently taken are squid, fish (greenling) and amphipods.

There is no inclination for steelhead to school on the high seas. Conditions such as the superabundance of forage fish might for a time bring a number of steelhead to a small area. But this is not a "school" in the classic sense where numbers of fish act as a single unit.

No experiments have been conducted on the steelhead's rate of ocean travel. Investigators studying the traveling speed of sockeye salmon have determined that their most efficient speed for the amount of energy expended was 1.1 miles per hour. It is felt the steelhead's swimming speed would be comparable. While this seems slow, it should be remembered that it represents the best functioning speed and can be exceeded many fold when the need arises. Even at this rate of travel. however, the constantly on-the-go ocean steelhead could annually cover thousands of miles.

CHAPTER FIVE

Steelhead By Area

The steelhead's range has been divided into six main areas. Most correspond to political boundaries, but still show a positive relationship by pointing out marked differences in the steelhead's life history from one area to another. They are: 1. California, 2. Oregon, 3. The Columbia River (Oregon, Washington, and Idaho). 4. Washington, 5. British Columbia, 6. Alaska.

The periods of pre-migrant residency were given as +, 1, 2, 3, and 4 years. In this chapter, the age "+" and "1" will be combined under the age "1." Just as some pre-migrants descend to sea shortly after emergence, some steelhead will ascend their stream after a few months at sea. We could then have a life history +/+—months in fresh water and months in salt water. However, such a life history does not exist among steelhead; returning fish would be little more than pre-migrant parr and hardly capable of spawning. The "+" period for ascending steelhead will also be combined with one year at sea. The youngest steelhead described will thus be 1/1 — approximately one year in fresh water and one year in salt water.

The pre-migrants can be any age from emergence to over four complete years, and the returning adults can be any age with up to four complete years in salt water. Combining these two we arrive at 16 age combinations theoretically possible—each of the 1, 2, 3, and 4 year fresh water age groups capable of combining with any of the 1, 2, 3, and 4 year salt water groups. Only one of these combinations, the 4/4 age class, is not found in nature. The 15 *first spawning* life histories are as follows:

1/1	2/1	3/1	4/1
1/2	2/2	3/2	4/2
1/3	2/3	3/3	4/3
1/4	2/4	3/4	

To what degree a river contains some percentage of these age groups determines the size and habits of steelhead in that river. These 15 ages comprise the majority of returning steelhead on almost all rivers.

There are also repeat spawning steelhead. Fish have been found that had ascended rivers to spawn five separate times. This is most rare for the percentage of repeat spawners decreases drastically after the second spawning. As a group, steelhead spawning more than once add as many as 18 additional life histories for a total cf at least 33. No river is known to have all 33.

Mentioned earlier was the ability of some stream rainbows to mature precociously and participate in spawning before migrating to sea. These are not counted in with the repeat spawning steelhead. The "repeaters" are only those having at least two periods of ocean residency in their life history.

1. CALIFORNIA

The most complete study ever conducted on steelhead was initiated in 1932 and progressed for more than a decade. The California Division of Fish and Game (now the California Department of Fish and Game) and the U.S. Bureau of Fisheries (now part of the Fish and Wildlife Service) worked cooperatively on Waddell Creek. This is a small coastal stream in Santa Cruz County felt to be typical of California's short-run anadromous rivers. A dam was constructed to trap all upstream and downstream moving fish. Here, stream pre-migrants and steelhead were counted, measured and their ages determined by scale analysis. No fish were killed and all of Waddell Creek was closed to angling. The principals who guided these research studies were Leo Shapovalov and Alan C. Taft.[1]

It was found that among ascending steelhead, an average of 82.8 per cent were spawning for the first time, 15 per cent for the second, 2.1 per cent for the third, and 0.1 per cent for the fourth. No steelhead were recorded spawning more than four separate times.

Waddell Creek filled 12 of the 15 first spawning life history categories though two represent less than 0.1 per cent and will be listed as + per cent. From greatest to least, they are as follows:

2/1	29.8%	18"
2/2	26.5	27"
3/1	10.5	21½"
1/1	4.9	15½"
3/2	4.4	27½"
1/2	4.2	26"
4/1	1.2	22½"
4/2	0.3	29½"
2/3	0.2	30"
1/3	0.1	31"
3/3	0.+	—
4/3	0.+	—
	82.+%	

[1] Shapovalov, Leo and Alan C. Taft, The life histories of the steelhead rainbow trout (Salmo gairdneri gairdneri) and silver salmon (Oncorhynchus kisutch) with special reference to Waddell Creek, California, and recommendations regarding their management. California Department of Fish and Game Bulletin No. 98, 375 pp. 1954

Lengths and per cents are averages bases on 3,220 steelhead examined over a nine-year period.

What creates steelhead with all their size and strength is the ocean environment. Pre-migrant residency by comparison has little bearing on the eventual size obtained. Taking from the above figures, we notice that $1/1 = 15\frac{1}{2}$", $2/1 = 18$" and $3/1 = 21\frac{1}{2}$". The weight ratio between the one-year and three-year stream fish when they migrate to sea is considerable, but after one year of ocean life the size advantage of these older smolts is reduced. If steelhead remain at sea for two years the differences are even less despite assorted total ages. Keeping the periods of ocean residency constant, we have $1/2 = 26$", $2/2 = 27$", and $3/2 = 27\frac{1}{2}$". The value of ocean residency is seen more clearly if we transpose the total ages for one year ocean fish. The result would be $1/1 = 15\frac{1}{2}$", $1/2 - 26$", and $1/3 = 31$". The total ages have remained the same but sizes have increased enormously. The four-year steelhead would weigh three pounds plus with a $3/1$ life history while his opposite number at $1/3$ would probably weigh 12 pounds or more. Clearly age alone does not contribute to size.

Looking at the first spawning figures again and realizing the importance of ocean residency, steelhead remaining in the ocean for one year before spawning constitute 46.4 per cent of the spawning total. In other words, on this and like streams, the angler can expect to encounter steelhead from one to three pounds—"half-pounders"—about half the time. Steelhead with a two-year ocean life account for 35.4 per cent of total run; fish in this category will average four to eight pounds with 12 pounds about the upper limit.

The only first spawning age group that could be expected to exceed 12 pounds are those three-year ocean steelhead, yet this group is so small as to be of scant angling value.

The reader has perhaps encountered the outdoor writer ecstatic over the prospect of catching one of those hoary giants ascending to spawn a second or third time and pushing the magic 20 pound mark. Knowing that about 17 per cent of all Waddell Creek steelhead are repeat spawners, we might presume the trophy fish would be found here. It does not work out that way. If two steelhead have identical life histories save for one having spawned once and the other twice, the first spawner will nearly always be larger. *The time required to ascend and spawn is lost as a growth period.* Steelhead remaining at sea are not so handicapped. First spawning figures showed the average size of $2/2$ steelhead to be 27 inches. At this length, they would weigh from six to eight pounds. The $2/1S.1$ steelhead is the same age but ascended to spawn in Waddell Creek at the end of one year at sea, descended to sea when spawning was completed, and is now ascending for the second time. Their average length was found to be $24\frac{1}{2}$ inches. This difference in length is slight but makes for a weight difference of two and a half pounds. The repeat spawner will average four to five pounds.

The following are the major percentages of repeat spawning steelhead found on Waddell Creek:

2/1S.1	8.1%	24½"
2/1.1S.1	3.4	29"
3/1S.1	2.2	24½"
2/2S.1	1.1	27"
1/1S.1	0.8	22½"
1/1.1S.1	0.6	27½"
2/1.2S.1	0.4	30½"
	16.6%	

The repeat spawners combined with the first spawning figures to give a 99+ per cent total. All other repeat spawning categories make up the less than one per cent balance.

The largest steelhead trapped on Waddell Creek showed the 2/1.2S.1 life history. It had spawned at the end of the first and second ocean sojourn and was ascending to spawn a third time. The fish was 32-33 inches long. No weight is available, but such a steelhead might weigh as much as 15 pounds. The steelhead was a female as were the vast majority spawning more than twice.

Two remaining steelhead ages seem capable of producing the great fish. First, those remaining at sea three years before spawning for the first time, then descending and returning to spawn a second time. Steelhead spending three years at sea showed as an extremely small percentage among first spawning steelhead. No repeat spawners were ever trapped that had in their life history three straight ocean years of growth.

The last possibility remains with the steelhead that has spent one year as a pre-migrant and two years at sea before spawning for the first time, weighing six to eight pounds. We know that some steelhead were found to have spawned four times. Attach this to the above described fish and we have 1/2.3S.1. As likely as this seems to be, no adults were found filling such a life history.

The oldest steelhead from Waddell Creek was 2/1.3S.1. A seven-year-old female, it was 31-32 inches long and spawning for the fourth time. Beyond seven years, Waddell Creek steelhead simply died of old age.

In summation, we can say that one per cent or less of Waddell Creek steelhead, regardless of their life history, will exceed 30 inches in length and 12 pounds in weight.

This writer is aware of some California steelhead larger than these figures. An explanation of these will be discussed later in this section.

California's great interior rivers like the Klamath, Trinity and Sacramento have steelhead similar but distinct from those in the short-run coastal river discussed. Generally the steelhead are smaller, more numerous and more active. Little work has been done on the comparative weight/length relationship, but it is this writer's opinion that steelhead on these interior waters weigh more for a given length than would ordinarily be found.

The Sacramento River begins at its Lake Shasta source and flows south, joining with the American River at California's capital, Sacramento. The two rivers continue on as the Sacramento, passing to San Pablo Bay and the Pacific.

A jack steelhead is examined and found to be one of a select group of former fin clipped pre-migrants. Such fish will usually be two or three years old and will have spent a year or less in salt water.

The findings from a study completed on the Sacramento[2] would be compatible with information in evidence on the Klamath and Trinity. While the sampling completed on Waddell Creek numbers in the thousands and on the Sacramento but a few hundred, the results are nevertheless remarkably similar.

A hundred fish examined for age determination gave the following results:

2/1	. . . .	30%
2/2	. . . .	26
1/1	. . . .	17
1/2	. . . .	10
2/1.S.1	. . . .	6
2/1.1S.1	. . . .	6
2/1.2S.1	. . . .	2
3/1	. . . .	1
1/1S.1	. . . .	1
1/1.4S.1	. . . .	1
		100%

The most notable difference between the Sacramento and Waddell Creek sampling is found in the 1/1 age category. On Waddell Creek, 4.9 per cent filled this life history while the Sacramento has 17 per cent.

[2] Hallock, Richard J., William F. Van Woert and Leo Shapovalov, An Evaluation of Stocking Hatchery-Reared Steelhead Rainbow (Salmo gairdnerii gairdnerii) in the Sacramento River System. California Department of Fish and Game. Bulletin No. 114, 74 pp. 1961.

This is more than made-up for by the almost total lack of Sacramento River steelhead in the 3/1 class. The run of half-pounders totaled 46.4 per cent in Waddell Creek and 48 per cent in the Sacramento.

Both total number of spawnings and ages of Sacramento River steelhead were remarkably like those on Waddell Creek.

Spawnings

83% spawning for the first time
14% spawning for the second time
2% spawning for the third time
1% spawning for the fifth time (one fish)

Total age

17% = 2 years
41% = 3 years
33% = 4 years
6% = 5 years
2% = 6 years
1% = 7 years

100 fish

We should notice that 100 per cent of the steelhead sampled had spent one or two initial years in ocean residency. This in itself is a size limiting factor. Only on the Sacramento and Oregon's Rogue have steelhead been found without three straight years at sea in at least some life histories.*

The two groups of one-year and two-year ocean fish are almost equally divided—47 per cent and 43 per cent respectively. Measurements were taken of 18,671 Sacramento River steelhead. The average length was found to be 18.7 inches. This does not mean much for it is actually mid-way between the two basic first spawning age groups. Those steelhead that had spent one year at sea averaged 15½ inches in length and just over two pounds in weight. The two-year ocean fish averaged 20½ inches—far shorter than steelhead of comparable age in Waddell Creek (2/2 = 27"). One possible explanation besides the "nature of the beast" is the early ascending time of Sacramento River steelhead. They are known to migrate upstream from July to mid-March, with September and October the peak months. There is no doubt the early ascending time could shorten by five months the rapid ocean growth period. This alone can hardly be totally responsible for their smaller size, but probably is a contributing factor. While these Sacramento two-year ocean fish are shorter than the average, they are heavier for their length, weighing about 4 pounds

*Future studies may well reveal additional rivers.

each.

During the Sacramento River period of study, 1952-1958, the largest steelhead recorded weighed 15½ pounds. Fish above 13 pounds were very uncommon.

Both Waddell Creek and the Sacramento River are felt to be representative of California's two types of anadromous rivers. On these waters, the detailed life histories gave steelhead a maximum weight of about 15 pounds or more. However, there have been steelhead of still greater weight ascending California streams. Howard Dunlap took a 21 pound 6 ounce steelhead from the Smith River on November 15, 1948. On September 26, 1926, Leslie Korth caught what is certainly the state steelhead record for fly tackle; it weighed 21 pounds 3 ounces and came from the Feather River. This could have been a resident trout though the size makes this rather unlikely. The Feather, I might add, is a tributary of the Sacramento, joining about 30 miles north of where the America River becomes the Sacramento. D. L. Ruff caught an 18-pound 6-ounce steelhead from the Smith River on December 30, 1948. An 18-pound 9-ounce steelhead came from the Klamath River in 1965. In Chapter 8 a number of Eel River steelhead are described in the 15-17 pound range.

With few exceptions, the best of California's steelhead will fall short of the 20 pound mark. But by what method do their steelhead exceed even 15 pounds? There are no scale readings for such fish. Nevertheless, we can make some good guesses. Repeated spawnings would not bring a steelhead to these weights. It is felt that in California any life history containing a three-year ocean period with no time off for spawning is capable of producing the 15-20 pound steelhead. While these trout represent a small percentage of the total population, they may seem more common if choosing to ascend at a particular time—such as toward the end of a river's steelhead migration period.

HOW FAR SOUTH?

Practically speaking and certainly from an angler's point of view, the Russian River, just north of San Francisco, represents the southern limit of the steelhead's range. Twenty years ago this honor would have gone to the Santa Ynez in Santa Barbara County only a hundred miles from Los Angeles. Between the Russian and Santa Ynez are dozens of little coastal streams that once provided excellent fishing and still manage to produce the occasional steelhead. When there was sufficient rainfall, when no water preserving dams blocked their passage, when the rivers were not diverted for farms, industry and homes, their continued existence was still critical. At times, only the headwaters remained a constant source of life; the main river was reduced to a trickle as the stilled lagoon became separated from the ocean by a tidal bar.

Fall steelhead were blocked from ascending while the smolts were trapped in the very waters sought by the adults. As mature fish congregated, surf fishermen with long whippy rods cast sinker weighted spoons or spinners far out between the rolling waves. There they hooked steelhead in the most foreign of settings. For many years, this was the only surf fishing done for steelhead where they were an intended rather than incidental catch.*

Other anglers ranged the canyons and fished pools holding the six to seven inch juveniles. These fish were often augmented by plants; almost from the angling beginning there was a mixing of steelhead races in these waters.

The separation of steelhead generations ended when torrents of winter rain soaked the Coastal Range. Waters rose overnight. Their faint trickling complexion became a muddy rampage that pounded the tidal bar and opened the river to the sea. The smolts escaped with it, passing adults seeking to sustain their race. More than a few of these mature fish would tarry long enough on their ocean return to perish when the rapidly dropping water imprisoned them in pools.

Some of the better known rivers south of San Francisco fitting this description would first include those leaving the Santa Cruz Mountains like San Gregorio, Pescadero, and Waddell, Soquell and Pajaro creeks. The largest river in this area is the Salinas running along the eastern side of the Santa Lucia Range and entering Monterey Bay between Castroville and Monterey. Just south of Point Pinos and by Carmel is the little stream of that name. Continuing out of the Santa Lucia's are the Big and Little Sur rivers, and Salmon, San Simeon and Santa Rosa creeks. North of Point Conception and the Santa Barbara Channel is the already mentioned Santa Ynez, once the best steelhead stream south of the Russian.

The realization that these were fertile rivers producing steelhead fully representative of California's best makes their loss all the more tragic. The California Department of Fish and Game attempted to sustain these runs with every means at their disposal and the few steelhead still caught are a direct result of their efforts. But there is really no present run of sufficient quantity to justify the name.

We may go still farther south to locate the steelhead's once most southern range. Well into the present century, steelhead were making fairly consistent runs up the Ventura and Santa Clara River and Ojai Creek in Ventura County. E.H. Glidden, a Southern California game warden during the 1920's, tells of seeing steelhead caught from San Juan Creek in Orange County and of fine runs in San Mateo and San Onofre Creeks in San Diego County. Glidden observed steelhead in these two streams for more than 20 years and claims that some of these sea-run rainbows weighed as much as 20 pounds. Alan C. Taft, when he worked for the Fish and Game Department in the San Diego area, recognized the value of these runs. During the rainless summer months, San Mateo Creek almost dried up and he devoted himself to rescuing pre-migrant steelhead from diminishing pools and liberating them in the ocean.

---

*Steelhead are sometimes caught by salt water anglers fishing for sea-run cutthroat. Surf fishing for steelhead off Whidbey Island, Washington, has become moderately popular in recent years.

Observers during the 1880's and 1890's report steelhead in the Smith Mountain tributaries that feed San Luis Rey River. Glidden, again, observed steelhead caught from the San Diego River about 1927, and saw two steelhead caught from the Tijuana River "on the California side of the international border." This last river meets the ocean near San Ysidro but a few miles from the border, meanders south, passes to Mexico at Tijuana and travels still deeper into Mexico. Since these substantiated reports seem to confirm steelhead in the Tijuana River, it is conceivable that in the past they wandered down the Baja to ascend unnamed streams. It should be pointed out that these coastal waters are relatively cool, and the algae, fishes and some invertebrates of the intertidal reefs of Northern Baja are of an even more northern assortment than are the corresponding types in the San Diego area.

The idea of steelhead ascending desert rivers in Mexico's Baja ia an intriguing one. Those reported in the Tijuana River may have resulted from unplanned rainbow trout stockings. Even were this true, it would not detract from the fact that steelhead once ascended a river that save for a mile or two is Mexican. Biologists have presumed these "Mexican steelhead" to be no different from those in San Diego County counted as typical of the migratory rainbow.

We can only say with assurance that steelhead once naturally ranged south to the Mexican border, and that they *probably* ascended a few rivers in Baja, California. Exactly how far south they once ranged may never be known.

To water poor Southern California, the smallest stream is a most valued resource. It is not a case of merely rehabilitating these rivers for anadromous fish; often the rivers have disappeared altogether. In their place are earth and rock dams, reservoirs, aqueducts, miles of steel pipe, millions of faucets and enough garden hose to reach the moon. The complete loss of these rivers and their steelhead was the price exacted by the ever burgeoning California population.

There is still the confusing and amazing appearance of *a* steelhead in these waters. They have been discovered when caught by charter boats working for yellowtail, barracuda and bonito. Two solutions are offered. Steelhead may sometimes straggle this far south with their ultimate destination more northern waters. Much more probably, trout planted in the few streams open to the sea are washed out with heavy rains and the few gaining access to the Pacific will seek to return in a year or two. This still happens periodically on the Santa Ynez River, though most of the year sees a dusty land scar in its stead.

2. OREGON

The one steelheading river that quickens the angling pulse at the mention of its name is, of course, the Rogue. It more properly divides California and Oregon steelhead than the 42 degree N. longitude border. Because Washington, Oregon and Idaho's Columbia River streams will be presented as a separate unit, only coastal Oregon is presently under discussion. This area too can be divided: the Rogue watershed and all other coastal Oregon waters.

Rogue River summer-run steelhead form a unique race. They are the only members of this grand species showing almost total uniformity in their salt water life. Most of the pre-migrants reside for two years in the Rogue before migrating to sea. Unlike other rivers where these trout can be expected to spend up to four years in salt water, the Rogue steelhead are peculiar for their return before one year. Most come back in four to eight months as scrappy half-pounders. It is believed they will spawn almost entirely in the lower main river and its tributaries. This part of the river is favored again as these fish ascend the following year. If spawning for the first time, they average between 13-17 inches, but may be no more than a few inches longer than the pre-migrants they were a few months before. These half-pounders generally show earlier than the older, heavier steelhead.

The tippet and line snapping five to ten pound fish arrive and continue through the lower river to the Grants Pass area. The greatest of these are best known for their September and October appearance, but large steelhead are still found ascending from summer to fall and winter.

One hundred four Rogue River steelhead were trapped upstream at Gold Ray Dam during July and August, 1964, by the Oregon State Game Commission. The fish measured 18-31 inches long. A scale analysis determined they had spawned one to four times, with most having spawned once or twice before.

Those who claim the Rogue steelhead to be a breed apart are probably right. We know now that the river is a constantly renewed acquaintance for these fish. Of course there is no way to prove that such singular habits manifest themselves to an angling advantage. But fishermen whose experience give us an expert's frame of reference claim the river never gained its enviable reputation because the steelhead were larger or faster or more numerous. Steelhead here, they say, won renown because they were great "takers" of established wet fly patterns. In the light of present information, the reason may point to the more residential character of Rogue steelhead.

The Alsea River draws from its Coastal Range headwaters to feed Alsea Bay at Waldport. At the request of the Oregon State Game Commission in 1954, the Oregon Cooperative Wildlife Unit initiated a comprehensive life history study of Alsea River steelhead.[3]

The river is average in volume and gradient and the steelhead are typical of coastal Oregon—winter-run fish that ascend, spawn and obtain a size more in keeping with what is really the majority of north country steelhead.

[3] Chapman, Donald W., "Studies on the Life History of Alsea River Steelhead," Journal of Wildlife Management, Vol. 22, No. 2, April, 1958, page 123-134.

The 978 first spawning steelhead trapped for scale analysis gave the following life histories:

```
2/2 . . . . . . . . . . . . . . . . . . . . . 52.5%
2/3 . . . . . . . . . . . . . . . . . . . . . 21.8
3/2 . . . . . . . . . . . . . . . . . . . . . 13.6
2/1 . . . . . . . . . . . . . . . . . . . . .  4.0
3/3 . . . . . . . . . . . . . . . . . . . . .  2.9
2/4 . . . . . . . . . . . . . . . . . . . . .  1.9
3/1 . . . . . . . . . . . . . . . . . . . . .  1.3
1/3 . . . . . . . . . . . . . . . . . . . . .  0.9
3/4 . . . . . . . . . . . . . . . . . . . . .  0.4
1/4 . . . . . . . . . . . . . . . . . . . . .  0.3
1/2 . . . . . . . . . . . . . . . . . . . . .  0.2
4/1 . . . . . . . . . . . . . . . . . . . . .  0.1
4/2 . . . . . . . . . . . . . . . . . . . . .  0.1
                                            100%
```

The reader will immediately recognize the vast difference between these life histories and any previously discussed. First, there are several four-years-at-sea categories not found in California. This group contains the ultimate in steelhead size, for there are four years of rapid growth before sexual maturation necessitates spawning. Most such fish will exceed 15 pounds with many topping the 20 pound mark. Just what the maximum size these steelhead will reach is difficult to predict, but 30 pounds would seem a reasonable figure. Whereas in California the three-year ocean steelhead represented a very small percentage of the annual total, they comprise a whopping 25.6 per cent on the Alsea. And the one-year ocean fish that made up nearly half the total on Waddell Creek are but 5.4 per cent of the Alsea's run.

Using years at sea as the critical size determining factor, the following percentages sum up the Alsea River's first spawning steelhead population.

```
 5.4% one-year-ocean fish
66.4% two-year-ocean fish
25.6% three-year-ocean fish
 2.6% four-year-ocean fish
100%
```

The repeat spawners formed 17 per cent of the annual run in 1954, 12 per cent in 1955 and 3 per cent in 1956. Almost 85 per cent of these were spawning for the second time and 15 per cent for the third. No steelhead were found that had spawned more than three separate times. The male to female ratio among these repeat spawners was 1/2.5.

Another important Oregon study was conducted by F.H. Sumner, the scale analyst for the Oregon State Game Commission at Corvallis.[4]

[4] Sumner, F. H., "Age and growth of steelhead trout, Salmo gairdneri gairdneri Richardson, caught by sport and commercial fishermen in Tillamook County, Oregon." Trans. Amer. Fish. Soc. 75:77-83 1945.

This was a two-pronged investigation into the relative age and size of steelhead caught commercially and by sport methods from Tillamook Bay and tributaries. Because most half-pounders are able to slip through commercial gill nets, the average size of the two groups differs considerably. Sport caught steelhead averaged 24.4 inches long and 5.9 pounds compared with 27.1 inches and 8.6 pounds for the commercial catch. Length extremes for each group were 11.25-34.5 inches and 21.5-36.0 for the gill net catch. Between 50 and 60 per cent of all fish examined fell into the 2/2 life history.

Fresh water/salt water steelhead histories from Tillamook Bay are similar to those on the Alsea. Among this sampling, though, were two that may be steelhead longevity records. The 702 steelhead commercially caught in the 1941-42 winter showed a male in his ninth year and a female in her eighth. Both had spawned four times.

The largest steelhead examined by Mr. Sumner while he was living in Tillamook County was a 41 inch, 25 pound male. Its life history is worth breaking down, for it offers a cycle not yet discussed. The five-year-old fish had spawned after two years in the ocean, had successfully returned to salt water, *but had not returned to spawn the next year.* It rather ascended during a second year of ocean residence. This is most unusual, for invariably steelhead annually spawn again and again until old age or predators overtake them. Of the many Tillamook Bay steelhead examined, only two had skipped a year between spawnings. No steelhead is known to have passed more than two years at sea before spawning a second time.*

3. THE COLUMBIA RIVER

Though the Columbia is our largest western river and its rivers are many and its steelhead number in the hundreds of thousands and call three states home, they are steelhead that show a remarkably clear summer-run, winter-run geographic preference. It can be said that nearly all steelhead passing beyond Bonneville Dam are summer-runs, and most below are the winter-run variety. The principal winter-run exception above Bonneville is Oregon's Hood. Important summer-run rivers below the dam are Washington's Washougal and Kalama.

The winter-run race will average slightly more in weight. As a maximum weight, the two are equal and either represents the largest of their races found in the United States with the possible exception of Alaska.

The first summer-run steelhead appear at Bonneville as early as February or as late as November while their greatest numbers pass the dam in June, July, and August. Most are bound for the upper Columbia and Idaho's great Snake River. To reach those upper Snake River spawning beds requires as much as 800 miles travel from the sea.

---

*The Tillamook Bay tributaries were closed to gill netting steelhead in 1957. See Chapter 6 — "Commercial occupancy of our rivers."

The majority of returning fish have spent two years in the Columbia watershed before migrating to the ocean where usually one, two, or three years will be spent. Though said to average eight to nine pounds, they actually fall into three divisions contingent on those one, two and three or more ocean years. One-year-ocean steelhead average 22 inches, two-year average 27 inches and seven pounds and three-year 33 inches and something over ten pounds. Commercial and sport fishermen have caught these summer-run steelhead weighing over 30 pounds and more than 40 inches long. Sport fish records are discussed in another part of this book, but it should be pointed out here that the American record for steelhead was a 35½ pound summer-run specimen caught from the Oregon side of the Columbia River just below McNary Dam on September 19, 1970, by Berdell Todd of Milton Freewater, Oregon.

No percentages are available on Columbia River four-year-ocean fish, but based on the outsized steelhead this river has produced, we can presume it is at least competitive with other Oregon and Washington rivers. A select group of 31.5-36.0 inch steelhead caught from the lower Columbia were aged by scale analyst F.H. Sumner. Four of the fish were found to have 3/4 life histories.

The slightly heavier weights of the winter-run are due more to the extra few months of sea life available to them before they spawn than to any other life history advantage.

The Cowlitz must first be mentioned when listing capital winter-run steelhead rivers. Others include the East Fork Lewis, Elokomin, Washougal and Kalama in Washington and the Willamette and Sandy Rivers in Oregon. The Cowlitz has been the principal beneficiary of the Columbia's great winter steelhead and at this writing it claims the Washington State winter-run record, a 32 pound 10 ounce steelhead caught by Clifford Aymes in 1971.

On February 14, 1963, Mike Bodine caught a 27 pound 15 ounce steelhead from the East Fork of the Lewis River. This trophy of a lifetime, unlike most such fish, had a scale sample expertly "read." It was only in its fifth year, having spent three years at sea for a 2/3 life history. The size this fish reached in three years is astonishing. The 2/3 life history is represented in California, but no fish of comparable weights have been found, yet further investigation will hopefully explain why.

4. WASHINGTON

Not only does Washington have its full measure of Pacific running rivers from Ilwaco on the Columbia to Cape Flattery in the Makah Indian Reservation, it has scores of rivers that first meet an interior sea. The Strait of Juan de Fuca separates the Olympic Peninsula from Vancouver Island and leads to the Strait of Georgia and Puget Sound. The "Sound Country" is an endless series of quiet bays and coves that tranquilizes metropolitan Washington. The statistic minded claim if Washington's coastline was drawn to its full length, it would reach from home shores to the Atlantic.

The many rivers that derive their source from either the Cascade or

Olympic mountains would be far better known in any other place—sheer numbers disguise individual assets. The Green River between Tacoma and Seattle offers a case in point. It annually blesses its ardent followers with 20 pound steelhead yet it is little known beyond Washington's borders.

It was the Green that served as a site for that most thorough investigation of Washington steelhead by Clarence F. Pautzke[5] and Robert C. Meigs[6] in 1940 and 1941.

The Green River is felt to be representative of Puget Sound rivers. A sampling of 1941 returning fish showed these percentages of ocean years:

> 12.8% one-year-ocean fish
> 65.0% two-year-ocean fish
> 20.0% three-year-ocean fish
> 2.0% four-year-ocean fish
> _____
> 100%

from year to year. If the three- or four-year percentage increased for any given year, anglers realized this increase by taking a greater number of trophy steelhead. There apparently is no pattern to this, but it definitely does exist. The year before, an identical sampling illustrates this difference:

> 8.0% one-year-ocean fish
> 61.0% two-year-ocean fish
> 28.0% three-year-ocean fish
> 2.0% four-year-ocean fish
> _____
> 100%

The three-year-ocean "trophy" category is almost 40 per cent greater in 1940 than in 1941. Allowing for this year-to-year variance, the figures for Washington's Green River are for all practical purposes identical to those of Oregon's Alsea.

Complete life history figures from a study conducted by Ralph W Larson and John M. Ward show a general statewide consistency.[7] The Green, Chehalis, Hoh, and Cowlitz were the rivers investigated, with the Cowlitz having a definite large steelhead edge.

---

[5] Pautzke, Clarence F., and Robert C. Meigs. Studies on the Life History of the Puget Sound Steelhead (Salmo gairdnerii). State of Washington Department of Game, Biological Bulletin No. 3, 1940 — 24 pp.

[6] Meigs, Robert C., and Clarence F. Pautzke. Additional Notes on the Life History of the Puget Sound Steelhead (Salmo gairdnerii). State of Washington Department of Game, Biological Bulletin No. 5, 1941, 13 pp.

[7] Larson, Ralph W., and John M. Ward, "Management of Steelhead Trout in the State of Washington." Transactions of the American Fisheries Society, Vol. 84, 1954. page 261-274

Steelhead By Area

Freshwater and saltwater winter checks on scales of steelhead trout caught in the sport fishery of the Green, Chehalis, Hoh, and Cowlitz Rivers. (Percentage of total sample in each group)

	Green 1940	Green 1941	Chehalis 1948	Hoh 1949	Hoh 1950	Cowlitz 1947	Cowlitz 1948
1-1	0.0	1.5	0.0	0.0	0.0	0.0	0.0
1-2	10.0	12.8	4.0	0.0	2.0	2.0	4.0
1-3	6.0	5.9	5.0	3.5	0.7	10.0	8.0
1-4	0.0	0.0	0.5	0.0	0.0	1.0	1.0
2-0	2.0	1.0	0.0	0.0	0.0	0.0	0.0
2-1	4.0	9.4	7.0	3.5	1.3	3.0	2.0
2-2	52.0	51.2	66.0	77.9	71.1	63.0	52.0
2-3	17.0	8.4	15.0	10.5	17.5	19.0	26.0
2-4	0.0	1.5	0.5	0.0	0.0	0.0	0.0
3-1	3.0	4.4	0.0	0.0	0.0	0.0	1.0
3-2	4.0	3.4	2.0	4.6	6.7	1.0	5.5
3-3	2.0	0.5	0.0	0.0	0.7	1.0	0.5

Three-year steelhead—2/1, 1/2—were found weighing from 2.5 to 7.25 pounds. Four-year steelhead—2/2, 1/3, 3/1—weighed from 4.75 to 11.25 pounds. Five-year steelhead—2/3, 3/2, 4/1—weighed 5.5 to 18 pounds. Finally, the six-year steelhead—3/3, 2/4—weighed from 5.5 (a single fish fully spent) to 20 pounds.

Investigation has shown that while not all four-year-ocean fish reach 20 pounds, the vast majority of Washington steelhead 20 pounds and over have spent four years at sea.

The largest steelhead caught during the 1964-65 Washington steelhead season weighed 28 pounds 6 ounces and came from the Wynooche River, a tributary of the better known Chehalis. A scale analysis completed on this fish revealed it was seven years old, having spent three years in fresh water for a 3/4 life history. The Larson and Ward study showed no fish of comparable age and the life history is atypical for Washington. This is not the case, however, in British Columbia.

5. BRITISH COLUMBIA

There is a marked change in the steelhead's life history when we go to the Fraser River and its tributaries. One is the Chilliwack, joining the mother river about 60 miles from Vancouver.

The principal British Columbia study of steelhead life histories was conducted on the Chilliwack.[8] Scale samples were collected by anglers at the request of the British Columbia Game Commission. The age composition of steelhead resulting from an evaluation of 784 different

[8] Maher, F. P., and P. A. Larkin, "Life History of the Steelhead Trout of the Chilliwack River, British Columbia." Transactions of the American Fisheries Society. Vol. 84, 1954, pages 27-38.

scale samples gave these percentages (first and second spawnings combined).

2/2	31.1%
2/3	30.7
3/2	17.7
3/3	17.3
1/2	1.0
1/3	0.8
3/4	0.4
4/3	0.4
2/1	0.3
1/1	0.1
2/4	0.1
3/1	0.1
4/2	0.1
	100+%

No figure less than 0.1 per cent is given even if this represents a single fish. Because all age groups are represented by at least this amount, the total per cent is actually 100.1.

Chilliwack River steelhead serving an ocean residency for one or four years comprise less than one per cent of the total. If the percentages for the years at sea are combined, the total steelhead population can be divided into two main groups:

1/2	1.0%	1/3	0.8%
2/2	31.1	2/3	30.7
3/2	17.7	3/3	17.3
4/2	0.1	4/3	0.4
	49.9%		49.2%

Average lengths and weights were 27½ inches and 7½ pounds, and 32 inches and 12 pounds. One-year and four-year ocean steelhead averaged 18½ and 35 inches; size extremes for the total population were 10-40 inches.

The size of Canadian steelhead can better be appreciated if we refer back to California for a moment. Waddell Creek: one-year-ocean—46.4 per cent, three-year-ocean—less than one per cent. Chilliwack River: one-year-ocean—less than one per cent, three-year-ocean—49.2 per cent. Because of this great increase in the three-years-at-sea category, which is at the expense of the half-pounder population, the Chilliwack River steelhead will average heavier than those in Waddell Creek, indeed, heavier than any river's steelhead yet described.

The other half of the steelhead's life history also shows some remarkable differences. While pre-migrants generally spend two years in fresh water before migrating to sea, there are still considerable numbers that stay a single year or descend shortly after their yolk sacs are absorbed. The Chilliwack is peculiar in the almost total absence of these groups. In their place are pre-migrants spending three years in fresh water. An evaluation of 770 smolts in downstream migration revealed that 2 per cent were one year old, 62.1 per cent two years old, 35.4 per cent three years old, and 0.5 per cent four years old. These figures clearly explain why there are so few repeat spawning steelhead in northern waters. Nearly 100 per cent of all pre-migrants spend two or three years in fresh water before migrating to sea. When this longer period of river residency is paired to the longer uninterrupted years of ocean life, we find that the steelhead are quite old when their initial spawning trip is completed. For example, almost 70 per cent of the Chilliwack's steelhead would be at least in their fifth year. Compare this figure with California's Waddell Creek where more than 75 per cent of all steelhead are four years old or less when spawning for the first time. The greatest repeat spawning success comes from steelhead spending one year at sea before returning to spawn. They will return to the ocean as either two or three year olds. But these are age combinations (1/1, 2/1, 1/2) almost totally lacking on the Chilliwack River. With rare exceptions, the life expectancy of a steelhead will be seven years. This would put a Canadian steelhead that has spawned at the end of a fifth year late in its sixth year if ascending a second time. Having initially spawned so late in life, old age simply overtakes most before a second spawning can be attempted.

The life histories listed in the first part of this section show no repeat spawning steelhead. Actually, the few steelhead shown as having spent four years at sea are all second spawners (2/4 = 2/3S.1S and 3/4 = 3/3S.1S). Because these fish were in their sixth or seventh year, no steelhead were found spawning more than twice.

However, steelhead seven years old (3/4, 4/3) at the time of their first spawning have been caught from the Alouette, Coquiltlam, Cheakamus, Seymour, Capilano and Cowichan rivers. This implies a widespread Canadian distribution of these older and larger steelhead.

HOW LARGE?

We have seen the life history trends as we proceed north and the size advantage that results, so it is the steelhead heartland, British Columbia, that must be searched for the ultimate steelhead. Alaska is not being considered because so little is known of its steelhead. Information available, however, indicates size laurels may still, in the final analysis, go to British Columbia.

Little scientific study has been done on rivers north of the Chilliwack, and here I speak of great steelhead waters like the Dean, Kispiox and Babine. The Skeena River area is the only known place where 20 pound steelhead can be angled for with any expectancy, and where there is a very real possibility of one over 30 pounds.

Call it artistic license if you want, but based on the range of latitudes and data that have led us from California to British Columbia, I will take what I would hope to be some competent guesses regarding the life histories of these steelhead. Any river consistently averaging steelhead larger than ten pounds could conceivably produce these fish in a variety of ways. The steelhead may be able to survive a number of repeat spawnings better than fish in other areas and thus live to a much older age. They have found an ocean area with a superabundance of food. The extra size is a genetic trait. Life histories have continued to shift toward longer periods uninterrupted by spawning. Of the four possibilities, I think the first three may be discounted. First, longevity records are not found in fish that are "old" when they spawn for the first time. Secondly, all high seas sampling at this writing has shown a general mixing of the races though further investigation may show some racial selectivity. And lastly, steelhead have never shown a true genetic advantage—at least life histories are not transferred when eggs are hatched in distant watersheds. More probably, "traits" in the river set steelhead for an expanded ocean residency.

Left with the fourth possibility, and working only within those life histories already encountered on other rivers, a reasonable explanation as to why these British Columbia steelhead reach such an incredible size can still be offered. These steelhead will tend toward a salmon life history: years in rivers, years at sea, a final migration, spawning, then dying before spawning again.* Repeat spawners will amount to a very small percentage of the whole. Life histories would likely be 2/3, 3/3, 2/2, 2/4, 3/4, 4/2 and 4/3. Popular California life histories such as 1/1 and 2/1 would be rare, if found at all.

There is no saying how large a steelhead could grow within the confines of three or four ocean years. Washington is not a place where world record steelhead are now found, and I know of but three western Washington rivers that have given up sport-caught 30-pound steelhead. Jack O'Neil of Seattle took a 30-pound 4-ounce steelhead from the Olympic Peninsula's Humptulips River in 1969. A steelhead just over 30 pounds came from the Quinalt River in 1970, and on January 1, 1971, Albert English landed a 30-pounder from the Skagit. Yet a discussion with an elderly Hoh River Indian revealed that years ago a 36-pounder was taken on a hand line from the Hoh and sold commercially. In a like manner, the Kispiox and Babine River Indians have gathered from their net a few steelhead over 40 pounds and claim to have caught them to 50 pounds (never substantiated).

If this seems a bit hard to believe, Robert T. Baade, a fisheries biologist for the State of Alaska Department of Fish and Game in Ketchikan, told me that dressed steelhead weighing 45 pounds have been incidental catches in the Alaskan seine fishery. Because it is unlawful to take steelhead by means other than rod and reel in Alaska, such fish usually go unreported and are served-up on the galley table.

---

*A fascinating scenario begins with 30-35 pound steelhead, showing 3/4 or 4/3 life histories, spawning and returning to the sea. While unable to ascend their natal streams again, they wait out their remaining months on the high seas, getting larger and larger and . . .

Winter steelhead angling on Washington's Puyallup River

Taking a deep breath and ready to duck the brickbats, I would give the top steelhead weights as 20+ pounds, California; 30 pounds, Oregon; 35 pounds, Columbia River; 30+ pounds, Washington; 40 pounds, Fraser River and southern British Columbia; and 50+ pounds, Skeena River and northern British Columbia.

There is always the possibility of a steelhead heavier than these weights. But year in and year out, they are the size ceiling, and while a number of outsized steelhead come quite close to the listed weights, they are weights almost never topped.

6. ALASKA

As might be expected in our sparsely settled 50th state, steelheading is little advanced in the settled areas and virtually unknown in the great civilization voids that is present day Alaska. This retardation is due more to city placement than any lack of angling enthusiasm. The Alaska panhandle is the British Columbia coast north of the Skeena River. Protecting this coastline and its many unexplored rivers are any number of coastal islands forming an Inland Passage. The Alaskan timber and salmon cities of Ketchikan, Wrangell, Petersburg and Sitka settle the islands. Only boats connect the cities or the cities to the mainland and the game is salmon unless the small island streams are fished. Even Juneau is no less remote—no roads leave to penetrate the interior.

Little scientific study has been accorded Alaskan steelhead. However, salmon surveys conducted by the Fisheries Research Institute at the University of Washington determined that spring, fall and winter-run steelhead ascended most of those Alaska sockeye salmon watersheds where lakes form part of the river system. On non-accessible lake systems or on rivers where there are no lakes to interrupt progress, the steelhead tend to ascend in the spring only.

57

A small number of scales were evaluated in the Ketchikan area and showed a predominance of 2/2 steelhead weighing an average of four to eight pounds. But older fish, repeat spawners and precocious males were reported. This sample population did not include representatives from mainland rivers that very possibly receive larger fish.

The information on mainland steelhead is scanty and the best of this centers on the Anchor River near Seward in the Kenai Peninsula. While I will be describing steelhead runs farther west than these, the Anchor run represents one of the most northern of all steelhead races.

This unpublished life history information was collected and sent to me by Sidney M. Logan, Area Management Biologist for Alaska's Department of Fish and Game in Seward. The classes encountered were as follows:

Age	Average length	Range in length	Average weight	Range in weight
2/0	17½ inches	15−18 inches	1.9 pounds	1.4−2.4
2/1	23 inches	21−26 inches	5.3 pounds	4.0−6.4
2/2	28 inches	23½−31½ inches	8.9 pounds	7.0−12.8
2/3	(one fish)	35½ inches	17.1 pounds	−

Here, the 2/1 category has been separated from the 2/0 age class—juvenile steelhead migrating downstream in the spring and returning in the fall.

Most smolts were observed averaging 6.5 to 9.0 inches at the time of downstream migration. The returning adults ascended in September and October with a few coming on in November. A true winter-run is not known to exist. Spawning took place in the spring with spent fish showing in the lower river from May 15th to June 15th.

Kodiak Island's Karluk River near the village of that name is understood to an unusual degree for that area, and may offer a reference for other Gulf of Alaska island streams and south flowing Alaska Peninsula rivers.

The Karluk is the major steelhead stream on Kodiak Island. Though the run has of late declined, the Karluk Indians have for years taken 3,000-5,000 steelhead annually for subsistence. An additional 100-200 are caught by sportsmen each year.

The U.S. Navy stationed on Kodiak formed the Kodiak Conservation Club and initiated an egg collecting, hatching and stocking program using Karluk rainbows. Besides the Karluk, lakes and streams throughout Alaska were stocked. Results were discouraging and the program terminated. This has been Alaska's only artificial propagation attempt devoted to steelhead.

Steelhead ascend in September and October, dividing themselves so that some continue to Karluk Lake and spawn in its tributaries while others spawn in the lower Karluk River. Spring for either group is late April and May; spent steelhead are encountered in June.

(Detailed 1953-1959 Karluk River field records with lengths and scale sample histories were stored in the main Kodiak office and lost to the May 27, 1964, tidal wave.)

Richard Marriott, regional biologist for Alaska's Department of Fish and Game sent me data that gives some idea of what ages comprise Karluk's steelhead. On 17 steelhead examined, 15 were females, a disproportionate ratio probably due to the late spring sampling. The fish ranged from 22.8 to 33 inches and were three to five years old. The majority had spent two years in fresh water, the remainder but one year. This is unusual because of the absence of three- or four-year-stream fish, the ages we would expect from a river so far north.

The Dog Salmon River on Kodiak also supports a fine run of steelhead that follows a like seasonal timetable. They are larger, averaging 32 inches and about 12 pounds. Steelhead ascend Ayakulik River and waters tributary to Saltery and Buskin Lakes; little specifically is known of these runs. The Paul's Lake system on neighboring Afornak Island supports fall-run steelhead. Undoubtedly there are other rivers on Afognak and Kodiak that support steelhead.

The Kodiak rivers are presently the westernmost waters positively identified as sustaining steelhead populations.

BERING SEA STEELHEAD?

Ed Clark's fishing camp is reached by first flying to King Salmon in the Alaska Peninsula. A bush plane takes 35 minutes to fly the balance of the trip to the 2,500 foot runway near Lake Illiama and the mouth of the Kvichak River. A boat transports anglers to an island lodge comfortably equipped with electric lights, oil heat, indoor plumbing, and two large freezers for trophy trout. The freezers are needed.

Illiama is a lake of legend. A few miles away, nature's more perverse efforts have created the Valley of Ten Thousand Smokes where acrid yellow vapor pours from ground holes and the land rests on geologic uncertainty. Here too, amid bleak desolation, is Katmai Crater, a mountain in 1912 that blew its top to dust with one cataclysmic effort. The skyborn outpouring of the earth's vitals trapped air and fell as pumice. There are miles of it. In this setting is the nearly sea level lake that bottoms more than 600 feet in places. At 100 miles long and about 35 miles wide, it is Alaska's largest lake. Hair seals live in Illiama, so do sockeye salmon, and a "mystery fish" that were the area better known would vie with the Loch Ness Monster, "bigfoot," and the Abominable Snowman in modern mythology. Below the lake surface swim shadows longer than seals; bush pilots stare in wonderment. Sharks, whales, sturgeon and pike for Finn McCool have been offered as explanations. Whatever, they are part of the Illiama scene, a scene that plays its best with the giant rainbow trout.

Biologists have long wondered if some of the lake and river rainbows are migratory steelhead. This separation, if there is one, seems academic to the angler at the optimistic end of a smashing strike.

THE STEELHEAD TROUT

"We catch steelhead as early as September 15th," says Ed. "Most of the steelhead come in from the Bering Sea and travel up the Kvichak River and into Illiama Lake. There are several small streams where they go to spawn. The main run of steelhead go up the streams between October 1st and November 30th. They seem to spawn in April and May, as do our rainbow trout.

"Over the last 18 years, the steelhead have averaged 12-14 pounds. We have caught steelhead up to 21½ pounds. My neighbor caught one of 22½ pounds, and we have lost many big ones which broke 20 and 30 pound test lines even though we had 265 yards of mono on our reels. During the fall of 1963, I had out a small party of three and we all broke lines. I played one for an hour and this beautiful fish jumped six times and looked like all of 30 pounds; that was my guess as I lost him on the sixth jump.

"Water in the Kvichak River is very cold. As the steelhead approach the lake, but while still in swift water, they jump and chase herring up and down the beaches.

"Two years ago we had an invasion of lemmings. They were migrating to sea. I caught a nice steelhead with six lemmings inside. Looks like they will hit anything that moves."

Several years ago I sent a number of flies to Ed—2's, 1's and 1/0's for the most part. They took many fish, and though tied on regular hooks, were either broken or straightened.

Ed Clark, who lives in nearby Naknek, Alaska, draws a clear distinction between his steelhead and rainbow trout. Biologists are not so sure there is such a difference, or that the area even contains steelhead.

The Fisheries Research Institute at the University of Washington is responsible for the best of what research has been conducted on Illiama and Kvichak River rainbow-steelhead.

If these rainbows are migratory, the steelhead's range can be extended to north of the Aleutians. This would be a radical departure from their presently understood ocean distribution. Investigators aboard high seas research vessels have noted a migratory consistency which keeps the steelhead south of the Aleutians. It would seem from their summer congregation in this area that a few must pass between the islands and beyond to the Bering Sea. Yet none have been netted there (see "Japan," Chapter 4).

There is a commercial fishery in Kvichak Bay. Steelhead ascending the Kvichak River in October and November, or spent and descending in May and June, should encounter this fishery. They do not. Their absence from ocean nets still does not preclude the possibility of a migratory species.

The most telling proof has come from a scale analysis of Kvichak River rainbows. They show ages and growth periods quite foreign to those associated with anadromous rainbows.

Scales from four Kvichak River rainbows caught in August and September, 1963, by Kline Hillman, Seattle, Washington, were evaluated by fishery research biologist Kenneth H. Mosher. The estimated ages were as follows:

1. 24 inch female, seven years old. The fish had apparently spent three years after hatching in a tributary of Illiama before migrating to the lake. It had spawned at least three times.

2. 32 inch female, seven years old. It had first spent four years in a tributary before moving to the lake. No spawning "checks" were found.

3. 32 inch female, 12 years old. The trout had lived six years in a tributary before moving to the lake. It had spawned at least four times.

4. 29½ inch male, 10 years old. It had a stream residency for five years before moving to the lake.

Their periods of tributary and lake residency are longer than our steelhead knowledge might accept. The age breakdown, though, is not unlike a steelhead's stream/ocean years. But scale annulus rings at no time show the broad spaces indicative of the rapid ocean growth found in the steelhead's life history.

There are several reasons why these steelhead colored lake rainbows move to the Kvichak River. Illiama is a sockeye salmon lake and supports great numbers of these fish in their pre-migrant stage. Like the rainbows of Idaho's Pend Oreille (though they are both land-locked), the Illiama trout feed ravenously on the young sockeye. In May and June these smolts begin their downstream migration. The rainbows follow, feeding as they go.

Fresh water herring also inhabit the lake. During the summer they migrate to the Kvichak River and there spawn. As Ed Clark pointed out, the rainbows are in hot pursuit the whole way.

The lake rainbows are naturally destined for the Kvichak River in the fall to spawn. It seems probable the rainbows are drawn from the lake proper as the summer proceeds. Those following herring and salmon will stay to join later arrivals and then spawn. This may explain why the Kivchak can at once contain rainbow-like rainbows and steelhead-like rainbows; a river spawning residency affects the lake rainbow's coloration much as it does the steelhead's.

Information presently available cautiously places the Kvichak rainbow in the resident category. Disclaimers to this theory may well have their day. Biologists are not ready to concede that among the Illiama and Kvichak trout there cannot be some Bering Sea steelhead.

CHAPTER SIX

A Trout And Salmon Heritage

1. AN AMALGAM OF THE BEST ENGLISH AND DOMESTIC

England's yardstick for angling excellence has usually been cost and social position. Most good waters being privately owned, the prospective angler needed to rent a "beat" or join an organization doing so. The expense depended on one's tastes and pocketbook. Generally there were, and still are, two primary angling routes which follow the two main classes of fresh water fish in England. "Course fish" that can be taken on rod and reel, whatever the bait and method, include tench, bream, barbel, rudd, dance, grayling and fish more familiar to American anglers: the carp, chub, perch and pike. They constitute the bulk of English fishing efforts. The other group, called "game fish," is the salmon and trout, occupying that angling niche reserved for royalty among people. Prime trout waters commanded a premium price; salmon rivers of note were beyond the means of any but the wealthy. The brown trout *(Salmo trutta)* in all its many forms, and the almost incomparable Atlantic salmon *(Salmo salar)*, form the English fresh water gamefish list. The developing efforts to catch these two species were the principal reason for fly fishing. Those techniques that evolved, and the myriad of fly patterns conceived, were the consequence and foundation of our own angling heritage.

Early America contained all the rivers England's landed aristocracy has been so chary to part with. We too had a trout and the Atlantic salmon. The trout—phylogenetically a char—became our beloved brook trout. They thrived in the many icy waters that once passed freely to the sea along our eastern seaboard. These fast flowing streams maintained trout averaging two pounds, a size that compared with today's "put and take" trout, seems beyond belief.

The brook trout had a shortcoming only too well appreciated: the terribly accommodating manner in which they struck bits of fur, feathers, and tinsel no matter what the arrangement. Fishermen caught them in appalling numbers while fly tiers, no longer inhibited by English rules of imitation, produced colorful wet fly "attractor" patterns that met both aesthetic inclinations and certain desires of the fish. The closest we have come to a renaissance of this gaudy dress period must be the boom in present day steelhead flies.

The eventual establishment of proper game laws would have done much to offset the results of such gluttony were it not for the ruination of the rivers themselves. Water powered much of the nineteenth century economy. It powered lumber mills that were the end result of massive deforestation, and textile mills that returned· the favor by pouring back tons of foul pollutants into the same rivers. Angling pressure, pollution and rising water temperatures resulting from a lack of streamside cover eliminated the beautiful brook trout from the angling scene.

If such manifestations of the industrial based eastern United States were to spell swift decline for fine trout fishing, it was also to mean immediate disaster for the Atlantic salmon. It is an anadromous fish, returning to the river of its birth to reproduce. The erection of but a single saw mill dam in the lower reaches of a river broke the cycle, for it blocked the two or three generations still at sea and those juveniles in the eventual process of downstream migration. Four to five years was sufficient to bring total extinction to a river race of salmon. The Denny River in Maine offers such an example. At the turn of the century, the Denny was considered the finest Atlantic salmon river in America, held in even higher esteem than the famed Penobscot and St. Croix. A large lumber mill was built in 1900 and put in operation at tidewater. The resulting dam blocked not only salmon, but also anadromous shad and alewives that had helped support local economies. The destruction of the river birthplace of salmon sport fishing in America, the Denny having produced a fly killed salmon in 1832, was complete by 1901.

To this gradually increasing sport fishing vacuum came the brown trout from Europe. Fred Mather, a New York conservationist and fish culturist, had first met German friend Von Behn while attending the 1880 International Fisheries Exposition in Berlin. Three years later, the two arranged for the exporting of 80,000 German brown trout eggs aboard the liner *Werra*. These safely arrived and were successfully hatched by Mather at Long Island's Cold Spring Harbor hatchery. Further importations followed to combine with transplants from the original shipment. This began establishment of the brown trout in New York and Pennsylvania. Possessing a greater tolerance for adverse water conditions than the native brook trout, the cunning "brownie" required more sophisticated angling methods, and fly patterns more in keeping with the naturals became a continuing trend.

While brown trout filled eastern streams and creels, fishermen waited for still another gift from the "old country."

The dry fly is English in origin and dedicated to the brown trout. Its genesis rests in the soft flowing chalk streams of the Hampshire district and came not as a sudden realization, but rather was the result of its propounders eroding the pureness of long established wet fly beliefs. Foremost iconoclast was Frederic M. Halford. He entered during dry fly infancy, fought for its begrudging acceptance and watched it flower to become embraced with a revolutionary fervor. Those once held in distain or as a curiosity now became the haughty elite of piscary.

In 1890, Halford received a letter from America's Theodore Gordon requesting information on this dry fly development. Carried with Halford's answer was a generous sampling of duns and spinners imitating the best of a carefully sexed entomological roll count. The flies sent, with floating qualities as ephemeral as the insects they represented, needed to be tailored for the more violent waters found in America.

Gordon was to convert many of our wet flies to dry fly status and, with Edward Ringwood Hewitt, George LaBranche, and others, develop completely new patterns that closely simulated or vaguely represented natural insects. Our dry fly beginnings start with these men, their experiences and developments.

2. A PROBLEM WITH NOMENCLATURE

The many stages of Pacific salmon and races of western trout were not initially understood and carried names bearing little in common with their ancestry. Early observers, like easterners years before, transferred nomenclature and angling *modus operandi* to the circumstances found prevailing. They named what they saw before them "trout" if the fish were trout-like and seemingly residential, or "salmon" if the fish were salmon-like and migrating upstream. That the two groups could overlap, that some residential trout were salmon, and some ascending salmon really trout were not commonly realized.

The pre-migrant salmon and rainbow trout, cutthroat, resident rainbow trout and usually Dolly Varden char were counted as trout. The salmon were the returning adults of Pacific salmon and the steelhead trout.

The trout were first labeled with location names. Those caught in mountains were simply called "mountain trout." "Brook trout" referred to any trout in small streams. Another means of identification listed the watershed in which a particular trout resided.

Western trout and salmon, however, were certainly not without their early scientific discoverers. The Pacific salmon were first distinguished by two exacting Russian naturalists, Steller and Krascheninikov, in 1731. Johann Julio Walbaum's continued study, 1791-92, of the salmon he encountered in Siberian waters put the different species on a sound scientific footing. And in 1861, George Suckly described the new genus for Pacific salmon, which he named *Oncorhynchus,* meaning "hooked snout."

The steelhead was first noted by Dr. Gairdner in 1833. He was a physician and promising young naturalist employed by the Hudson Bay Company operating at Fort Vancouver along the Columbia River. The specimen gathered from this river was sent to noted English naturalist Sir John Richardson. It was first described and listed as a new species of trout in Richardson's *Fauna Boreali-Americana,* published in 1836. To honor Dr. Gairdner, the trout was named *Salmo gairdneri.* *

*Richardson gave it the vernacular name "Gairdner's salmon," and thus compared it with Salmo salar, the Atlantic salmon. Confusion arose when S. gairdneri was thought of in terms of Pacific salmon.

Fauna Boreali-Americana was also the first scientific mention of the cutthroat trout *(Salmo clarki)*. Thus by the second half of the nineteenth century, the two trout and five species of salmon indigenous to western North America had been carefully observed and officially categorized.

Other discoveries were to follow but they confused rather than clarified the nomenclature. The next was by Dr. William P. Gibbons of San Francisco and came on March 19, 1855. Dr. Gibbons, founder of the then fledgling California Academy of Sciences, received three trout, each about five inches long, from Mr. Nevins. The fish had come from San Leandro Creek near the present town of that name in Alameda County. Because of the obvious lateral line of iridescent pink, the fish was given the name *Salmo iridea* (changed to *irideus* by David Starr Jordan in 1878), which roughly translated means rainbow trout.

For almost half a century following Gibbons' discovery, the rainbow and steelhead were considered individual species. Early California game laws drew a clear distinction between the two; seasons and creel limits were separate for each. A few did think they might belong to the same species. David Starr Jordan and B. W. Evermann in their monumental work, *The Fishes of North and Middle America,* published by the Smithsonian Institution in 1896, mention that *Salmo gairdneri* is "perhaps not seperable from *Salmo irideus.*" But at least into the 1900's, *Salmo irideus* was California's pre-migrant and coastal "resident" trout and *Salmo gairdneri* her migratory steelhead.

An interesting story concerns a San Bernadino, California, angler in 1909. He had been arrested for taking trout on a Bear Valley stream in April, a month open to steelheading but closed to trout fishing. The gentleman contended the fish were steelhead, the prosecution could not prove otherwise, and his case was dismissed.

Another California "rainbow species" that must be mentioned is the "Shasta trout." First described by David Starr Jordan in 1894 from McCloud River specimens, *Salmo shasta* became the rainbow trout of the fish-culturists and for years was propagated by state and federal agencies. Many Shasta trout were stocked in California's coastal rivers simultaneously with steelhead smolts. Californians gradually understood that returning steelhead were the same species as the stream dwelling *Salmo irideus.* What was not appreciated was the percentage of these trout destined to mature in salt water. Just as early biologists could not conceive that *all* salmon died after spawning, 1900 observers would not believe that *all* coastal rainbows migrated to sea. Certainly a considerable number must remain behind to take up permanent residence. It was these "stay-behinders" that stocking supposedly augmented when introducing the Shasta rainbow. We now realize that not only do all coastal rainbows migrate to sea, but so do resident Shasta rainbows or any race of rainbows if given a sufficiently open and obvious route to salt water.

Any confusion or vacillation among biologists over the proper identification of our trout sometimes reflected itself as a lack of vernacular consistency among anglers.

Because laymen first placed the steelhead with our salmon, the common name "steelhead-salmon" was most appropriate. *S. gairdneri,* was sometimes called "Gairdner's trout," a name of limited application appearing for the most part in textbooks. And almost from the beginning, the steelhead was nicknamed "hardhead." A number of other names, fixing themselves to both trout and salmon, came into early use.*

The Columbia River fishing industry helped perpetuate the term "salmon-trout." Originally it extended to include any large trout in coastal waters and the steelhead canned for export. In time it applied to just about all our fish that could possibly be called salmon. Like steelhead-salmon, the salmon trout term was descriptive for any fish that appeared salmonlike. But it worked the other way too. Puget Sound commercial fishermen once used it when marketing (surely on a very limited basis) pre-migrant chinook and silver salmon. Salmon-trout also described those trout that followed or were believed to follow ascending salmon for their loose spawn. These were the steelhead grilse and sea-run cutthroat. Though this steelhead age group is no longer called salmon-trout, the cutthroat is, especially in the fall. I might add that in Oregon the cutthroat was and still is called a "harvest trout" because their upstream migration coincides with that time of year. The Dolly Varden as a sea-run variety were called salmon-trout in Alaska. Salmon-trout and "land-locked salmon" once referred to rainbows in Oregon's Williamson River. Even today the term salmon-trout sometimes refers to under legal size salmon caught in salt water.

Before migrating to sea, the pre-migrant steelhead was usually called a rainbow. When the trout season opened, spent steelhead could be caught in large numbers. Because of the coloration change a spawning steelhead undergoes, it was thought of as simply a very large resident rainbow trout. Washington followed just such a nomenclature route.

"Rainbow," in Washington, referred to either pre-migrant steelhead or steelhead caught during the trout season no matter what their size. The ascending steelhead was called a steelhead-salmon by many anglers and commercial fishermen, but was listed as a salmon-trout in the fish and game laws. On July 12, 1914, A. A. Cass caught a 26½ pound "rainbow" from Washington's Skykomish River. It was listed as a rainbow trout record and stood for many years. Obviously it had matured in salt water and qualified as a steelhead but was considered a rainbow because of the season. That record was exceeded on January 6, 1930 when E. E. Ames took a 29 pound steelhead from the Chehalis River. This, however, was a steelhead record, again because the season determined the "species." So Washington once held two all tackle world records for the same species.

---

*The origin of the name "steelhead" is not clear. The extremely hard bones in the skull and coloration of this trout when it is a fresh sea-run fish have been both suggested as origins of the name. However arrived at, the name was in common usage in the Nineteenth Century.

Only three discoveries pertaining to the rainbow trout have been discussed. There were many more during the period. Jordan and Everman's *The Fishes of North and Middle America* lists almost 40 species of western trout and char. The three, though, came to be considered "type species" — all other rainbow and steelhead species were descendants of these. To sum up the rainbow's taxonomic position by 1920, we can say that there were three major divisions: 1. *Salmo irideus* was the coastal rainbow trout south of the Rogue River. Steelhead over the same range were considered "steelhead of the *Salmo irideus* type." 2. *Salmo shasta*, the Shasta trout or Shasta rainbow, represented California's interior. It was the type species for all resident rainbow trout in California. 3. *Salmo gairdneri* was the steelhead with a range from southern Alaska to Oregon's Rogue. Some biologists included all permanent lake and river residents under *S. gairdneri*. A principal exception and point of argument for many years was the Kamloops trout, first described by Jordan in 1892.

Our salmon too, were blessed with a colorful variety of local names. Two that early applied themselves to the largest species included first, "quinnat," originally a non-specific Indian name referring to all the salmon ascending the Columbia River. It gained particular favor in California long after becoming archaic in its place of origin. The other is the more familiar "chinook." Those Indians with this anglicized tribal name dominated the Columbia River inter-tribal salmon trading "industry" and sought this fish for its great size. Both "quinnat" and "chinook" were in common usage by the 1880's.

"Sachen" is an Algonquin Indian term meaning chief or chief of a confederation. It periodically referred to the chinook until the 1900's.

A Columbia River commercial title for the chinook came about as an incentive to purchase the cans which contained the epicurean delights. No longer chinook, but ROYAL chinook, the can's testified. This early bit of marketing genius was undoubtedly appreciated more by vain anglers than shop-wise housewives. Used in the early years of the present century, it is rarely heard today.

The chinook was "king" to Washingtonians because it described the largest of our salmon; it was not an outgrowth of "royal" chinook. King is also the name the chinook goes under in present day Alaska. British Columbia prefers "tyee," a Siwash Indian word meaning chief. Spring salmon, another name for the chinook of Canadian origin, is now widely used where they are found ascending rivers in the spring. The Tyee Club of Campbell River is more definitive in the use of tyee; they apply the name only to those salmon exceeding 30 pounds.

"Silver" salmon is shortened from the original vernacular name "silver-side" salmon. The silver is also called "coho," in British Columbia.

Briefly reviewing the remaining species, we find the pink (flesh color) salmon called "humpback" because of the disfigurement its body undergoes as spawning approaches. The chum salmon has the lowest market value of our five species. It is often referred to as a "dog" salmon which alludes to the canine-like teeth that develop just before spawning. And finally, the sockeye of the Frazer River and Puget Sound, the Quinault salmon of that river in Washington, the Columbia River blueback salmon, and the redfish, red salmon, and red Alaska salmon are all terms applying to the same fish.

As more species of western trout were discovered (as late as 1930, 40 species of trout and char were listed in the U. S. Bureau of Fisheries *Check List of the Fishes and Fishlike Vertebrates of North and Middle America),* they were placed in one of three "groups": rainbow, steelhead, and cutthroat.

It became increasingly clear during the 1930's that steelhead occured wherever rainbows had access to the sea, no matter what the species. To be sure, this theory did not meet with universal acceptance, but California had first considered it such with *Salmo irideus*. In this regard, the name steelhead was more properly a *characteristic* than an actual species. Many felt there were but two rainbows: *Salmo irideus*, representing the coastal pre-migrant and returning steelhead, and *Salmo shasta*, the non-migratory rainbow. "Steelhead" could then relate to any trout or char that contained a salt water stay in its life cycle. Steelhead chars from British Columbia's Nass, steelhead cutthroat from Washington's Skagit, and steelhead rainbows from Oregon's Nestucca or California's Garcia would serve to identify the habits of the species. This maddening piece of taxonomic juggling left some nomenclators complacent and the angler's lexicon a general disaster area. Fortunately, the name steelhead survived to relate only to anadromous rainbows.

There was a general agreement after World War II that decided upon the single species concept and reverted to the first scientific name for the steelhead, *Salmo gairdneri* (containing the numerous non-migratory rainbow races). The term was not chosen because the rainbow was this "type" or that "true species," but because *gairdneri*, as a scientific name, applied first and was adequately described by Richardson.

3. COMMERCIAL OCCUPANCY OF OUR RIVERS

Laws to protect and perpetuate our fish were a natural reaction to their capture. The salmon's commercial value was an unassailable fact over a century ago. So, too, was the knowledge that it would never be economically feasible to capture pre-migrant trout and salmon on a large commercial scale. Two groups then, not just trout and salmon, but commercial and non-commercial came into early existence. Fish favored commercially are not necessarily incompatable with an angling minded citizenry, for salmon, shad, and striped bass are taken in satisfying numbers by both parties. The criteria for placing the fish in one or both groups should be plain. Will the fish have sufficient market value? Does the gamefish have greater value to the state if caught by sporting methods than on a so much per pound basis? And where will the fish be intercepted by either fisherman? Gradually, rivers became the sole property of the state's residents while the sea showed no such discrimination. Past prejudices and no viable method of commercially securing juveniles, placed stream trout in the gamefish column. There, as a non-commercial fish, they were subject to all the protective measures a state's conservation-minded agencies would enact at the behest of their conscience and constituency.

Long before our salmon's sporting qualities were appreciated, industry had filled millions of cans for export in the Sacramento and Columbia River commercial trades. So no teeth knashing was required to place the salmon under regulation, thereby protecting them from either interest group. The steelhead was quite another matter. Initially, they had little sporting value. When netted with salmon they violated no revered angling trust. Their commercial capture ran contrary to fishing interests only when their full value was realized: taxonomically — they are not Pacific salmon, and practically — the steelhead are great gamefish.

Except for the Sacramento, California's inland commercial salmon fisheries were negligible. Small coastal rivers put to commercial use with drift and set nets usually served only those immediate local needs. Much the same can be said for our coastal towns. Troll caught salmon were quickly marketed fresh, for lack of refrigeration prevented their transportation to distant areas unless salted or canned — and the fishing was too seasonal to support canneries. An exception to this could have been the Eel, the one river that rivaled the Sacramento in size and fecundity.* But by the time an increasing population would have made practical a Sacramento size industry, and the railroad had tied the area with trade arterials (the Eel was too shallow to negotiate by ship), laws had already been passed putting the possibility in the realm of permanent conjecture. California's legislature, with remarkable foresight for the time, aligned itself behind the steelhead. Laws were established for their preservation, any type of net on rivers were outlawed (I think state-wide by 1915), and stocking rivers with pre-migrants was started.

Washington and Oregon had much in common regarding the steelhead's status. Both states had recognized its commercial value through long years of successful netting on their mutual Columbia River border. And each was slower than California in coming to recognize the steelhead's angling value. These states classed the steelhead a food fish if taken by commercial license, or a sport fish if caught on hook and line. Because of the commercial emphasis, steelhead were called "steelhead-salmon" and placed with salmon in their fishery management programs.

The Rogue River was almost unknown beyond Oregon's borders in 1910. By that year, however, residents in the area of Grants Pass to Gold Beach had begun to appreciate this great river as an angler's haven. Even though it had been the site of at least one Hume cannery,** the Oregon legislature declared the steelhead-salmon a trout on the Rogue

---

*Apparently a weak start was made at salmon canning on the Eel. In 1883, 920 dozen cases of salmon were exported from Eureka.

**William, John and George Hume with Andrew Hapgood started the Columbia River fishing industry in 1866. By 1890, these four Maine natives were operating 20 canneries on the Columbia alone.

Photograph by Eric Carlisle

in 1914. As a trout, the steelhead was now protected under the trout creel limit of 30 fish per day or 20 pounds. The latter weight limit would hold a daily catch of fall Rogue steelhead to approximately four fish per angler.

The salmon to trout move did much to establish the myth of Rogue River steelhead supremacy. Anglers came to feel that somehow intrinsic in the water and geography of the country were contained intangibles only this salmonoid race was able to exploit. Admittedly, steelhead in this river enjoy certain peculiarities in their life history not found elsewhere, but they are no more "steelhead" than other anadromous rainbows.

As an Oregon salmon, the steelhead was not protected — other than on the Rogue — until 1917, when a three fish a day limit was established for any species of Pacific salmon caught on hook and line.

Following the Rogue, there was a general tightening of commercial fishing laws and a gradual reduction in the number of rivers open to netting. The Nestucca River after March, 1927, was closed to commercial fishing. The Rogue was closed to all netting in 1935 because of the difficulty in taking only salmon and not steelhead — both ascend during the fall. It did not prohibit all commercial fishing. Chinook salmon could still be caught on lures until 1938 when the river was closed altogether to commercial interests. The Salmon and Umpqua Rivers were closed to commercial fishing in 1947. As laudable as this trend was, it still allowed for the seasonal plundering of steelhead on many fine rivers. Finally, a 1957 state-wide initiative petition was passed that closed all Oregon rivers except the Tillamook and Columbia to commercial fishing. The Tillamook, open only for chum salmon, was closed in 1961 after that salmon's numbers had rapidly declined. In all fairness it should be pointed out that chum salmon are given to considerable population fluctuations. Their decline in the Tillamook — and the resulting closure — possibly was not due to commercial netting.

From 1890, steelhead in Washington landings were always recorded as steelhead-salmon and for many years were an important addition to the commercial salmon industry. A sharp curtailment in 1921 left only the Indian reservations and the Snohomish and Skagit rivers still open to steelhead netting. The 1925 legislative session closed all rivers to Whites for commercial purposes by declaring the steelhead and salmon gamefish "above a point established by the director of fisheries as the mouth of any river or stream."

The steelhead's conversion from salmon to trout, from food fish to gamefish, is now nearly complete.

On the Columbia, where it really all began, one can still see boats seeking the steelhead and salmon. Laws prevent us from pressing all but this river into commercial service. Netting steelhead here should also be a non-returnable passing.

4. PACIFIC SALMON AND THE FLY

More than a few moving West took along their fishing equipment and angling acumen. Unnamed rivers and uncountable trout awaited their arrival. With high hopes, they put rivers to the fly — bright colored brook trout dressings that would find a permanent place on these waters while going into decline on the new brown trout rivers of their origins. The rainbow found the attractor patterns to their liking and complemented the fishermen's efforts.

Our pre-migrant steelhead were consistent in their small size, yearly spring abundance, and summertime decline. On many of these early streams that became a traditional meeting ground for angler and trout, the complaint was often heard that they were "fished out" by summer. Most of those legal fish escaping the best angling offered had migrated to sea, resulting in an obvious but then puzzling depletion of waters which had abounded in trout a few weeks before. The one trout that initially seems to have been angled for and taken with traditional techniques was the sea-run cutthroat. So sporadic in its anadromous habits as to approach residency on some waters, the cutthroat offered anglers a type of coastal angling that was quickly comprehended. More than the steelhead, they showed a willingness to strike the attractor patterns then being introduced.

If the trout occupied the angler's efforts, the salmon occupied his thoughts. The salmon by the very nature of his ascending habits was easily secured by every foul means. Yet to "properly" angle for these fish, and this meant with the fly, was a terribly unsuccessful experience. Alternate methods, thought by many to be only slightly better than the "Dupont spinner," were used.

71

An eating spoon which accidently dropped off Julio Buel's fishing boat into the clear waters of New York's Lake Bomoseen in 1834 apparently proved fascinating to a nearby pickerel. Buel's reaction to the accident brought about a patent in 1838 for a lure appropriately called a "spoon." The lure became a favorite in the more remote regions of the West for it could be fashioned out of any shiny metal. The Wilson and Kewell-Stewart spoons from San Francisco became local adaptions of Buel's original. Using this lure, chinook salmon were "spooned" for on many California rivers and a few Columbia River tributaries like the Willamette.

The spinner was designed and refined by John Hildebrandt in the 1890's and did not initially become popular for salmon, possibly because of the spoon's better casting qualities. It was, however, a mania on the Rogue in two distinctly local methods. But again, salmon, by name alone, implied the use of the fly. The road to success meant persistence, experimentation and empirical development of effective patterns which involved new methods. In other words, the fault lay not with the fish but with the fishermen. When the right combination was found an angler's Valhala would be realized. All these efforts were directed at the chinook salmon that by way of its size was referred to as "king of the salmon" and "big brother to the Atlantic salmon." It had been made a member of the scientific community under *Oncorhynchus* years before, yet the chinook's supposed close relationship to the Atlantic salmon persisted and is seen in the laymen's early use of *Salmo Quinnat.*" An example of man's eagerness to transplant name from the old and familiar to the new and unknown? Yes. But westerners were finding to their woe that fly striking habits do not transfer in a like manner.

All dressings then in vogue for either trout or Atlantic salmon were used in a futile attempt to raise chinook to the fly. In the last decade of the nineteenth century the spoon's use surpassed that of the fly in salmon fishing. Its sometime success and the salmon's lack of interest in flies seemed all the more paradoxical. Indeed, once interest in the spoon was a proven fact anglers felt they were on the right track. They reasoned that if a spoon worked then certainly a zealously tinseled fly like the Silver Doctor or Dusty Miller would also attract. It should have but did not. The use of trolled baits in salmon fishing began in the 1880's. The realization that salmon would strike a salt water bait and not a fly suggesting bait in fresh water was an additional dose of bitterness.

One hope did prevail. There were very few west coast fishermen with any first hand experience in taking Atlantic salmon. And the fly methods used in capturing this gamefish differed in many important respects from those employed for trout. What was needed was a man expert at this other game. When all the right moves were made success would naturally follow and this dour Pacific giant would be elevated to its proper place atop fly fishing's hierarchy. To this purpose came noted New York attorney and famed Atlantic salmon angler Henry P. Wells.

He had fished the great rivers in Canada and New England, authoring his knowledge in *American Salmon Fishing,* 1886, and *Fly Rods and Fly Tackle,* 1885. Also, it was Wells in 1878 who gave us the Parmacheene Belle trout pattern.

Henry Wells worked our rivers in the Atlantic salmon manner with all the skill at his command, but the quinnat salmon he had traveled so far to catch were unresponsive. Even so, his trip was not a complete failure. July 12, 1889 found Wells on "Klalamas Creek," a tributary of the Columbia some eight miles from Portland, Oregon. Above a weir by the Clackamas Station hatchery, a school of "steelhead-salmon" was found. They rose freely to the fly, and a dozen averaging eight pounds were caught. Wells was not impressed either by the salmon's appearance or performance — they were but a poor consolation. He returned East convinced quinnat salmon would not rise to a fly no matter how it was offered, and that steelhead were anything but members of the *Salmo* family in the great Atlantic salmon tradition. But it had been an odd stroke of luck that had permitted Wells to even take the steelhead. The weir completely blocked the river; it held chinook salmon in one convenient spot until they could be netted and stripped of eggs for the nearby hatchery. Its closure apparently followed the year's main steelhead run. When they reversed themselves to begin their return to the sea, downstream escapement stopped at the weir and the steelhead had languished for weeks. They were starved and their capture was like shooting ducks in the proverbial rain barrel. Nevertheless, Henry Wells' trip did indicate that at least one Pacific salmon, the "steelhead-salmon" was not above taking a swipe at a fly.

The most publicized attempt to take quinnat salmon with a fly took place the same year Wells was on the Clackamas. And ironically, Rudyard Kipling fished the same river. Kipling traveled the wild West in his discovery of America and being a fisherman and Englishman to boot, he saw to it these Pacific salmon he had heard so much about were given a good go with English flies and techniques. The reported results of his trip differed considerably from those of Wells. Kipling had fished for the quinnat salmon with a fly and the fish had avidly struck the offering. The story created great excitement among fly anglers who had long dreamed of harnessing this enormous fishing potential. That a man not a westerner should accomplish this feat was bad enough, but to have an Englishman do it was an ego shatterer for chauvinistic locals. Questioning the veracity of Kipling's claims was the initial reaction, wondering how he did it the second. It seems Kipling was either the victim of some fine though unauthorized public relations work, or the degree of paranoia among anglers ran high enough to let the fly part of his adventures become paramount. For years the story was told and retold but contained some mention of a spoon or fly attached to a spoon being used instead of a fly alone. Wishful thinking? Mr. A. N. Cheney, editor of New York published *Forest and Stream* wrote about Kipling having taken Pacific salmon with a fly "and the suspicious admission that a spoon was later lost in the game." The article was read by R. B. Marston, editor of the London *Fishing Gazette.* He clipped the story out for republication. First, though, he sent the clipping to

Kipling for any comment the writer might like to make. Mr. Marston received the following reply:

> Dear Mr. Marston:
> In the language of the immortal Jorrocks, Spoon! Spoon! Spoon! "Fly" is a slip of the rod. Those brutes won't rise to it.
> I return the cutting.
>
> Sincerely,
Rudyard Kipling

This correspondence took place in 1899, 11 years after the actual event.

It was to be pointed out by Thurston L. Johnson, Dr. F. Cauthorn, president of the Multnomah Rod and Gun Club, Harry Eldridge, C. F. Sliter and others residing in Portland, that if Kipling had only persevered, he certainly would have succeeded in rising salmon to the fly. They had done it a number of times and would like to make a correction in Kipling's story. The fish Kipling had caught, and the fish they too had caught in the spot mentioned, were not quinnat salmon, but spent steelhead-salmon. Johnson and Sliter had hooked ten of these salmon about the time Kipling was there. "The fish were," said Johnson, "from two to three and a half feet in length and weighed from 15 to 40 pounds, and it took a person from 20 to 40 minutes to land one if he was lucky enough to do so." Johnson is surely heavy in his weight estimates. But this is really not the point. While the circumstances encountered by both Wells and Kipling were most unusual, their efforts would not have been rewarded were it not for the steelhead . . . salmon.

As the recipient of such attention, the Clackamas gained local fame as a place where "salmon" could be angled for with flies. A letter by W. F. Burrell of Portland is included in Mary Orvis Marbury's *Favorite Flies and Their Histories, 1892,* and illustrates this point.

> Salmon fishing with a fly, in the Clackamas River, a tributary of the Willamette, was a new experience for us last spring. My brother, Herman J. Burrell, now of Moscow, Idaho, was quite successful in fishing there, and if you ask him, he can perhaps give particulars about the kinds of flies and tackle used. It was the first time salmon had been known to take the fly in Oregon or Washington fresh waters."

It is interesting to note that the fish are called "salmon" and no specific species is given. However, when a species was recalled it was the steelhead, the only salmon that would cooperate when using a fly.

Angling for salmon in salt water began and matured in the early 1880's. Steelhead sport fishing developed ten years after the salmon sport fishery, however it was met with and paralleled the equal enthusiasm on the part of westerners.

Two writers of letters, each residing in San Francisco during the

1890's, corresponded by writing of their experiences and submitting them to the editor of *Forest and Stream* magazine. Their comments allow us insight into the early development of steelheading as we know it today. It was common practice in the somewhat false modesty of Victorian times to write under names often indicative of their theme yet dramatically mysterious. A few of the era appearing in *Forest and Stream:* Juvenal, Special, Tunero, Hackle, Grizzly King, Senor X, A Social Tramp, John Leasure, Lone Angler and Starbuck. One of our writers, representing the average western angler still trying to fit his fishing into eastern molds, is called Pogers, his actual name. The other gentleman is urbane, experienced, and unusually well informed about the scientific conceptions then in vogue. He goes under the cryptic and most apropos non-de-plume of "Steelhead."

Concerning that burning question whether Pacific salmon would take the fly, Pogers, in August, 1899, wrote to *Forest and Stream* relating his experiences on the Navarro River. It was then an almost unknown river meandering through California redwoods and meeting the sea near Albion. Pogers thought he might have taken salmon on the fly; his letter elicited the following reply from Steelhead:

> "His story is certainly interesting to all fishermen, but did he catch any salmon in the Navarro River? That is the question. I am satisfied that he thinks he did, but I believe he was taking steelhead trout, and not salmon. The writer has never fished the Navarro River, but has fished the estuaries of similar coast streams to the north and south of the Navarro, and believes that he is familiar with the fish that run in these waters."

At this point we may marvel at our writer's understanding of steelhead as a *trout*. But wait, Steelhead continues:

> "The steelhead *(Salmo qairdneri)* is the most common of all the Quinnat salmon *(Oncorhynchus tshawytscha)*. The salmon of California does appear for a very limited time in the Navarro River in late November or during December, according to the season."

"Quinnat" is the chinook salmon *(O. tshawytscha)* and a generic term encompassing all Pacific salmon and the steelhead. As Steelhead continues, "quinnat" becomes specifically the chinook.

> "The steelhead trout, which is known to more people as salmon, enters the estuaries of all the coast streams as early as September, and is found in all the streams during the winter months. The steelhead is a large salmon-like fish, running in weight from a few pounds to 20 lbs. The Quinnat salmon that enters Mad, Eel, Matole, and Navarro rivers average 20 lbs. in weight. The run of Quinnat salmon in the Eel River greatly exceeds the run in any other California coast stream save the Sacramento. Their run in the Navarro is insignificant, while the run of steelhead trout is large. The fish taken in that river with nets are sent to

the San Francisco markets, and very few Quinnat salmon are to be found in these shipments.

Now, the steelhead will take the fly both in the estuaries and in the streams from September to February, though very few of the large steelheads can be taken in that way, while I have never known but two Quinnat to be taken with the fly in the Eel River. I have visited that stream several times, and have talked with many fly fishermen who go there every year, and can only find authentic testimony of the capture of two Quinnats with the fly. They will occasionally take a spoon and I have seen many of them taken that way in the Eel River and in the headwaters of the Sacramento and McCloud rivers, and in Battle Creek. I have never known a Quinnat to be taken with a fly in the Sacramento or McCloud, or in Battle Creek, save for a few grilse from the McCloud River, and they seldom exceeded 3 lbs. in weight.

From Pogers' communication I am of the opinion that he caught steelhead trout, and not salmon, and would suggest to him that next time he catches fish in the Navarro River he send one of them to Dr. Jordan or Dr. Gilbert of Stanford University, and let them determine the species, for even so accomplished a sportsman as Podgers could easily mistake a large steelhead trout for salmon."

Steelhead mentions that steelhead were most commonly called "salmon." They were also called "steelhead-salmon" in California. However, continued use of either salmon or steelhead-salmon was not of the extent found in Oregon and Washington. This, as we have seen, was because of the longer commercial importance of the *steelhead as a salmon* in these states.

Pogers quickly answers in a letter dated October 18, 1899. Addressing his comments to the editor of *Forest and Stream,* he writes:

"After reading his experiences in fishing for salmon in the waters of California, I think it is quite possible that his conclusion is correct. The distinction he explains is not generally noticed, as we are so much in the habit of calling the fish salmon without investigating the points of difference in variety. To the non-scientific fisherman this nice point of difference does not detract from the sport of catching them, for they are fully as gamy and afford as much sport as would result from capturing the bona fide slamon.

"But when it comes to a question of Pacific Coast salmon taking the fly, I am willing to admit that Steelhead has apparently the best of the argument, and that is the question under discussion. Steelhead's experience is certainly greater than mine, as I have fished for salmon only in the Navarro and St. Cloud rivers. In the latter I only used salmon roe for bait, never having tried the fly there except for trout. Whether the so-called salmon I caught in the St. Cloud were real salmon or steelhead I am not sure, since reading Steelhead's article. Whether it is the salmon proper that I have been catching can be easily settled by acting on his suggestion by submitting a specimen to Dr. Jordan the next time I visit the Navarro if I be successful. I am curious now myself to learn what variety I have been catching. Not that it will detract from the sport if I find that my salmon are proven to be steelhead, for I shall enjoy the fishing just as much, and it is only the question under discussion whether the Pacific salmon do or do not take the fly. From

Steelhead's experience I am beginning to waver in my belief that they do – at least only in exceptional instances.

"In all my fishing I have given little heed to the scientific question of variety of the differences between tweedledee and tweedledum – as great a shock as the confession must be to the scientific sportsman. I don't mean to admit that I don't know the difference between a chub and a trout; but when I hook a 10 lb. steelhead and he is giving me lots of fun I do not lose my interest in him by stopping to consider whether he is a real salmon or only first cousin of the aristocrat. He has all the habits. He fights as well, eats as well and I stand up for him, even if he may be considered a little off color by the scientific fisherman, who scorns to fish with anything but a Leonard rod and a 12 dollar reel and babbles of the Ristigouche as the fisherman's Mecca. There is a good deal of good fishing outside of the Ristigouche, and good rods that Leonard did not make, and good flies that have not high-sounding names; and here, too, is where I'm going to shock the scientific fisherman by declaring that I never want a better fly nor any other variety than a red hackle with a peacock body, and a miller, for all-round work. I have tried all the fancy varieties, and settled down to these, and I never get left.

"I remember reading in the *Forest and Stream* an article about salmon fishing and suggesting that a larger fly would perhaps be an inducement to them. I tried that dodge. I had Conroy make me up a lot of large flies, assorted, and with as great an assortment of colors as you see in a woman's bonnet, but although I tried them all I never had a rise. All the salmon (I beg Steelhead's pardon for so calling them) were caught with the old reliable brown and red hackle and I bless the chanticleer that grew the hackle. The time was when I spent money on a gorgeous array of flies, and expensive fly books, but I have discarded the lot and left to the moths. In all books of flies there is one or more of the red ibis. I have heard fishermen say they have caught fish with them, but in thirty years fishing I have never caught a fish with one, and likewise with many of the other fancy flies, the like of which are never seen in nature, and which trout look upon with wonder and omit the experiment of trying them. All of these beliefs will of course shock scientific fishermen, who will set me down as unworthy to be called a true sportsman. Nevertheless, I manage to bring home a basket pretty well filled without a financial transaction with a small boy with the proverbial tow string and pin hook, or without calling at the market on my way home."

Fishermen (even "scientific fishermen") were being required to evaluate past prejudices and Podgers has done this. His defense of steelhead at the cost of sounding like a heretic to the "true salmon" fraternity indicates angling of evolving values.

Steelhead's reply is quite long. He explains what he knows about each of our Pacific salmon and trout, and then ends his letter with these remarks to Podgers:

"The salmon of the East or of Monterey Bay, where you find him at his best on the Pacific Coast does not equal a fresh run steelhead – a fish that has just entered fresh water from the sea – as a game fish. No, Podgers, when you hook and are playing a steelhead, don't lose your interest in him because he is not a salmon, for he fights better, "eats at will," and you are right to "stand up for him," for none of the sportsmen that I know consider him a "little off color." He is a worthy object of pursuit and the angler who lands one on light tackle may well be proud of the achievement, and when he has brought him to gaff or "beached" him should remove his hat and say, "Steelhead, you have no peer in fresh water," for not even his full brother, the rainbow trout, over which the scientists have so long puzzled their brains to find a distinguishing difference, is more game than he. And again, Podgers, let me tell you that no section in America offers you better sport in fresh water than your own California, when it permits you to take the steelhead in tidewater with hook and line at any time. Have you ever been surprised that so few of the anglers in California know anything of this fishing?

The Quinnat salmon is never so game and interesting a fish to fish as the steelhead. In my opinion, none of the Pacific salmon are game fish. True, many of us enjoy trolling for them in Monterey Bay, but they are "not in it" with fresh-run steelhead. There is more sulk in the Pacific salmon than fight. No Podgers, it does not detract from the sport you so enjoyed on the Navarro to find that you were taking the steelhead and not the salmon. I almost envy you the recollection of that trip, but you are welcome to all the remembrances that come to you from catching the Pacific salmon, for I have caught a few of them in different waters on the Pacific Coast and I would swap all of them for one good play with a clean-cut and immaculately pure steelhead.

And one thing more, Podgers: Don't neglect that red ibis fly when you go for steelheads, for they are fond of it – especially towards evening. This past season it was a prime favorite on the Eel River. I have used it often, and next to a large Royal Coachman it has attracted the most fish. And don't be afraid of using large flies for the steelhead; but, as Mr. Mather would say, "That is another story."

We see in Podgers the last gasp of eastern bias. Steelhead's pragmatic approach to his fishing promises Podgers he is on the right track. Those that followed discovered the steelhead in much the same way.

5. A STEELHEADING HERITAGE

The Eel River anglers of Eureka, California, gave us our steelheading birthplace. They were the first to set their calendars according to the steelhead's ascending habits, and the first to intercept them with flies of their own design that were of lasting importance. As a consequence of these efforts, the Eel became the first of our western waters to gain a national reputation specifically as a steelhead river.

The Eel's dressings were, in the main, the result of local tailoring done on standard eastern patterns which in turn were a curious medley of the conservative English and the flamboyant New World. The flies from this admixture, made their way across the continent and underwent further testing. They breakdown into three basic types: English flies with added brook trout exuberance, English flies unchanged from their tradition-bound beginnings and flies that evolved

78

as products distinctly American.

The Royal Coachman originated by John Haily in 1878 would head any list of western trout patterns in 1900. Any order after this is debatable so the reader may judge the merit of the whole list and not the ranking of individual patterns. I would pick Henry P. Wells' Parmacheene Belle next. It was first used the same year that the Royal Coachman originated. Close to these two in national esteem was the Scarlet Ibis, named for the bird whose feathers contributed to its construction. A fly of indeterminate lineage, the all red Ibis begot a multitude of bastard creations as the tastes of the intended gamefish and fly tier demanded. These three were domestic inventions; the balance is English and English inspired. It includes first the Coachman, developed by Tom Bosworth during the 1830's. The oldest of all flies is the hackle variety and variations are legion. Westerners preferred the Brown or Grey Hackle to supply their needs. The Professor was given to us by John Wilson of Edinburgh, Scotland, about 150 years ago. His brother, James Wilson, is said to have first named the Grizzly King at approximately the same time. The Governor, an English fly brought to America in the nineteenth century, completes our list. These, then, were the best of an eastern fly heritage sent West. Our first Eel River steelhead patterns were the result of alterations within these color combinations, with the first four on our list predominating.

The sizes used were the same as those most commonly employed for trout over much of the country. Though anglers on many hard fished waters were beginning to appreciate the value of "small" flies in sizes 12 and 14, 8's and 10's were most in demand, particularly in the remote regions of the West. These were to become the "Eel River size" for steelhead flies. Larger flies were then not nearly so effective, probably because of the Eel River's unusual clarity.

John S. Benn, creator of the famed Benn's Coachman, was born in Malta, County Cork, Ireland in 1838. At the age of 17 he immigrated to America and settled in San Francisco. Sometime in the 1890's Benn moved to Eureka and had a home built on the Eel a bit upriver from Scotia. He was an ardent steelheader and spent his spare time tying flies commercially for Eureka residents, a trade learned while living in San Francisco. His dabbling in fly design led naturally to the Coachman, perhaps because of "old country" affiliations. Benn felt the fly needed more red and to this end added a scarlet hackle tail and middle wing of red. Using this dressing, called Benn's Coachman, he took many steelhead and the first fly caught chinook salmon from the Eel. This last feat, coming at a time when it was felt that hooking salmon on a fly was impossible, did much to set the pattern apart and elevate it to required fly status when fishing the Eel. Though there is no positive connection, the two "quinnat" salmon mentioned by "Steelhead" as having come to a fly on the Eel were probably caught by John Benn. The pattern was first used in the late 1890's and headed all Eel River fly lists during the 1900's.

Another Benn steelhead fly was the Martha, named for his daughter. It remained very popular for more than 30 years. Not until the advent of hair-wing patterns in the 1930's did this fly's use decline.

It is fitting that a man born and raised in Eureka should have originated the first great western steelhead fly. Sumner Carson, son of lumber magnate William Carson, used the Royal Coachman for his basis of change. Just as Benn had done, he added a third wing of red between the two of white for a Parmacheene Belle appearance. The tail was changed from one of wood duck to golden pheasant tippet. Called the Carson Royal Coachman and later shortened to simply Carson, it was in use by about 1900.

Sumner Carson's heritage was Eureka's and needs telling. His father was born in New Brunswick, Canada, in 1825, where he was the son of an exporter of lumber to Liverpool, England. William grew up to join his father's business. Such a familial status quo would have remained intact had it not been for the California gold rush. Joining with other young seekers of fortune, William Carson embarked on the ship *Brazilian* from The Ledge, New Brunswick, on September 18, 1849. The trip to San Francisco lasted until April the following year. After temporary employment in that city, Carson departed for Sonoma, Mexico, to gather horses that would carry supplies into the gold fields. He summered and searched for gold in the Trinity River area. When winter drove him from the diggings, he turned his efforts toward supplying Martin White's new Humboldt Bay sawmill with logs. After one more uneventful prospecting season, Carson returned to the more lucrative lumber business. He moved to Eureka in 1854. Nearby flowed the Eel River with a watershed that passed through the greatest stands of timber the world had ever seen. With a keen understanding of the lumber business and a deft handling of frontier trade, William Carson contributed more than any in establishing the Redwood Empire.

Sumner Carson lived in the city his father built. The Eel River was his backyard; he came to know all its moods, strengths, and shortcomings. Most importantly, Carson understood, as only a fervent angler can, the habits of the fish that yearly ascended his river. The Carson pattern was an outgrowth of this long residency.

The affluent of Eureka who possessed like fishing interests formed a private organization called the Sand Bar Club. Each Wednesday they took the Northern Pacific to Scotia and met at their club house just up, from famous Fernbridge Pool.* Mr. Soule, president of the Bank of Eureka, was a member and had developed a steelhead pattern that won immediate acceptance. The fly was called the Soule and differed little from the Parmacheene Belle. Like the Carson and Benn's Coachman, it had a middle wing of red primary strip. Several years later the Soule was altered by leaving red out of the tail and wing, and omitting the yellow floss body for one entirely tinseled silver. The Soule dressed in this manner was called the Silver Bell. Its originator is unknown. The

---

*Then called Gregg Pool in honor of the Gregg party that first discovered the river many years before. The party happened upon a small band of Indians collecting eels from this section of the lower Eel and named the river accordingly.

Soule was first used in the early 1900's and remained a popular Eel River pattern for many years.

Josh Van Zandt, well known Eureka sportsman, originated the Van Zandt, a 1900 steelheading standard on the Eel. It had a Coachman peacock herl body but was otherwise identical to the Scarlet Ibis.

From the fly book of "Mr. Soule" — the earliest steelhead flies known to the writer; years are approximate. Row 1, Soule (1890), Martha (1900), Humboldt Railbird (1920); row 2, Silver Bell (1915), Van Zandt (1890), Kate (1925).

Two other early Eel River steelhead flies bear little relationship to our original dressings, but then neither was ever intended for use on eastern trout. The first is the now familiar Railbird. Two men had a hand in its development. John Benn tied the original while living in San Francisco. The name Railbird came from the use of clapper rail flank feathers as a winging material. This was a dove size marsh bird then plentiful in the Bay area. The fly had a red tail, claret wool body and yellow hackle, probably tied palmer. It came into use about 1890, though perhaps earlier. At the time it was a trout fly and not specifically intended for the little understood steelhead. When Benn moved north to the Eel, the pattern's continued development was taken over by Jim Hutchens of Eureka. Because the clapper rail was not normally found so far north, drake mallard flank feathers were substituted. The tail was changed from red to yellow and jungle cock hackle sometimes shouldered the fly. The dressing's tail has remained its least consistent feature. Today, the fly is often called the Humboldt Railbird and has a red or claret tail, claret body palmered with claret hackle, a yellow hackle face and wing of either mallard or silver squirrel tail. The Jim Hutchens version, one which made the pattern famous for steelhead, was first fished about 1900. More than a decade passed before it became an Eel River favorite.

The last of the flies under discussion is the Kate, a nineteenth century Atlantic salmon fly used in Ireland and England. It was invented by Mr. Flynn, a game keeper for the Duke of Devonshire, whose responsibilities included overseeing the Duke's water on the Black River. The fly was used on the Eel unchanged from the original. Almost never tied locally, it was exported directly to Eureka from Hardy Brothers in Alnwick, England. The Kate was found in most Eel River fly boxes from about 1910 to the 1930's.

These flies were the new standard of excellence by which the taking properties of other patterns would be compared. The men who developed them and the water upon which they were used, became the fountainhead of our modern steelheading heritage.

6. OREGON

"The rivers and streams of water in said territory of Oregon in which salmon are found, or to which they resort, shall not be obstructed by dams or otherwise, unless such dams or obstructions are so constructed as to allow salmon to pass freely up and down such rivers and streams."

This paragraph from Oregon's 1848 territorial laws clearly shows the value put on salmon. Idealistic and positive in tone, it set the course for future management.

From earliest pioneer beginnings, Oregon won the unqualified devotion of hunter and angler. But more than Washington and far more than California her commercial fishing advantages have come in conflict with gamefish considerations. "Commercial occupancy of our rivers" described the excruciatingly slow placement of a commercial ban on Oregon rivers beginning with the hypocritical steelhead salmon-to-trout status of the Rogue rainbow in 1914. A remnant of this problem can still be seen in the commercial netting of steelhead on the lower Columbia, an annual practice looked upon with dismay by upriver Idaho steelheaders. This separation of the steelhead as a game and food fish began with Oregon's first general conservation act, "an act for the protection of game and fish," effective January 21, 1873. Game was offered a modicum of protection, and by amendment the following year, a closed season for the taking and selling of trout was legislated. It did not prohibit the sale of "brook" and "mountain" trout, residential or migratory, and only gave a closed season for the commercial taking of these fish during their spawning months.

There was no bag or size limit until 1899 when minimum size was set at five inches and a daily creel take limited to 125 trout. That same year the first Oregon fishing license, a $10.00 non-resident, was required. When the first statewide license was effected in 1909, the non-resident fee was dropped to $5.00 and resident license set at $1.00 for men only. Women were not required to have a fishing license until 1923.

The sale of all game was prohibited in 1905. This included the rainbow but not the steelhead. The trout limit reached more conservative proportions with the reorganization of the Oregon Fish and Game Commission in 1910. Daily limit was then set at 30 fish or

20 pounds.

Beginning with the legislative protection of trout in 1905, groups affiliated with the Oregon Fish and Game Commission began working toward the establishment of gamefish hatcheries. Though Washington and California maintained an active hatchery system to aid trout populations, Oregon had refused to spend a single cent for this purpose. It was not until 1912, when Oregon already had 18 salmon hatcheries and its citizens had for three years been financially supporting its game commission, did the legislature vote money for a trout hatchery.

The best Oregon fishing in 1906 from the standpoint of fish size and degree of angling endeavor was that practiced by spoon fishermen on the Columbia River streams, especially the Willamette and its tributary, the Clackamas. The latter was the site of Oregon's first government hatchery in 1877, with Livingston Stone its superintendent. (The first hatchery in Oregon was built by the Oregon and Washington Fish Propagating Company in 1876. It went out of business in 1880, probably as a result of the new government hatcheries supplying the same service without direct cost to commercial interests required to replenish salmon runs.) The Clackamas sport fishery had gone a long way towards discovering the steelhead – epitomized by Henry Wells and Rudyard Kipling – but the river was most ardently worked for its spring and fall runs of chinook salmon. Electric streetcars carried fishermen from downtown Portland almost to the river bank. And when the fish were in, many a businessman ended his day spooning for Clackamas salmon with an eight foot split cane bait-casting outfit.

An angling method unlike any other evolved on the Rogue late in the past century. Tackle consisted of a tremendously long bamboo pole of some 20 feet with guides tied in place and a reel taped about three feet from the butt end. To the end of the line was attached a six foot piece of gut which tied to a brass spinner. The lure was extended by violently jerking the rod back and forth until the desired distance was reached, sometimes more than 100 feet. The spinner would fall on the water, drift downstream, and swing across the current. When a strike occured, the fish was hauled out and dispatched with a minimum of fanfare. Originally devised as a deadly way of taking steelhead, the bazarre method's future was assured when Rogue steelhead could be caught commercially only by hook and line.

The lower Rogue contained a basaltic river bottom where water and time had eroded long grooves. Conventionally drifting spoons or baits through these slots was impossible. To catch chinook salmon here a distinctly local type of "plunking" developed. Piers, called "salmon boards," were built 20 to 30 feet out from shore. The same bamboo steelhead outfits were used, except fishermen changed to a large star drag reel. A triangular shaped "spreader" with a loop at each corner was tied to the reel line. One loop secured four feet of line to a heavy sinker and six feet of gut connected the remaining loop to a brass spinner. The spreader kept the lure and lines from tangling and the long rod correctly placed the whole affair in the mill race channel that worked the spinner furiously.

Both of these colorful methods are no longer used. Toward the end of their era, they were held in special contempt by visiting anglers. Those who had come so far and expected so much were thoroughly deflated when watching locals armed with these outfits snatch fish after fish from the river that sportsmen "owned" by way of expensive equipment and endeavor.

7. WASHINGTON

Crisp weather in March, 1907, made the April 1st opening of trout season a propitious one — streams were without melting snows to flood and discolor. Fishermen had put their equipment away when the season closed November 1st, so the enthusiasm for wetting a line increased during the five month angling lapse covering Washington's wet and blustery winter. Now warmer rains and a higher sun would help make trout fishing the fizz in springtime's effervescence.

Favorite fishing grounds were sought. Seattle anglers with families in tow could take a short streetcar ride to Lake Washington. Large, stocked, and available, it was the state's most popular lake. A fishing hike from here reached Squak slough connecting Lake Washington to 14 mile distant Lake Samamish. A highly regarded rainbow stream also serviced by streetcar was the little Cedar River. The Duwamish was searched for its early season Dolly Varden. And the more energetic might ride to the Green River and hike several miles up from Auburn to fish Suise Creek where some of the finest strings ever seen in the state have been caught.

None of these waters were solicited by the trophy angler. Those who desired monster-size "rainbow trout" traveled to the Skykomish River. They could go by horse or train, the latter by hitching a ride since the "Sky" was not a scheduled stop. S. Phillips was an experienced regular at this. Several years back he had left by train in the early hours and returned that evening with a huge rainbow just over 16 pounds. Many saw the fish for the lucky angler had hung his prize outside the freight car door! In the season of 1907 his best from the Skykomish was but 14 pounds and he was "somewhat disgruntled" over the small size. Modest Mr. Phillips would admit to nothing except to say the fish were all caught on a small spoon. This gentleman, however, would bow to W. H. Finck regarding the skillful use of the spoon. Finck was a Seattle resident who made his own highly effective spoons using all sorts of materials but favoring dull brass for large early season rainbows.

These "rainbows" were of course steelhead, spawners for the most part. Identification was made easy by the fact that they reverted to the definite spawning colors more typical of resident and pre-migrant fish. One may wonder why the steelhead was not fished for when they were ascending rivers from the sea. A "salmon-trout" season was established during that period when the regular trout season was closed. But there were very few who tried this winter fishing and those who did found the results most disheartening. Generally it was felt the rainbow and this other fish were separate species. All understood that "salmon-trout" of the game laws and "steelhead-salmon" in the commercial landings were the same fish, though most anglers lumped steelhead with salmon and favored steelhead-salmon as a vernacular name.

State sport fishery personnel certainly had a clear understanding of Washington's trout and listed only three: steelhead, "cut-throat," and Dolly Varden (char). *Scientifically speaking, there were no rainbow trout in Washington at this time* — not if we consider rainbow trout *Salmo irideus,* and the steelhead *Salmo gairdneri.* The name "rainbow" was borrowed from California anglers and applied here to the pre-migrant steelhead and spawning adult.

About 1910 a unique method for taking steelhead originated that in principle was a primitive form of spinning. It involved the use of a heavy duty fly rod, single action fly reel with enamel fly line, and a short piece of gut from line to hook. Because casting directly from the fly reel is impossible, a shallow basket was tied about the waist. Line was stripped from the reel into the basket before casting. Following a side arm throw, the small ball of salmon eggs and whatever weight used, carried line from the basket. The bait was allowed to bounce along the bottom at current speed with more line fed into the "drift" if necessary. This line holding stream appliance later became known as a "stripping basket."

The basket was an outgrowth of fishing techniques both crude and conventional. Most of the fishing line used was treated silk. It was very stiff and needed to be soaked overnight in water to make it pliant enough for casting. Its redeeming features were lasting wear and low cost. Early Washington anglers sometimes wound this line on a coffee can, placing a stick through the closed end. Baited hook and sinker could be swung around the head and sent flying while coils slipped off the can. We can only imagine what happened when a large fish was hooked. Using a conventional outfit, the stiff line was soaked on the reel and covered with a wet rag while the angler was enroute to the fishing grounds. Just before fishing, line was stripped from the reel and attached to something solid. The fisherman then backed off and stretched the line, removing all kinks and coils. The stripping basket-fly rod was, by comparison, rather simple and soon became a medium by which many were first introduced to the steelhead.

These were tackle exceptions. The Washington angler was a fly fisherman. His rod was split cane, his reel the automatic type; rainbows and cutthroat were the gamefish sought. A variety of eastern patterns were used: Brown, Gray, and Black hackles, Professor, Black Gnat, Queen of the Waters, White Miller, Royal Coachman, Grizzly King, and Parmacheene Belle.

Captain Leslie A. Beardslee U. S. N. whom the reader will meet shortly, visited Port Angeles, Washington, in 1896 as a Rear Admiral commanding the Pacific contingent of our fleet. From this Olympic Peninsula city he traveled 20 miles to Lake Crescent. The beautiful landlocked steelhead he caught today bear his name. The Beardsley trout is peculiar to this lake and a much prized trophy. They have been brought to net weighing more than 20 pounds.

8. BRITISH COLUMBIA

British Columbia had by 1900 gained international renown among sportsmen for its great tyee salmon. Many salmon rivers were held in favor, but none excited the imagination like a small river on north-eastern Vancouver Island called the Campbell.

Salmon oriented Englishmen were naturally attracted and a Campbell River stop became a must on itineraries, whether following a Cassiers grizzly hunt or the beginnings of a trip which would terminate with Southern California sea fishing. Arriving in Vancouver, the sportsmen proceeded to Nanaimo on the east coast of Vancouver Island by steamer. A second steamer was boarded for Comox, the next port of call. This still left 20 miles to go on foot—18 by trail and two miles breaking brush. For the affluent, boats were chartered at Comox to take lord, lady and entourage directly to the Campbell River camp. And camp it was! There were few substantial dwellings. The Willows Inn under construction would be a modern departure from the crude facilities. Most took along large mountain tents and set them up on the beach. The best salmon were found in August through September and tents provided all the protection needed.

The river entrance was also a Siwash Indian village. Indians in their ocean canoes worked Discovery Strait, trolling for salmon they would sell commercially or smoke for their own use.

The visiting angler could rent a boat — oars only — for $2.00 a day. A boatman hired to row, clean fish, and cook meals cost $3.50 a day. The best time to fish was during the current calm between tide changes; the current's peak velocity when the tide was moving made rowing and effective trolling difficult.

Gray Griswold's 1908 trip to the Campbell might be described as typical. He fished a total of 15 days beginning August 1. The lure used was a five inch spoon trolled deep with an eight ounce lead weight addition. Statistically, Griswold caught 47 tyee averaging 43 pounds and running from 30 to 63 pounds. Five spring salmon (immature tyee) about 20 pounds each and 45 coho salmon were also killed. Total weight for the tyee alone was 2,179 pounds. What to do with such a harvest? Along with the boatman's fee usually went whatever fish were caught — not counting a dinner salmon or two. Guides took the salmon to the Valdez Island cannery which paid one cent per pound for tyee and 10 cents for each coho and humpback.

Americans visiting the Campbell used rods much the equivalent of present day heavy duty drift rods made of split cane rather than glass, eight to nine feet long and weighing 10 ounces. When matched with appropriate reels, they allowed hooked tyee enough restrained freedom for the maximum degree of sport. The English favored still longer rods. Attached beneath each was a smooth running, narrow arbored, direct drive reel. In general appearance they were not unlike a two handed salmon fly rod. The "Murdock," 11½ feet long, and made of greenheart by Hardy Brothers of Alnwick, England, was an example of the type used in this fishing.

A few Englishmen could be seen casting an Atlantic salmon fly with a two handed fly rod, while aboard a pitching rowboat. A coho was only occasionally caught this way — and then when schooling and feeding on candlefish or herring.

The General Money No. 1 and General Money No. 2, patterns developed by Brigadier General Noel Money of Qualicum Beach, Vancouver Island, British Columbia. (Fly tier: Harkley & Haywood)

Compared to coastal salmon fishing, the trout sport fishery remained rather insignificant. This is not to say that trout were not sought; they were, especially the Kamloops on interior lakes. But the steelhead fished for with singular effort did not come into real maturity until the 1930's in the interior (tributaries of the Frazier and Skeena) and perhaps 15 years before this on Vancouver Island. The most advanced river during the 1900's was Vancouver Island's Cowichan. At least one early fly pattern developed peculiar to the river. The Cowichan Coachman had a claret body ribbed with gold tinsel, claret hackle, and white wings divided by a claret center wing. Bearing no resemblance to any fly in the Coachman series, it was in use on the Cowichan by 1900.

9. ALASKA

Anglers dream of finding themselves in a wilderness where armed only with the latest tackle and finest lures, they meet unsophisticated gamefish that take freely and fight with splendid abandon. Considerable latitude is allowed for one's sense of the dramatic, but the outcome will be personal perfection. The component parts for just such imaginings were there when Captain Leslie A. Beardslee U.S.N. sailed to U.S.S. *Jamestown* to our new Territory of Alaska in June, 1879, and anchored in quiet Sitka Harbor. Captain Beardslee came to Alaska with both the knowledge of a skilled angler and the trappings of this pastime. A wonderful assortment of Orvis rods, reels and flies equipped him for this virgin country. From his initial experiences to his departure almost two years later, he wrote a diary commentary for *Forest and Stream* magazine. Years later, his Alaskan observations were included among the essays comprising *Fishing with the Fly*, 1886, edited by Charles Orvis and Nelson Cheney. These two sources are almost the only in depth angling records we have of pre-twentieth century Alaska.

Astonishingly enough, the results of his Alaskan experiences are quite unlike the utopian visions conjured up in angling dreams. Captain Beardslee opens his essay, "The Salmon and Trout of Alaska," in *Fishing with the Fly*, with the following sentence:

> "From the great salmon of the Yukon, to the tiny fingerlings, which in innumerable quantities throng in the various creeks of Alaska, and are as ambitious to seize a single salmon egg as are their larger brethren to appropriate great masses of the same, however illy the bait may cover and disguise the hook which impales it, there is not, I am convinced, an Alaskan fish, which through any merit of its own, is entitled to an introduction to the angling fraternity through the medium of this volume, and to the companionship of the beautiful fac-similes of the flies, which in life they scorned."

A new adventure awaited his every move with rod or gun whether exploring coast or interior. The many rivers he saw and crossed were filled with ascending salmon from May until fall. And they were salmon, so a finely crafted cane rod was gathered and exquisite flies correctly propelled. The salmon were foreign to his teaching; Captain Beardslee despaired. It was bad enough that the salmon proved immune to his offerings, but they became hideous looking mindless wanderers before dying. We may imagine the Captain overjoyed in anticipation. Fates had allowed him a chance at what visually appeared to be the greatest in fishing mother lodes, yet actual sampling had brought only bitter frustration. He was such a traditionalist that when forced to turn to the sea and use herring to catch salmon, he makes no mention of their game qualities. Such a method in the realm of angling etiquette was analogous to cheating. Not only had the salmon degraded the sanctity of that other heritage, but by the use of bait they had brought a "fly only" believer to their level; it was demoralizing. Redemption did not come from any pristine acts by trout in behalf of the good Captain's conscience. When migratory he saw them tainted by their close association with ascending salmon — they gorged themselves on salmon spawn. In such a sated state any fly not resembling a little orange ball was refused, and Orvis, sadly, did not market a little orange ball fly. These trout were first the Dolly Varden, and Beardslee called them by their latin specie names *spectabilis* and *malma* when temporary residents, or salmon-trout if silvery mature and ascending. The cutthroat was referred to as "Clarks trout" and *Salmo purpuratus*. The small smolts of either species had identical gastronomical vices. Spawn leavings were eagerly seized and then they too, judged the flies presented as of dubious value. The largest Dolly Varden taken on rod and reel measured 21 inches and came to the "salmon spawn fly." Two larger than this were secured with the aid of a shotgun blast.

Alaska offered Captain Beardslee *Salmo gairdneri* to right the uncivilized wrongs dealt him. But the straw was fleetingly grasped and then cast to history with no lessons learned. His discovery might have advanced the cause of steelheading a quarter of a century. Of all the fish observed, *gairdneri* is the only one to have elicited a favorable response.

"My acquaintance with this species is very limited. The first one I saw I took in Sawmill Creek, well up to the head, in September, 1379. Seeing that it differed greatly from the *spectabilis*, I preserved it in alcohol, and it was subsequently identified by Professor Bean. It measured a trifle over ten inches, and was very plump, weighing seven and a quarter ounces. In my notes, I describe it thus: Body, dark green on back, but in general colors very much like a steel head or quinnat salmon; covered with round, black spots, from one-sixteenth to one-eighth inch in diameter; these extend considerably below the median line, and the tail and dorsal fins are covered with them the second dorsal adipose, but less so than that of the *fontinalis*, having a slight show of membrane, on which there are four spots. ventral and anal fins, yellowish in centre, bordered with red; belly, dull white; tail nearly square; scales, quite large, about the size of those of a fingerling chub; flesh, firm; and the skin. not slimy. No signs of ova or milt."

Captain Beardslee finds the specimen attractive. He might have wondered if this trout was a hint of better things to come if he correctly judged the absence of ova or milt due to the fish's immaturity. The following spring he discovers proof of such a relationship.

"On the 28th of April, 1880, I made a note: The first salmon of the season made their debut today – that is, if they are salmon, which I doubt.

Five beauties, from thirty to forty inches long, were brought alongside, in a canoe paddled by a wild-looking and awe-struck Siwash, who, with his crouching Klootchman and papoose, gazed upon our ship, guns, and us with an expression that showed them to be unfamiliar sights. He was evidently a stranger. and was taken in, for he took willingly two bits (25 cents) each for the fish, and no Sitka Siwash but would have charged treble the price. Through an interpreter, I learned that he had spent the last seven months in a shanty on the western side of Kruzoff Island, and that well up, among the foot-hills of Mount Edgecomb, there was a little lake, from which there flowed a small stream into the Pacific, and that in the headwaters of this stream he had speared these fish, which run up the stream in the fall, remain all winter in the lake, and in the early spring spawn in the head of the outlet.

All of this militated strongly against the theory that they were salmon, and when, on being dressed, the females were found to be full of ripe ova, said theory was upset completely. My ten-inch specimen of last September supplied us with a clue, and it was soon decided that these magnificent fish were indeed trout; for in every respect except size, and size of spots, some of which were a quarter of an inch in diameter, the fish were identical. Whitford, the oldest inhabitant, confirmed the Indian's story, and gave me in addition the Indian name for the fish – *Quot*, and that of the Russians, which I forget, but it meant 'Mountain trout,' and said that they are found only in the lakes, high up in the mountains, and that in winter the Indians spear and catch them through holes in the ice.

We found the flesh very delicious – far more so than the best of the salmon. The process of cooking, both by broiling and boiling, had a curious effect, for the flesh, which when uncooked, was a very bright red, blanched to pure white.

The trip to Mount Edgecomb, in the early spring, involved hardships and danger; and although several of us resolved that we would undertake it, for the sake of such fish, somehow we never did, and I have thus described all the *gardneri* (sic) that I ever saw."

Captain Beardslee, so unknowingly close to the promised land of his angling goals, fatalistically put his cherished flies aside and pursued the Alaskan trout with the degrading "salmon spawn fly."

He ends his essay with an almost laconic expression of discovery biologists would have done well to heed.

"Since the body of this paper was written there has been on exhibition by Mr. Blackford, of Fulton Market, New York, a number of trout, pronounced to be the *salmo irideus*, one of which weighing fifteen pounds, was sent to the Smithsonian Institution, and there identified by Professor Bean as being *'Salmo gardneri*, the great trout of Edgecomb Lake.' I, studying these fish in their glass tank, did not form this opinion, for Blackford's trout had a broad red band extending from just back of the eye to the tail, covering the operculum, a marking not existing on any of the Edgecomb trout I have seen. But the Professor assures me that 'color on the lateral line is not a specific character.' On comparing my notes of descriptions of these fish, I find that in all other respects they did appear identical, hence that the conclusion arrived at by Prof. Bean, that 'the *gardneri* and the *irideus* (or rainbow trout of McCloud River) are identical seems well founded. If so, and my crude supposition that *Clarkii*, obtained in Piseco Lake near Sitka are also identical with *gardneri* turns out to be correct, there can be a condensation of nomenclature, which will lead to at least one valuable result from this paper."

The separation of *irideus* and *gairdneri* as individual species, or combining them into one species was a decision that bedeviled biologists for years to come.

Captain L.A. Beardslee lived in Alaska commanding a lonely floating outpost. Twenty years after he left, the salmon's economic importance was establishing a viable future, linking together coastal Alaska with a series of canneries that by themselves were no less remote than the U.S.S. *Jamestown*. The discovery of gold gave growth its greatest push, and enough remained when pans showed no color to call this territory

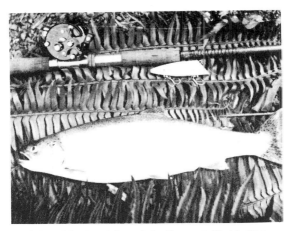

A Beardsley trout from Lake Crescent, Washington.

ours by occupation rather than by purchase. But not all regarded our ownership of Alaska an advantage. Captain Beardslee relates that when the Scotch Admiral of an English squadron at Victoria, British Columbia, was told of our acquisition, he replied, "Dom the country! let 'em have it; the blausted saumon won't rise to a floi." Fortunately, he had never heard of the "great trout of Edgecomb Lake." Could discovery of the steelhead have changed the course of history?

CHAPTER SEVEN

The Golden Age Of Steelheading

Zane Grey first heard about steelhead while visiting Long Key, Florida, where he had gone to angle for bonefish. What he was doing there or any of a hundred other places constitutes the most remarkable chapter in the history of American sports fishing. He was a novelist and fisherman. His writings were a reincarnation of a fabled past which perpetuated our western myth of how such times should have been. All the women were demure, milk-skinned virgins barely capable of breathing without effort. His men, mesmerized horse kissers in their presence, were otherwise fearless, flinty-eyed giants of good who could have eaten railroad spikes had they the mind to. The public loved these Guineveres in homespun and buckskinned Lancelots representing the romantic best of a lost "when men were men and women were women" era.

He cranked his books out at a prodigeous rate — one a month when working at top speed — and they became enormously popular. In the 1920's and 1930's only the Bible and McGuffy's Reader exceeded Grey's books in national sales. His critics, numerous and vocal, considered much of his work inept despite its vast readership. But as an angler he had no peer, he was the supreme master, the greatest fisherman America has produced.

Royalties ran into the millions. With money and time available, the incredibly robust Grey began a three decade odyssey in pursuit of all the world's great gamefish. While writing bankrolled him to 20 lifetimes of fishing, his was not a leisurely pursuit from the strains of occupation. He savagely devoured the sport with intense dedication. Gamefish records fell like wheat from Grey's onslaught; at one time he held nine all tackle world records.

Mr. Lawrence, an easterner big on Atlantic salmon, was the Long Key fisherman who put Grey onto steelhead. He described them as rainbows that grew strong in the Pacific before ascending a little known Oregon river called the Rogue. The big ones jumped once when hooked and then could not be stopped on their pell-mell race downstream.

Broken lines and rods accompanied angler and fish. These were stories to fire the imagination and the scorch the soul! Time and the gods permitting, Grey would seek out this river of legend and engage its fish and bring them to heel as he had done to countless denizens cn a dozen seas. Realities have a way of tempering such grandeur, even to as formidable an angling personage as Zane Grey.

Author and river met a short time later with the river getting the best of it; not a single steelhead was caught. When accomplishments are many and failures so few, the refusal of the Rogue to do his bidding must have affected him deeply. He gathered from the challenge a lasting love for the river. True, the heroic hyperbole so characteristic of his writing found its place here too, though with an underlying feeling of serenity without the primitive gut-fight abrasiveness seen in his duels with billfish, tuna and tarpon. These were fish fought to a standstill or lost. They took the bait or did not, and the choice lay more with the vagaries of contributing tangibles: movement of boat and movement of fish with Grey an interested third party until the fish was hooked. During the mortal test, where a bending of wills determined the outcome, Grey excelled. He had heart enough for ten. But one does not fish for steelhead in this light. The river is fished and the fish its reward. It was the Rogue that must bend Grey to its will if he was to succeed. The successes he eventually realized were most satisfying; he came back again and again — while some great fishing grounds saw his presence for but a fleeting trial.

Zane Grey returned to the Rogue in 1922 following a late summer trip to the Campbell river for salmon. In September he and his entourage arrived in Grants Pass and went to Joe Wharton's ("the sage of Grants Pass") sporting goods store. They checked on river conditions, purchased flies and had their tackle evaluated. Most of the rods were considered too light and the reels too small. But Grey traveled with a whole battery of tackle so that by selecting a heavy split cane rod and Hardy Brothers salmon fly reel it was possible to put together a proper Rogue River steelhead outfit. The river, they were told, was full of fish and they should proceed at once.

Grey's companions were brother R.C., friend "Lone Angler" Wilborn — a former captain of the University of Pennsylvania track team and college confederate during Grey's troubled days there — and a pint-sized Japanese cook. This trip might have been marked like his first Rogue failure had it not been for the addition of Fred Burnham by chance encounter. Burnham was then probably the greatest of our western fly fishers. A successful San Francisco broker, he traveled north when business permitted which was often enough to be considered a regular on the Rogue and North Umpqua. It is difficult to get a fix on Burnham. He was not a writer or fly tier and his leavings smack more of the fireside legend than the cataloged reference. Most oldtimers from the Oregon country have stories of Burnham: his great casting ability, how the fastest water posed no problem when wading, or the many steelhead wooed by his methods. Zane Grey was quite taken with this gentleman and the two became fast friends. On the river together,

Burnham was the patient teacher and Grey the humble student. Grey's mentor took fish after fish while Burnham's student caught nothing. Days later a fish finally did come and Grey would relish its capture. It was his first. No other steelhead would ever rate so high.

Between Grants Pass and coastal Gold Beach the Rogue cuts through the Coast Range. This part of the river was rarely visited then, so of course Grey had to float it. Mackenzie boats (Atlantic dory type) carried the party down the river. Enroute, a prospector who owned Rogue River land and a riverside cabin was met. Across from the dwelling was a productive drift. As was the grandiose Grey manner, the cabin was purchased and for years Winkle Bar was a favorite retreat from the writer's permanent Altadena, California, home.

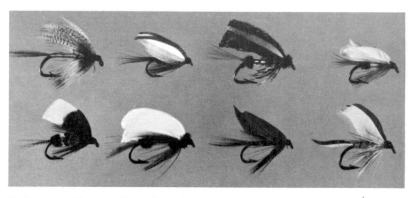

Early Rogue River steelhead flies (circa 1925) tied by Al Knudson. Row 1, Grizzly King, Benn's Coachman, Silver Doctor, Royal Coachman (yellow body); row 2, McGinty, Royal Coachman (with ostrich herl head), Scarlet Ibis, Parmacheene Belle.

Zane Grey wrote about his fishing. His eight *Tales of* . . . series represent the greatest angling autobiography ever written. Such was the popularity of these books that while serving to introduce the world's fishing, they brought anglers to areas previously unknown or known but locally. From 1915 to 1925 the Rogue gained enormously in western prominence. Such recognition was hard won and deserved, yet the river still remained a western property rather than a national shrine. Grey changed all this. Through his imagery, the Rogue became the promised land and its steelhead a will-o-the-wisp known little better than the satyr and centaur. They were born in the turbulance that was the Rogue, nurtured by water thought to originate in Crater Lake and tempered by the Pacific. Grey viewed their return as the animist; all the forces of land and sea made the meeting greater than the singular triumph of man over fish.

His Rogue exploits were related in *Tales of Fresh-Water Fishing,* Harper and Brothers, 1928. Those reading about the steelhead for the first time would see the fish as Grey did. A visit to the Rogue then became a necessary pilgrimage. Girded with strong rods and line packed reels, the angler would cap a career by testing his mettle against America's greatest trout.

There were fine steelhead that did not ascend the Rogue and skilled anglers who followed the sun to other waters. Four outstanding rivers, equally divided between California and Oregon, evolved as a kind of steelheading breadbasket. All were rivers where the fly reigned supreme and all held great numbers of steelhead. Beyond their ability to fit into the fly angler's mold, differences were marked. Size of Klamath fish seemed the most seasonally consistent, the Eel built to a late fall and winter peak, the Rogue saw its largest fish from October on and Umpqua waters produced two separate summer runs capable of ten pound June and September steelhead. The experienced angler matriculated to a river's heritage for an incidental sampling or prolonged stay depending on the fish it held. The Klamath need not deal a fatal blow to one's plans if the Umpqua, Eel or Rogue was running hot. Connecting highways and the automobile made possible the change in a few hours. Thus was born the steelheading circuit rider, a fisherman here for all seasons.

Some fishermen of the period tell us that the 1922 Rogue River Zane Grey first fished successfully and the river in 1932 had all too little in common, and that today's Rogue remains but a shadow of its former talents. Such pessimistic reflections are, of course, natural; the old and unretrievable are revered. To those whose age does not permit this point of reference the Rogue is still considered a great river, for it continues to draw them and their generation each year.

A 1922 Oregonian did have much to savor in his Rogue River ownership. The river was impressive. It churned and brawled from a Cascade source, then quieted enough in the Grants Pass area to be highly fishable. Here at Joe Wharton's Sporting Goods, the Rogue mystique was first tasted. Wharton had designed many local steelhead patterns that, while not surviving the test of time, found their way into almost every Rogue fly box. With the flies went the advice about how when and where to fish them. He was both seer and supplier for the visiting angler.

Though its chinook salmon once averaged 30 pounds (so it's told), and its silver salmon ignited many a spoon casters line, the river won fame for its steelhead. They began appearing in late May or early June. Numerous half pounders mixed this early return and the fish still averaged six pounds with a 15 pound limit. These really are the fish of Rogue River folklore. Sleek and fat, they are the greatest river travelers of this race. Once in the river proper, the steelhead moved rapidly through the coastal range's wild canyons and could be counted on appearing in Wharton's bailiwick the next month. Close to their spawning destination, the fish began emulating the summer river by hiding in its diminishing volume and drawing sustenance from its passing current. No thoughts contained them but neither would flies move them whenever the sun touched their darkening flanks. Slanting rays and September rains brought the last explosive outburst of the summer-run, heretofore so ill disposed to do the angler's bidding.

In those passing months, steelhead breached the river mouth many times. The older and greenest fish racked their bodies to reach the smallest tributaries of their origins. Later and smaller arrivals spawned

Three grandmasters of Rogue River lore discuss what fly pattern to use. From left to right, I.R. "Russ" Tower, Frank Lowrey and Bob "Big Fish" Savage.

farther down until the October and November steelhead, heavy with milt and spawn, were pressed by the urgencies of reproduction to seek no more than the lower river. Angling activity then switched to that end for those larger, less perilous steelhead. A few were caught weighing over 20 pounds; Zane Grey was told of one 42 inches long and 12 inches deep. Such a fish might weigh 30 pounds, an incredible size for Rogue steelhead.

There were expert fishermen who annually returned to the Rogue. Some eventually built small summer cabins along the river. A few "cabins" as monuments to their owner's station in life, were palatial lodges where guests could be lavishly accommodated. In this category must first go Fred and Huie Noyes who in the 1920's built a beautiful home along the Rogue. Fred and Francis Burnham followed with one of their own and in the early 1930's, Frank Madison, Andrew Welch, Nion Tucker and Cappy Black joined the resident aristocracy. A regular here by virtue of his lifelong Rogue devotion was Toggery Bill Issacks. Herbert Hoover is to this writer's knowledge the only U.S. President to have sampled steelhead fishing. He did so on the Rogue and his boon fishing companion was Toggery Bill.

Every sport has its masters, those redoubtable builders of lore who in retrospect become the hall of famers. Each summer saw these experts congregate for the June opening of the Rogue River steelhead season. New flies were tried with last year's acquaintances or regulars of a decade. Talk in town and around campfires told of other years when fish came easier, when a yard long steelhead cleaned a reel and broke a rod, when it was discovered the distinguished looking gentleman working a fly was Zane Grey. Zane Grey legends abound. To see him was to meet him, to actually meet him was to know him and anglers claiming some inner knowledge of Grey were numerous. His river experiences have sired so many retellings to the new generation of rookie anglers they remain a large slice of the Rogue Story.

This vacation assemblage of course included Fred Burnham, perhaps up from his San Francisco home or over from the North Umpqua. Whatever, Burnham would be there as assuredly as the changing season. John Dose made the Rogue a required summer stop. He was an early commercial fly tier and a genius with fur. Several patterns of his became favorites on the Rogue and one Dose dry fly is still in use, surviving because of a remarkable floating quality made possible by deer hair in its construction. Ed Lamport, who owned Lamport Sporting Goods in Medford, Oregon, was a Rogue regular. Lamport's store stocked the best selection of English flies found in Oregon. Some were snelled and others tied on hooks with extra large eyes to accommodate the "required" loop knot at the end of one's tippet.

These men fished the wet fly, quartering down and across so the fly rode near the surface. All had their own individual style for working the fly. Harold Preston stood alone in using the dry fly for steelhead. He selected heavily hackled bivisible-type flies for this purpose and was quite successful. One year he caught 140 steelhead, all on floating patterns.

It might seem strange that so few flies originating on the Rogue during the 1920's and 1930's survive today. John Dose and Joe Wharton developed highly popular patterns for Rogue use, yet none are presently tied. One reason is the continually evolving habits of fly dress. This often changes the old beyond recognition, or produces entirely new flies which by their effectiveness leave former standards obsolete. Another cause is the rather atypical Rogue fly design. The "average" fly here for summer-run steelhead was small, size eight to ten, with fours to twelves the upper limit. Because of the hook's short bite and gap, double hooks were used. Dark colors dominated, involving browns and greys instead of white. The standard red, orange and yellow steelhead colors found their way into this "basic brown," but sparingly. And of the three, yellow was preferred. Many flies found so effective on the Eel or Stilliguamish or a dozen other rivers usually did poorly on the Rogue, while Rogue patterns rarely made it beyond their origins.

The favorite flies included Wharton's Fancy, Dose's Imp and Dose's Perfection. The Golden Grouse and Golden Pheasant were quite popular. Both are English in origin and were favorites with Zane Grey. Hackle flies, Brown or Gray, tied with a yellow body, were often employed. The Royal Coachman and Coachman were the only white winged flies that commonly saw Rogue service. After 1930 the Golden Demon and this fly's look-alike, Cuenin's Advice, wedged their way into this elite group. If forced to name a second line of defense commonly carried, it would include the Silver Doctor (with many local variations), Governor, Black Gnat, Professor, Grizzly King, Preston's Perfect and Rogue River Special (original).

Because they were effective on the Rogue and could be purchased in a few of the better tackle stores, imported English Atlantic salmon flies also came into play. The Thunder and Lightening, Dusty Miller and Jock Scott are three that were commonly used. Although many colors are incorporated in these beautiful flies, brown and yellow dominate and thus follow the Rogue fly dressing fashion.

The steelhead limit was as commonly accomplished on Oregon's North Umpqua as the Rogue. While the Umpqua held fish from source to sea, it was the north fork from its point of departure to some 50 miles east in the Steamboat area, that drew anglers from all parts of the country. Felt by many to be a better river, if big summer fish are the measure of excellence, the North Umpqua's steelhead divided to make two distinct runs. They first arrived in June. Populations then steadily tapered off until September when a second seasonal race ascended. Both afforded fine sport for the fly angler. The fly's use was not total, though it so dominated the sport that North Umpqua water was set aside on a "fly only" basis.

Peculiar to the river were fishing camps committed to an angler's sporting and spiritual needs. Steelhead arrivals and departures were known because so much of the river was under constant scrutiny. Recent successes ordained daily fly choices, most productive waters and best angling methods. Actually, proper pattern selection rarely required the reading of tea leaves necessary elsewhere. A single fly named for the river produced so well one could do no worse to stick by it and probably no better by changing. The Umpqua and Umpqua Special — "special" for its jungle cock cheeks — was *the* fly of choice like no other pattern on no other river. It had first appeared about 1930 and seems never to have gone through the feather to hair-wing transition. Forty years later, it is still a popular Umpqua dressing.

North Umpqua flies have always been more gaudy affairs than those on the Rogue. The Parmacheene Belle, Coachman, Royal Coachman, Black Dose, Gray Hackle, Brown Hackle, Cumming's, Cumming's Special and Skunk were all early favorites. Just as with the Rogue, several English salmon patterns were usually found in use.

The two best known Umpqua River personalities were Major Mott and "Umpqua" Vic O'Byrne. Each owned and operated fishing camps in the Steamboat area. The Major's was located opposite the former Forest Guard Station. Zeke Allen was Mott's guide, cook and general man about camp. The two received anglers from as far away as New York and Pennsylvania, men raised on brown and brook trout who came to hear their reels scream during the steelhead's first endless run. Major Mott died on the river and left the camp to Allen who gave way to Clarence Gordon. He continued to operate the site as a concession from the Forest Service. It should be mentioned that Gordon was partially responsible for developing the Cumming's pattern, named for and designed with Ward Cummings, a well known North Umpqua steelhead guide in the 1930's.

Umpqua Vic O'Byrne's camp was just up from Steamboat at the "old fish rack riffle." He was the Umpqua's angler philosopher and would discuss at great length the merits of individual flies, rods, lines and those techniques necessary for their effective use. Though the river was his home for many years and he respected the many hazards of wading this most treacherous of western waters, it still claimed his life. Umpqua vic's passing was grieved by hundreds who had come to know this river through his teachings.

Fred Burnham and Zane Grey have frequently been mentioned for their Rogue River exploits. They came to the Umpqua too, though not necessarily together. When Burnham arrived, he stayed at the Circle H Ranch and fished the river between Bogus Creek and Susan Creek. Despite Burnham's fame, he might have passed unnoticed — many fished this stretch of the North Umpqua. Zane Grey's arrival *could not* go unnoticed. A Grey party is said to have numbered as many as 20, and Steamboat buzzed with their every move.

There is a rock in the North Umpqua that centers on a fine fishing riffle. A delightful little legend has it that Grey's guide secured this fishing station each morning at the crack of dawn. He did not fish or in any way bother steelhead that might be holding there. His purpose was to ward off visiting anglers who might want the place for themselves. If the guide's presence did not prove discouraging enough, money would change hands to assure the angling great of an undisturbed piece of water for his fishing. True or not, "Zane Grey's Rock" is a very tangible monument to the writer's happy North Umpqua days.

1. THE EEL RIVER IN 1936

The Eel received her usual *complement* of rain and anglers during the steelhead season that got underway in September. Storms raked the coast as they had for countless millenniums, though as the year progressed it seemed they were less frequent and gentler than in times past. Many steelhead had come to visiting and resident anglers. Few bettered ten pounds. The river's quiet flow held constant in November, and the lower 25 miles remained clear. Located here are the great fish producing pools that balloon from the river's convoluted course like so many connected lakes. Moving towards the coast there is Pollard, Long, East Ferry, Gully, Jetty, Pleasant Point, Harris, Palmer Creek, Grand Pit, Weymouth, Fernbridge, Snag, Lytel, Ellery, Dungan and Fillmore pools. Some are a mile long and require a boat, but their easy manner allowed silk lines to plumb pool depths and bring the attached fly near resting steelhead. Now the balmy weather made fishing a slow game. The little activity experienced came on tidewater pools where the occasional bright fish could be hooked. Once in the river a day or so they became unresponsive, dourly finning in channels to the consternation of anglers who through the clear water could view this rejection. On November 26th, K.D. Roberts took a 14 pound 14 ounce steelhead from Dungan Pool using a Red Parma fly (red body Parmacheene Belle). It was the largest so far and finished the season on a happy angling note. Heavy December rains had traditionally closed the river and sent rods to the closet shelf. It was known that some wonderfully large fish entered during the month because bait accounted for a few, but when ascending high and muddy water, they were not for the fly man.

Days passed and still the weather held. Tourists had long since departed and concerned themselves with the yuletide in distant cities. Optimistic Eel River residents prepared for an expected steelhead run. Would fish now be available at a time foreign to the angler's fly fishing experience? Answers were soon forthcoming. Mrs. Ralph E. Luick caught a 16 pound 1 ounce steelhead by using a number eight Queen of the Waters on December 5th. Like many earlier arrivals it came from Dungan Pool. Anglers hoped this was a single impatient fish that had entered the Eel in spite of low, clear water. Enough rain fell two weeks later to color lower pools and bring in the awaited winter run. A 16 pound 10 ounce steelhead hit a Polar Shrimp for B.R. Harris at Fernbridge Pool on Christmas Eve. The next day, the size was pushed still higher. While waiting for the Christmas turkey to cool enough to carve, Clark Varian, who lived on the Eel, took a five minute fishing walk from his house and was quickly fast to a steelhead. Varian delayed his return long enough to beach the 17 pound 4 ounce trophy. The Golden Demon was the fly used, a new pattern which had been introduced two years before. It was not an original with western tiers; Fred Burnham and Zane Grey had brought the dressing back with them from New Zealand in 1933. It had been the rage throughout the Eel's 1934 season, a popularity scarcely diminished two years later.

On Christmas evening a respectable rain began to fall and lasted most of the night. By morning the river was rising fast under an overcast sky. Walter J. Thoresen in company with Fred Blair and Frank Tooby traveled from their Eureka homes to fish Dungan Pool. Only two miles from the Pacific, it had, during fair weather, been the one productive spot. Now rain made effective fishing difficult. They moved several miles upstream and rented boats at Fernbridge Pool. Anchored on the river, Thoresen started casting. and he was well equipped for steelhead: a Hardy Perfect reel matched his nine foot, seven ounce Leonard rod while an Ashaway silk line carried his fly out. To a nine foot leader was attached a new fly by C. Jim Pray. Thoresen and Pray had been good friends since the latter's arrival in Eureka a few years before. When the Depression wiped out a real estate business Pray owned, he had turned his hand to professional fly tying. He opened his own shop. Jim Pray had become Eureka's most respected commercial tier. The flies he gave

Steelhead optics were developed by C. Jim Pray for use on the Eel River. The Pray-type short shank optics pictured above were tied by Lloyd Silvius, a longtime friend of Jim Pray. Top, Red and Yellow, Cock Robin; bottom, Red, Black.

Thoresen were all on number six hooks with the pattern carrying those proven Royal coachman colors. On this day, on this river, the fly was a killer; Thoresen soon hooked and boated an 11 pounder and a matched pair a few ounces over 10 pounds. A commotion on the beach then momentarily drew his attention. A young boy who had been fighting a steelhead for many minutes was now gaining the upper hand. While his father nervously watched and gave instructions, the youngster slid his fish to the river's edge where it could be grabbed. Hoisted aloft, it looked huge. Proudly carrying his steelhead, the boy and his father headed for their nearby car. Thoresen resumed casting. A slashing strike and heavy, powerful weight announced he had hooked an exceptional fish. The struggle was long, the steelhead well hooked, and when immediately weighed after being boated, it brought the scales down to the 18 pound mark. One final steelhead of 10 pounds came to Thoresen on this day of days. His California limit of five was filled; their weight totaled 60 pounds. His largest fish was entered in the annual *Field & Stream* fishing contest and won first place. Jim Pray now had a name for the fly Thoresen had worked to such advantage. To honor his friend and the event, the pattern was called Thor. It has become one of the greatest in the steelhead fly fishermen's repertoire of standard dressings.

The boy Thoresen observed and the boy, incidentally, who watched Thoresen battle his fish, was Gene Silvius. His steelhead weighed 14 pounds 14 ounces and took first place in the Junior Division of the same contest. Gene's father, Lloyd, was an amateur fly tier and baker by trade. The fly used had been designed by Lloyd and was called the Silvius White Bucktail. Most fishermen know it today by the name it was later called, the Nite Owl. First tied in 1930, it was the earliest hair-wing steelhead fly to win fame on the Eel River.

Lloyd Silvius retired from the baking business in 1946 and opened his own fly tying shop. That same year he invented what has probably come to be the most popular winter steelhead pattern from California to the Skeena, the Fall Favorite. He resides in Eureka today as a kind of grand old man of Eel River angling. Not that Lloyd is old — he's in his 60's — but he has simply spent almost all his years in Eureka and steelheading's historical best has passed before his observing eyes.

What of the other catches described on the 1936 Eel River? Those mentioned filled the first five places in the list of top ten North American rainbows caught that year. It would be almost 30 years before another river in a single season so dominated the steelhead angling scene. I refer here, to a Skeena River tributary, far north of the Eel. The 1936 steelheader did not know and would not have believed that a little river with the unlikely name of Kispiox, would produce a steelhead twice the size of Thoresen's record catch.

2. THE STILLIGUAMISH RIVER

The "Stilly" flows like a miniature Eel, holds North Umpqua size summer-run steelhead that fight as hard and jump as high as those on the Rogue. When Washington in 1939 set aside the Stilliguamish as a summer, "fly only" river, it told that angling discovery here was following the same cherished paths already realized in Oregon and in California. It is a river deserving the protection it has received.

Washington had lagged behind other states in developing her steelheading; "true" steelheading was enjoyed only on those rivers to the south. The reason for this paradox is found in the steelhead's habits. Chapter 5 discussed the various river race life histories. Two broad generalizations can be made relating these life histories to angling methods and seasons in vogue. First, there is a tendency as we go north for the winter-run steelhead to dominate the total run with the climax of this trend found in Washington. Moving into Canada and Alaska, fall-run fish dominate. For example, the Klamath River and those rivers tributary to the Skeena in British Columbia both produce their largest steelhead runs in early to late fall. But British Columbia and Alaska must be discounted; they were little more than angling potentials during the period under discussion. Thus within the realm of 1930 knowledge, steelhead runs extended later into the year as one traveled north. Washington tackle, seasons and prejudice favored the summer trout. A fishing season that closes in November offers nothing towards the capture of December to April steelhead. The trout season can not offer a fishery for winter steelhead either, for when it opens the last of these fish will have spawned. Admittedly the gradual realization that winter trout ascended Washington's rivers led to a winter season, but it had few followers. "Trout" meant April to November, all states saw to that. The season was first European, British in origin, then adapted in the eastern United States, and it was a resident trout season. Washington's migratory winter rainbows fell outside its limits. It comes as no surprise to find that tackle was first an extension of resident trout thinking. Fly rods with floating silk lines or short baitcasting outfits were poorly suited for winter steelheading.

That trout fishing methods were originally designed for resident fish is the second point. Those anadromous trout coming closest to approximating resident trout habits were the first to receive a close angling examination. Moving north through Oregon. there is a greater percentage of steelhead with an increased number of uninterrupted salt water years. It is this that produces great size, for ascending steelhead are not growing. We would expect to find our smallest steelhead spending short periods in salt water and the largest living years as an ocean resident. This is true, but the angler pays a penalty for size. The longer a steelhead stays in the ocean, the less likely he is to duplicate the shallow or surface fly striking habits of his resident counterpart.

The returning steelhead shows an increase in size and an attractive change in coloration. But he is still very much the trout that was rising to insects a few months before and the angler with insect irritating flies does well by him. At the opposite pole is the fish that spent two, three or four salt water years. It returns as an ocean fish whose catholic diet and long years away make for a dim fresh water memory. The steelhead will not show the same fondness for the surface swimming flies in use.

The Stilliguamish with an available and cooperative summer-run steelhead race came closest to matching angling conditions prevailing on more southern waters — the "big four" — that were the 1939 status quo.

Just as California had San Francisco as its focal point of angling development, Washington had Seattle. And her rivers were the Skykomish, Stilliguamish, and Skagit. They became the mainstay of Washington steelheaders, particularly for those preferring the fly. The "Sky" had been a favorite since the 1900's. Deer Creek, a tributary of the Stilliguamish, was known as a place to take steelhead as early as 1915. Beginning in the 1920's, the Skagit became an important water for steelhead. The mid-1930's saw a steady increase in the number of winter anglers afield, and the first real effort to take winter steelhead on a fly.

Steelheading was becoming less and less the sole domain of those California and Oregon rivers. Though residents in these states were experimenting on less famed waters, it was Washington generally, and those Seattle rivers specifically, that became the next steelheading paradise.

An interesting and enlightening series of statistics can be found in *The American Angler* by A.J. McClane. The author, long associated with *Field & Stream,* compiled lists of the 50 largest rainbows caught on any sports tackle and caught by fly only methods. The "open" 50 is completely dominated by Idaho's Pend Oreille Lake. But of the nine steelhead that are listed, eight came from Washington. Pend Oreille-like lakes are not attuned to the fly, so most of the rainbows listed in the 50 "fly only" division are steelhead. They breakdown in the following manner: Idaho-4, British Columbia-6, Oregon-8, Washington-14, California-18. Of the five largest steelhead, three came from Oregon and two from Washington. McClane's figures were gathered from the annual *Field & Stream* fishing contest and cover a ten year period from about 1945 to 1954. Were similar lists compiled from the previous decade, Washington would scarcely win mention. The trend, quite obviously, was discovery north. One final fact may be gleaned from the fly category: the best river in North America for prize winning steelhead was the Skagit. This river is credited with 10, one more than the Eel.

What of the pioneering anglers who first cast a fly on these rivers and came up with such steelhead? Five men were responsible for nine fish, five men who introduced many techniques and fly patterns for Washington's winter steelhead. Judge R.O. Olson must be mentioned first. He did his fishing on the Skagit near Concrete, produced the Lady Godiva pattern and caught four of the nine steelhead. (His wife accounted for one of Washington's 14 lunkers, and was the only woman to place on the list.)

Al Knudson, an Everett, Washington angler, captured two. He was the first to cast a fly on these winter waters and fathom the mystery of this race. In terms of experience and what the "gentle art" should epitomize, he is without peer. His Wet Spider and Al's Special have long been favorite steelhead flies throughout the steelhead's range.

One fish each goes to Ralph Wahl, Wes Drain and George McLeod. Ralph Wahl of Bellingham was another early devotee of winter fly fishing; a whole series of compact, fast sinking flies have resulted from his experiences. Wes Drain, a Seattle professional fly tier, claimed a 20 pound 7 ounce steelhead that topped the Washington list and was for many years the state record. The list of men, fish and Washington's early anadromous rivers is complete with the addition of George McLeod's Skykomish River steelhead.

George McLeod and father Ken conceived much of what is particularly Washington in steelhead fly fishing. Ken developed fly casting methods for use with the stripping basket. The long casts and drifts possible with the basket necessitated an extreme forward taper line. Years before the term "shooting head" was coined, he had attached silk casting line stiffened with melted paraffin to a silk fly line "head." Ken found that untreated casting line tended to kink, while early monofilament had too much character to properly lay in the canvas stripping basket. The McLeod Ugly Bucktail is his, and with the help of son George in 1940, the Skykomish Sunrise was born. Both are

Original steelhead patterns tied by Al Knudson of Everett, Washington. Left, Al's Special, Hot Shot; middle, Hot Orange Champ; right, Wet Spider, Black Bear.

popular Washington and Canadian steelhead patterns.

Others important for their lasting influence include Enos Bradner, whose book *Northwest Angling,* is one of the best on Washington fishing. His Brad's Brat, first cast over 30 years ago, remains a favorite for lake and stream. Sandy Bacon, who loved the Stilliguamish and often fished it with Bradner; Pauline and Lawrence Gallager, a much admired husband and wife fishing team during the 1930's and 1940's; Cal Hollingsworth, a North Fork "Stilly" regular; Bill Fay, a dry fly purist on the same water; and Roy Patrick, a popular Seattle professional fly tier are a few more of the many who have helped to uncover the secrets of Washington's migratory trout for the benefit of their fellow angler.

Besides the trophy fish these gentlemen caught from home waters, some were to travel north and repeat their successes on rivers that may well be the steelheader's final happiness.

Wes Drain and a fly caught steelhead; note stripping basket.

CHAPTER EIGHT

Steelheading Comes Of Age

Steelheading as a sport had been growing steadily in the decade of the Depression. Each year greeted an increase in the number of fishermen afield, exclusively devoted to the capture of this anadromous trout. New waters had become seasonally mapped, and places of past successes marked with colorful legends. Eagle creek Drift, Dead Injun Riffle and Claybank Hole carried certain expectations beyond the reputation of the river itself. Such rivers were waters that had come of age, for blind prospecting and chance interception was reduced to a minimum. This phenomenon is not unlike the settling of a town. A few must precede the many to explore, name and lay the cornerstone of local chauvinism.

The necessities of war intervened to deny the scientific advances beginning to appear in forms useful to anglers. Glimmerings of the better fishing life were to reveal synthetic lines, spinning reels, fiberglass rods and fluorescent dyes and paints. By the end of World War II there were more anglers than ever before taking advantage of these products and promoting *their* angling causes.

Our western rivers have seen any number of exotic woods turned into steelhead rods. Southern canes, hickory, dagama from Cuba, greenheart from Africa and South America, bethabara (also called washaba) from Africa, and bamboo from India and the East had either singly or in some multiple combination fallen in, then out, of favor.

English army officers had first brought bamboo lances back from India in the 1700's and converted them for fishing use. However, it was the American innovation of using cane strips to construct sensitive, light and strong rods that gained bamboo a permanent place on our salmon and trout rivers. For more than half a century, bamboo in strip constructed fly and baitcasting rods was preferred above all other materials for steelheading.

As the 1940's drew to a close, rods were marketed in solid glass, copper-beryllium, tubular and spring steel, and hollow glass, the latter the final rod material choice among steelheaders. Glass rods won quick acceptance for their low cost and astonishing durability — they do not show fatigue or take a set and have been subjected to temperatures from -70 degrees F. to +270 degrees F. without damage. When these rods were matched with spinning reels, proficient casters were all beginners and steelheading ceased to be a sport of experts.

Spinning reels were not new; the first patent for a fixed spool reel was taken out by Peter D. Malloch of Perth, Scotland in 1884. And a spinning reel closely resembling modern design was patented by England's Alfred Holden Illingworth in 1905. They were in use in this country by the 1930's and were being seriously investigated during the war years. Their lack of immediate acceptance lay not in any shortcomings in the reel's design. Until Dupont nylon became available in continuous lengths, the mechanics of spinning wore raw silk badly and were terribly incompatible with gut and treated silk.

Many first noticed these strange "coffee grinders" when home returning soldiers brought them back from Europe to begin years of successful domestic service.

These basics spelled an increased steelhead take. Three advancements, either inspired or developed by westerners, were to play additional roles of importance in this fast expanding sport.

1. LURES

For half a century steelhead lures had primarily been the spoon and spinner. To these, flies had been attached, an assortment of metals and finishes employed and different sizes and weights cast. These developments created variety. Plugs were of little value during most of these years. The Helin Flatfish came into specialized use in the 1940's and 1950's as a still fishing (plunking) lure. Here, current kept the light, well balanced Flatfish wobbling enticingly.

Lures left to drift with the current and containing little or no action began as embellishments of salmon or steelhead spawn. Eggs singly or in clusters were the one universal "lure." Some 40 years ago anglers began tying on their eggs with red thread or yarn. The color was less noticeable than say brown, and gave the eggs a bit of attraction when they had become current bleached after prolonged use. This simple addition remained unchanged for many years. As fluorescent yarns became available in the late 1940's, steelheaders eagerly substituted this brighter material. In the natural course of their angling, they discovered that the new colors had fish-taking qualities all their own. From this realization came the "red rag" lure we know today as the yarn fly. Even though yarn was usually used in conjunction with eggs, it nevertheless stands as our first lure specifically for steelhead.

At about this time a lure was developed that in years to come would surpass all other types combined. I am speaking of the bobber, an invention of Mr. Willis "Willie" Korf.

Willie Korf is a native Californian. After World War II he came to Bremerton, Washington, soon to be discharged from the Marines. What might have been a fleeting visit became a permanent residency when he met and married a Seattle girl. He was a barber by trade and worked first at Fort Laughton and a short time later in his own Ballard shop. It became a habit for him to market fishing tackle in his shop, a sidelight that served to introduce Willie to all the lures in use for both trout and salmon.

The Flatfish and spoon were the two popular clear water steelhead lures in Korf's area. When rivers turned high and muddy, eggs were employed to the exclusion of all else. A cheap lure effective under almost all water conditions was needed. An aquarium tank was installed in his barber shop so he could experiment with lure designs and view their qualities underwater. Willie's first try consisted of an egg shaped plastic body with a cork cylinder in front, each pierced with a wire shaft that attached to hook and line. The cork had a beveled and scooped out face which made the lure wiggle and work toward the bottom. A desire for flash led to the addition of a large spinner blade in front of the cork. It was by then becoming a bit cumbersome and the plastic body was dropped. Korf then noticed that the heavy spinner blade would normally swing back and forth rather than spin. Feeling that this would supply action enough, the cork cylinder was finished in a rounded shape. He wanted to paint his lures with fluorescent paint, but its sole manufacturer, Switzer Brothers (Day-Glo), tightly controlled sales. Willie, however, knew a sign painter who had produced a rather crude fluorescent paint. The painted lures were smooth and shiny as opposed to the deeper, flat paint he prefers today. It was poor in other respects too. The paint had a tendency to crack and the colors were not bright enough. But a dozen of these unnamed lures were made and offered for sale. Customers viewed them as a joke — buy one and invite a second clipping? He decided to spend three weeks testing his lures; if results were poor, he would forget the whole idea. The first weekend, Korf hopped into his Model A truck and drove to where the Wallace River joins the Skykomish. After rigging up, he cast his fluorescent invention, now called the "Fireball," and was rewarded with a healthy strike. The fish was lost but others followed to give a limit. A downriver fisherman and his son walked up to determine what had caused all this luck. The beached fish offered proof enough that the unusual looking Fireball was effective, and there on the river the first sale was made. It was 1952 and for better or worse, Willie Korf was in the lure making business. The gentleman practically tested the lures by hooking three steelhead and landing one. Other anglers came upon this scene of joy and bought out all the remaining lures. One fellow was a purchasing agent for a Seattle based sporting goods firm, a fact not announced at the time. Monday morning the phone was ringing. After a bit of haggling it was decided the manufacturer should handle production but Korf would receive 50 per cent of the profits from finished lures sold retail. They were marketed under the name "Korker," as a kind of cross between the inventor's name and material used.

The next weekend again found Willie afield trying to develop public interest in his Korker. The Ballard Locks connecting Lake Washington with the Pacific is a popular plunking spot among steelheaders. When he arrived the area was jammed with fishless fishermen, a situation quickly rectified. A lure loaned to a fellow angler brought a steelhead to net. Willie followed suit. With the lure still in the fish's mouth, he walked by the long line of fishermen, a bit of showmanship that would have done Barnum proud. Two dozen Korkers were sold on the spot. Soon this group of anglers were casting the new lures. Lines crossed, lures tangled and when the slow current had gobbled-up half a dozen of the bright red Korkers to produce a floating raft of cork and hooks, one angler was given to exclaim, "Look at all those cherries bobbing there!" From this chance remark was born the name "Cherry Bobber."

The company that was supposed to be producing these lures and giving Korf 50 per cent of the profits, gave him nothing because they "weren't selling." He pulled out, took a copyright on the lure under Cherry Bobber, and attempted to obtain a patent on it. A great new lure stands about as much chance of going unimitated as keeping the discovery of gold a secret. This first year of use saw the Cherry Bobber take fish in the Seattle area, become the rage on Tacoma's Puyallup River and come into use for both steelhead and salmon on the Columbia. Perhaps because it was so copied, or because the lure involved the use of a spinner blade, his patent application was rejected. But the Cherry Bobber did lead Korf to establish Wills Tackle Manufacturing Company.

Several years after its introduction, it was noticed that steelhead fishermen in the Samish River area were taking those Cherry Bobbers intended for trout and substituting a larger treble hook. the switch made for an excellent clear water steelhead lure. These miniature facsimiles inspired Willie to make still other modifications. Trebles were exchanged for a large single hook holding a few strands of yarn, and the spinner blade was dropped altogether. Dubbed Samish River Special, it was shortened in the course of nicknaming to Sammy. A copyright compromise decided upon Sammy Special. Desire for still smaller bobbers led to the Little Sammy.

Full credit is given to Willie Korf for inventing the bobber and adding to it a fluorescent finish. It must be pointed out, however, that he was not the first to use fluorescent paint on steelhead lures. This honor must go to the Martin Tackle and Manufacturing Company in Seattle, Washington. They had a direct line with Switzer Brothers in Cleveland, Ohio, the one major firm handling this paint. It was first used by Martin Tackle in the late 1940's on salmon plugs, then on spoons (which brought it into service for steelhead fishing), and during the early 1950's, on steelhead lures as a result of Korf's work.

Maxwell Manufacturing Company in Vancouver, Washington, marketed a fluorescent lure called the Fire Cluster in 1948. Its impact should not be compared with the Cherry Bobber or the Maxwell lures of later years. Their Firefish was first used in 1954 and looked like a scoop-faced pile of plastic eggs wiggling like Flatfish. As successful as any Maxwell lure and a most popular drifting lure for steelhead, is the ubiquitous Okie Drifter; it was introduced in 1956. Another Maxwell addition in 1963 was the Korky. Similar to the Cherry Bobber is the

Cherry Drifter created by Luhr Jensen and Sons of Hood River, Oregon. It was brought out in 1952 following Willie Korf's success with the original.

One of the best steelhead lures in recent years has been the Spin-N-Glo. This odd appearing and deadly bobber has propeller-like rubber wings which make the lure revolve on its wire shaft. It is a favorite among plunkers, but is also used in drift fishing and trolling. It began as the Spinning Fly, a small Spin-N-Glo with the treble hook wrapped with hackle. The Spinning Fly was and is used under all trout fishing conditions. Both lures are the invention of Howard L. Worden, owner of the Yakima Bait Company in Granger, Washington. Because of the Spinning Fly's original design, Worden was granted a patent for it in 1932. The Spin-N-Glo, always a fluorescent lure, was introduced to anglers in 1954. Two other typically exotic Worden lures were the Wobble Glo, initially marketed in 1957, and the Apple-Nocker, in 1963.

The use of fluorescent paint on steelhead lures had by 1952 become sufficiently accepted, that famous name manufacturers painted their lures accordingly and began participating in this rapidly developing market. Charles Helin of "Flatfish" fame introduced a flame copy of this favorite in that year while Lou J. Eppinger, manufacturing the world-famous Dardevle spoon, brought out a flame version called "Glo-in" in 1954.

Estimates of steelheading's increase are in most instances based on visual activity, fishing license sales and a gross estimate of the fishing tackle sold specifically for steelhead. Such an investigation would tell us there were more anglers afield and that they were better equipped than ever before. That, however, is concrete evidence only of a trend. The revealing figures that follow were gathered from Washington steelhead punch card records. While numbers are for the total winter-run catch (Washington did not have an all-season punch card until 1962), this still represents the vast majority of steelhead caught.

	1947-48	1953-54
Bogachiel River	74	1,881
Chehalis River	3,244	6,943
Cowlitz River	1,938	12,328
Hoh River	636	1,602
Humptulips River	684	3,863
Kalama River	221	1,718
East Fork Lewis River	384	2,816
Nisqually River	154	4,597
Puyallup River	1,771	16,886
Quinault River	402	1,545
Skagit River	3,712	16,170
Skykomish River	272	5,584
Toutle River	118	3,056
Washougal River	152	2,324

These figures clearly show how the steelhead take increased during the six-year period chosen. There are three reasons for this. First, many rivers were being stocked with pre-migrant steelhead. Secondly, there were more fishermen who were angling for steelhead. The final and principal reason remains with those tackle and lure advancements that paralleled steelheading's increase and helped create the enthusiastic following so typifying our present sport.

The search for new and better steelhead lures goes on. In researching this book, it was my pleasure to correspond with Paul B. Evans of Glen L. Evans, Incorporated, Caldwell, Idaho. His company has been manufacturing fine fishing tackle since 1922. The Cherry Buoyant introduced in 1955 and Loco Lure brought out a decade later have been well received by steelheaders. The first is a bobber and the other a spoon; both were designed with steelhead in mind. Yet Evans states that during the 1965 winter season, his company was besieged with requests from steelheaders for a lure that was unlike these two. Their hottest lure on the Snake River for those migratory rainbows was a black maribou jig! Possibly it represents food pursued in salt water. Whatever the reason, the lure is a boon to anglers. The jig requires no additional weight, is almost snag free, and can take any color incorporated in steelhead flies.

We have bobbers that spin, swing, wiggle and clack. Spinners and spoons are marketed in new designs and colors. Now jigs have been added to the growing lure list. All are changes unknown but 20 years ago.

If advancements improved the drift fisherman's lot, they were to revolutionize the fly fisher's world.

2. SHOOTING HEADS AND SINKING LINES

Near where the Seine River joins with the cold English Channel waters is picturesque La Harve. When the last agonies of World War II saw Germany's troops pursued to their homeland and France reoccupied by Allied forces, the population of La Harve swelled from the influx of American G.I.'s. One of the many was Sergeant Jim Green, tournament fly caster extraordinary.

Fishing and wars do not seem compatible. But it was a "hurry up and wait time." Spanish mackerel were seen along the shore. Jim sought to make the best of both. Shopping around he located a spinning reel, gut line and a bamboo "blank." Guides were unavailable, so using "yankee ingenuity," he fashioned some from wire and taped on the crude efforts. The makeshift outfit worked well enough to provide a pleasant interlude.

Jim did not like spinning as an angling instrument — fishing to him meant fly fishing. Nevertheless, the ease in which line left the reel spool was impressive. From this an idea was born. Perhaps, thought Green, gut could be attached to a tournament fly casting line. Instead of running line laying in loose coils on the casting platform, it could be replaced with hard, frictionless gut and carried on a spinning reel.

At war's end he began experimenting with the new combination. The fly line he was using was a specialized forward taper variety. Made entirely of silk, it contained a heavy 50 foot front section called a "head" that tapered at both ends. This was followed by a short level diameter holding line, spliced to a narrow level diameter running line. Gut was replaced by monofilament and attached to the end of the holding line. The new line was cast and at its completion, wound back on the spinning reel. It did not work as expected. As the heavy fly line shot forward, the point where the monofilament tied to the holding line tangled at the butt guide. After several casts, the force broke the silk holding line almost at the head itself. Rather than take time to splice in a new holding line, the monofilament was tied directly to the 50 foot head. Previously when casting such a line, the head had cleared the rod tip before releasing the holding line. Now this method was duplicated using monofilament. After several false casts, the head passed beyond the rod and was released. It bent into the tight curve which typifies a working shooting head, and nearly shot out of sight. He was dumbfounded. Again and again they cast and watched in amazement as the line sailed to distances once thought unobtainable.

He soon discovered the spinning reel that started it all was a useless incumbrance; line left in loose coils on the platform had enough body to prevent tangling.

Jim Green shared his discovery with fellow Golden Gate Casting Club members and in the following weeks all became proficient in its use. This was a most auspicious time for such a discovery; the club was soon to attend the 1946 National Casting Tournament in Indianapolis, Indiana. They swept the field and Jim captured first place. The defeated casters did not forget *how* they were beat and the new method quickly gained wide acceptance.

When back in San Francisco, Green, attorney, Charlie Barfield, and other club members set themselves the task of tailoring heads to a length practical for steelhead fly fishing. The length eventually arrived at, with no loss of distance, was around 30 feet. Heads were prepared in the following manner: any level line beyond the front taper, some two feet, was cut off. Thirty feet was measured back from this point and a second cut made. To the large diameter end, assuming a double taper, a ½ inch 50 pound loop of nylon line was spliced in place. A clinch or double jam knot was used to connect the monofilament running line — or shooting line, as it is now called — to the braided nylon loop. The leader was attached in any manner favored.

Once a shooting head selection was made, the question still remained how to best cast it under actual fishing conditions. Prior to casting, a fly line was hand held and either coiled together lasso fashion or individually looped on each holding hand finger. Either proved difficult when tried with monofilament. It tended to take a set off the reel and always had more character than silk or nylon fly lines. Trial and error showed that a few huge coils made the safest release. The fast escaping fly line quickly straightened sets and easily gathered and controlled the shooting line. This held true even if the coils were dragging in water, often the case in deep water wading.

Somewhere in false casting, enough monofilament must be released for a shooting head to clear the rod. Some space from rod tip to shooting head butt — "overhang" — is necessary for a smooth release and a distance eating cast. The monofilament's fine diameter makes it extremely difficult to hold coils yet with the same hand release the right amount of line can be thrown into a back cast. The only part of the anatomy left to hold reserve shooting line while moving arms prepared a cast was the mouth. This radical departure from any technique previously used looked most bizarre, but worked. Following the cast, a fisherman would strip retrieve shooting line in several large coils, placing the edge of each between his lips. The mouth opened as line shot forward in the next cast.

Petaluma, California, is the home of Sunset Line & Twine Company. A manufacturer of fly lines for many years, Sunset quickly came in contact with the shooting heads being perfected in nearby San Francisco. By 1950 they were producing silk shooting heads on a limited custom production basis for Golden Gate tournament casters. Sunset's first regularly manufactured shooting head came in 1952. Paradoxically it was designed for spinning rather than fly fishing use. Called "Spin-A-Fly," the line was only 14 feet long and worked with a spin-casting reel. The idea was to allow the spinning enthusiast a crack at fly fishing with the simple and inexpensive expedient of buying a single fly line. To safeguard their right to continue using the term "shooting head," Sunset applied for and received a copyright on it the same year "Spin-A-Fly" came out.

The many advantages of using a shooting head were not fully realized until lines designed specifically to sink came on the market. Synthetic float lines will do one task well: float. Shooting heads cut from these enable the angler to cast farther but little else. Sinking lines are quite different. They will sink slowly, fast like a stone. One would stagger under the load were he to carry an extra reel spool for each line of different density. How much simpler to carry a shooting head assortment. If a situation dictates increased depth, the fisherman needs only to change heads by cutting off the one and tying on another a process almost as easy as changing flies.

Another asset of shooting head sinking lines is what they will do after cast across a river. If a long, deep fly drift is required, and it is in much of winter steelhead fly fishing, there is nothing that will do the job as well as the sinking head. A conventional sinking line cast quartering upstream, across, or downstream will soon develop some degree of whiplash — "drag'. — because of the uneven current force exerted against it. And the deep, straight downstream drift we seek is lost. The shooting head offers no such problem. For example, let us say we want to drift a fly 50 feet across from our casting station. A 70 foot cast is made in an upstream direction. The current has less line to work on from the beginning. Nevertheless, line begins to belly as it starts downstream and we gather in shooting line while the fly sinks. As the fly passes, line is in the shape of a cresent which constitutes drag. Were we to hold on, the fly would begin to surface and our drift would be complete. Instead, we start releasing line gathered at a rate needed to keep the fly running straight downriver. Some 20 feet of shooting line is slipped before the fly swings around. Actually, few are content to release only the amount gathered. More line is held in ready and fed into the drift. Counting only the fishing part of a drift as that point when the bottom is reached, cast after cast can be made to cover 100 feet.

In 1953 Sunset again took the lead and came out with the first fast sinking fly line. "Stream King" in double taper, weight forward and 30 foot shooting heads was nylon but had metallic yarn woven into the line weave. Its specific gravity was about equal to our fastest sinking present synthetic lines.

The same year "Stream King" was introduced, George McLeod, a sales representative with Scientific Anglers, discussed the feasibility of marketing a sinking line with company president Leon Martuch. Scientific Anglers had been in operation for only eight years and initially had not manufactured fly lines at all, selling instead magnesium rod cases and other fishing sundries. When they did produce a fly line, it was a floater called "Air Cel" and an immediate success. Along the way they had dabbled in sinking lines, experimented with the results, but had not tried to market them. Martuch and McLeod felt the time opportune and in 1954 Scientific Anglers introduced the now famous "Wet Cel." It had a thin level nylon core covered with a tapered plastic finish, was fast sinking and almost indestructable.

Some credit for the line's quick popularity must go to George McLeod. When he caught a fly record steelhead on October 6, 1955, Wet Cel was the line used. The rainbow placed first in *Field & Stream's* fishing contest and Wet Cel gained many followers as a consequence.

Wet Cel and the still faster sinking Wet Cel Hi-D are now marketed in shooting head form (called "shooting tapers").

Diagrams Of Typical Fly Lines

Courtesy of Scientific Anglers

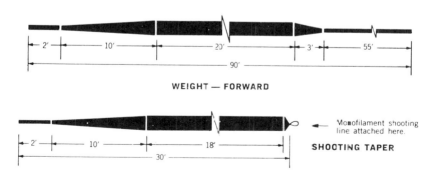

2' — 10' — 20' — 3' — 55'

90'

WEIGHT — FORWARD

2' — 10' — 18'

30'

→ Monofilament shooting line attached here.

SHOOTING TAPER

Ashaway in 1954 and Gladding (then South Bend) in 1955 got on the sinking line bandwagon with dacron. Tapers were braided in the dacron and the lines protected with a thin plastic covering. the remaining need was for a fly line that would give an extremely rapid sink on those deep, very swift rivers. Chosen for the job was lead core trolling line.

Lead core as a fly line is a phenomenon of sorts. Its period of use in any form is most recent and its conversion to fly line use dates to the early 1950's. Yet who first used it in fly fishing is unknown. We may only be sure the gentleman in question was brave beyond reason; false casting lead core is simply suicidal. The narrow line diameter coupled with high weight make for a great wind cutter and builds terrific velocity on the cast. It is axiomatic that the fly following is traveling at the same speed. Hardly a comforting thought, for lead core was unbelievably poor casting qualities.

A lead core shooting head is the most specialized of fly lines and its use is presently quite restricted. Only in California does it enjoy more than meager popularity. Its most noteworthy fresh water use is on Northern California's Smith River. The lower Smith runs so strong that no other line will get a fly down to its fall ascending chinook salmon. Lead core has made fly fishing for these brooding giants possible and a whole new sport fishery has unfolded. Salmon of 50 pounds or more are caught each year with Monti Rio's Bill Schaadt often taking top honors.

Potentially, lead core promises to open steelhead water heretofore denied the fly fisher.

No one person is responsible for lead core's conversion to a fly line though two well known California anglers have assisted in its growth. Myron Gregory who helped introduce the "head" to fellow tournament casters also expounded on its virtues in the lead core form. Larry Green, an outdoor writer from San Bruno, described the many lead core advantages in "A New World of Fly Fishing," in the February, 1964 *Outdoor Life*.

The first lead core these gentleman used was Ashaway's "Catfish." But Gladding's plastic covered "Special Mark V" proved superior for fly fishing and they switched when it became available in 1955. A few such heads have found their way to Scotland's Atlantic salmon rivers and proved effective when a deep sink was needed.

Lead core will probably never gather a large following until some method is developed to produce a more pliable line in lighter weights. The present stuff can be handled only by an expert caster owning the strongest of rods. For example, the lightest lead core line, testing 18 pounds, is the equivalent weight of a G4AG line under the old scale or weight 12 on the present fly line scale. As a shooting head it would weigh nearly 400 grains, enough weight to either badly overtax or break the average steelhead rod. Sunset's idea of a metal yarn woven into the line was an excellent one. If a durable covering was applied, such a line might supercede lead core as the line of choice among bottom bangers. A lead "putty" or "dough" now seen on the market might well be incorporated into some type of metal core line and sink like present lead core but without the ghastly casting properties inherent in that line.

DISTANCE VALUE OF THE SHOOTING HEAD

Internationally known tournament caster, Myron Gregory, sent me these figures regarding the distances that relative lines will cast. Myron used three different line tapers all of the same density. The weight 11 line had a nine-foot leader and was cast with a nine-foot rod. Results were as follows:

Shooting head

1. Roll casts were 58 to 64 feet with 61 feet the average.
2. Distance casting using the left hand pull, 128 to 135 feet, with the average cast about 130 feet.
3. Distance casting with no left hand pull and no "overhand.' 95 to 105 feet with about 101 feet the average.

Weight forward

1. Roll casts were 60 to 65 feet, with 61 feet the average.
2. Distance casting using a left hand pull; all casts were about 95 feet.
3. Distance casts with no left hand pull. All casts fell between 75 and 80 feet, with about 77 feet the average.

Double taper

1. Roll casts gave distances up to 70 feet.
2. Left hand pull or no left hand pull gave distances of 75 feet, and as Gregory says, "This was work and plenty of it."

These results were obtained at a casting pool furnished with a casting platform raised 18 inches above the water. Distances would be less under actual wading conditions.

Casting distances are substantially greater when using a shooting head. This is obvious. But the methods used to gain this distance are worth noting. *The shooting head gives the greatest distance with the least amount of effort.* The casting cycle begins when enough head has been retrieved to grasp the butt end with the retrieving hand. The rod is then raised and brought down hard to roll the remaining line clear of the water. The back cast starts as the head straightens. About 10 feet of monofilament shooting line escapes through the fingers while the hand goes to the stripping guide. The running monofilament is stopped when the head and several feet of shooting line have cleared the rod. As the forward cast is made, head speed is increased by pulling shooting line down from the stripping guide ("left hand pull"). Shooting line is then released when the head passes at its peak velocity. The cast had been accomplished with no false casting. One false cast is sometimes used to build up line speed *if lead core is not used.* False casting with lead core, besides being dangerous, creates a hinge effect that soon breaks the line's lead center.

THE SIX TYPES OF FLY LINES

Type	Reaction to water	Construction	Manufacturers
F	Floating	Floating lines are made with a taper braided nylon hollow core with a thin plastic finish, or they are made with a level braided nylon core with a tapered plastic finish containing air bubbles.	Ashaway – Fly-Buoy Cortland-333 Gladding – Aerofloat Gudebrod – 6-5 Newton Scientific Anglers Air Cel Supreme Orvis Shakespeare – Wonder Float – 4390 South Bend – Banshee Sunset Stream Queen Royal Coachman Silver Doctor Western W-80
FST	Floating with 10 feet of sinking tip		Scientific Anglers – Air Cel Syncro Taper Wet Tip
SS	Slow sinking or floating when greased	It has a taper braided silk core with a coating of oil that is impregnated into the line	Gudebrod – Gudeking Newton – Streamline Ashaway – Fly Sport – Golden Western W-40 Miller – Hollow Line Orvis
MFS	Medium fast sinking	This line is made with a taper braided dacron core with a thin plastic finish or with a nylon or dacron level core with a taper weighted plastic finish.	Ashaway – Griffin Cortland Gladding – Aqua Sink Gudebrod Sink–R Dacron Shakespeare – Sinking 4322 Sunset – Stream King Stone Nymph Caddis Nymph

FS	Fast sinking	This line has a level braided nylon core with a heavy tapered heavy plastic finish	Scientific Anglers – Wet Cel Wet Cel Hi-D
VFS	Very fast sinking	It has a level braided nylon core over lead and has a thin plastic finish.	Gladding – Special Mark V

FLY LINE STANDARDS

"Lines of the same calibre are not always the same weight, and the weight of the line is much more important than its diameter."

George M.L. LaBranche

Silk was the universal fly line material from its late nineteenth century appearance until World War II. Fishermen then could expect nearly the same weight from two lines of like tapers and diameters. Because of this consistency, the method devised to designate line sizes was based on diameter. Lines began with "I" at .020 of an inch and proceeded at .005 increases to "A" at .060 of an inch or some multiple of A: 2A, 3A, 4A. Any line marketed would be called by one or more of these letters. From this system came such familiar combinations as HDH, GAF and B for double, forward and level taper lines respectively.

Even during silk's prime days, however, there were a few like George LaBranche, *The Salmon and the Dry Fly*, 1924 who recognized the system's inadequacies.

As tournament casting lines came into angling use, diameter designations became less meaningful. Silk can be spliced to give a desired casting quality. This was accomplished first and then matched to a suitable rod. These early multiple diameter lines, such as those created by legendary tournament caster Marvin Hedge (Hedge 7 Taper), perplexed the "man on the street" and added to fly fishing's mystique.

The first nylon fly lines appeared on the angling scene at the end of World War II. The advantages were their maintenance free nature and "float forever" ability; nylon quickly secured a permanent place of high popularity. It was now possible for a person less intense in his piscatorial pursuits to enjoy fly fishing without the tribulations of silk. Nylon was not without its disclaimers, and on some California steelhead rivers it was held in particular dispair. It could not be spliced, would not sink, and when dressed to shoot, the dressing quickly worked free. Nylon also made it more difficult to correctly line a rod for it was generally a letter lighter than silk when both were the same diameter.

When dacron and specially prepared nylon sinking lines became available, the letter diameter system became completely obsolete. Dacron for a given diameter was heavier than silk; a HEH dacron, HDH silk and HCH nylon were all about the same weight. What to do when the rod was stamped, "Use HDH." HDH what? Obtaining a correct line became a trial and error process. Experts recommended that before a purchase was made, the prospective buyer first try out the line with his rod. This was possible if a friend had a line identical to the one under consideration, or when the tackle store had facilities to render this service. Usually neither was possible, and a great number of mismatched outfits resulted.

New innovations in fly line design had been conceived by tournament casters, so it is fitting that long needed changes in the fly line standard were initiated by this same group.

Myron Gregory, representing the National Casting Association, approached the American Fishing Tackle Manufacturers Association with a resolution that called for dropping the diameter letters for a number system based on line weight. AFTMA turned the problem over to its line division. The membership of Leon Chandler, Bob O'Connell, Jack Dougherty and L.R. Crandall appointed Art Agnew their chairman. Because Gregory and Agnew live in the same California area — Oakland and Petaluma — it was convenient they should get together to work out the details.

They first requested samples from all the major fly line manufacturers. Using these as their basis for change, they next contacted Ted Trueblood and A.J. McClane of *Field & Stream*, and Jason Lucas of *Sports Afield*, as well as tournament casters Ward and Sutphin. After considerable correspondence they arrived at a definite decision to use only "weight" in the new standard. Final study by Gregory and Agnew led to the idea of establishing weights based on the first 30 feet of line less any level line beyond the front taper. This opinion was circulated among the group, agreed upon, and in 1961 submitted to AFTMA. The new standard was quickly adopted. It is as follows:

No.	Weight in grains	Weight range
1	60	54-66
2	80	74-86
3	100	94-106
4	120	114-126
5	140	134-146
6	160	152-168
7	185	177-193
8	210	202-218
9	240	230-250
10	280	270-290
11	330	318-342
12	380	368-392

Identification symbols used with the new system:

L – Level
DT – Double Taper
FT – Forward Taper
ST – Shooting Taper (shooting head)
F – Floating Line
S – Sinking Line

Fly lines are labeled with some combination of these numbers and symbols. Manufacturers list the taper first, weight next, and whether it floats or sinks last. For example, a DT6F line has a double taper, weighs about 160 grains and floats.

Most generally, the old letter diameters from E to A correspond to the present weight numbers 5 to 9.

An angler can now choose whatever weight line recommended by his rod manufacturer and be assured of having a correctly balanced outfit.

3. FLUORESCENT FLIES

Joe Switzer started the "fluorescent" story in 1933. While thumbing through a magazine in his father's Los Angeles drugstore, he spotted an article on "black light" (invisible ultraviolet light). Intrigued, he set about building a lamp that would emit these invisible rays. Though crude, the improvised result of his efforts worked. The night following its completion, Switzer returned to the drugstore and moved his "light" about the darkened room. To his surprise, he noticed that a few drugs glowed brightly when hit with the beams of black light. The significance of this anomaly was not lost on Switzer, for as an amateur magician he could, quite literally, see its immediate application. He mixed the chemicals with shellac, painted the result on some stage props and gave a show at his high school. There in the darkened auditorium, the props eerily appeared as ultraviolet light played across their surface. His classmates were dumbfounded and the "magic" was a huge success. At his brother's suggestion, they decided to market the paint commercially.

The operation remained small until Joe Switzer and Dick Ward, chief chemist in their employment, developed black light fluorescent ink. First used on theater posters and billboards, it was in constant demand when World War II airplane and ship charts, manuals, dials and navigation tables had to be read in total darkness. Just before the war they invented daylight fluorescent colors that today form the bulk of their business. These colors were initially paint additives for signal panels and later, when fluorescent dyes were produced, were found in all types of fabrics where increased visibility was important: Army, Air Force and Navy wind socks, parachutes, aerial tow targets, semaphore flags, and signal flags that helped guide planes in on carrier decks.

Carrier decks were almost nonexistent in 1942. The Japanese had reduced our flattop force to one lone ship, the U.S.S. *Enterprise.*

Aboard her was AP's roving correspondent, Eugene Burns. Carrier warfare was Burns' specialty and here he first noticed the bright fluorescent colored signal flags. As a lifelong fisherman, he wondered if the same colors could be incorporated into fishing lures.

After the war, he had not forgotten his discovery of fluorescent materials and now sought to find where the dyes originated and to determine if they had a practical application in fishing. Burns succeeded on both counts. Beginning with trout patterns, he called his first creations "fireflies" — standard dressings save for fluorescent yarn bodies. He then got together with a small group of businessmen and in May, 1948, formed the Firelure Corporation. The corporate membership included Bob Switzer, who would supply the dyes, and John O. Gantner, president of a company that had used these same dyes in manufacturing bathing suits and sweaters. Since Gantner was already using fluorescent yarn in his products, it was an easy step from the loom to the fly tying bench. Actually prior to Firelure, Gantner had distributed materials to a few fishing tackle manufacturers. Now Firelure was to have complete control of this end of the business. In deference to Gantner, fly tying yarns and flosses were marketed under the trade name "Gantron." Fluorescent paint for spoons and plugs was also sold.

The Firelure distributing shop was set up in San Francisco. Professional fly tiers all along the Pacific Coast were next contacted and became part of the "Gantron Program." The fluorescent material was sold at a nominal cost but with it went tags at one cent each per 10,000 or two cents each per 1,000. One of these had to be attached to each commercially made fly. Most of these specially dressed patterns were fair traded at 35 cents each.

Two tiers who joined the program were Polly Rosborough of Chiloquin, Oregon, and Wes Drain of Seattle, Washington. Rosborough began Gantron's use on steelhead by converting the popular Van Luven. The fluorescent chenille version was an eye catcher, produced well and since has become an Oregon standard.

Wes Drain, an inventive and imaginative fly dresser, conceived a pattern quite unlike any other before or since. An orange Gantron tip set off a neon magenta (cerise) body and the fly was framed with a grey squirrel tail wing and purple saddle hackle. Only the tail of golden pheasant tippet smacked of tradition in what was otherwise a most incongruous series of colors. As with Rosborough's Van Luven, the fly was first used during steelheading's 1948-49 season. Nameless until February 4th, it was then christened in a most glorious manner. Drain was fishing the lower Skagit and searching its waters with his favorite outfit: a nine and a half foot E.C. Powell rod balanced with a Pflueger Medalist reel and GAF (FT9S) Ashaway Crandall American Finish fly line with a 12 foot leader tapered to a remarkably fine four pounds. The steelhead that came to his fly that day weighed 20 pounds 7 ounces and was recognized as a new Washington fly record. To bestow honor on both his pattern and good fortune, Wes named the effective new creation Drain's 20. His catch was only recently bettered by Ralph

These exquisite dressings are by Wes Drain of Seattle, Washington. Top row, Drain's 20, Muddy Waters; row 2, Steelhead Bloody Mary, Steelhead Kelly.

Wahl of Bellingham. The new state record was caught in 1965 from the Skagit River, a steelhead of 20½ pounds.

Firelure lasted but a few years. Other companies were able to develop their own dyes and dilute a still limited market. In 1949 Herter's Incorporated, the country's largest fishing tackle supply house, established their own line of fluorescent fly tying materials under the trade name "Radiant Color." They sold not only yarn and floss, but chenille, fur and feathers as well. Steelheaders will remember Eugene Burns for introducing fluorescent materials to their ranks. The many who followed Wes Drain and Polly Rosborough continued to substitute the new colors. Such established patterns as the Fall Favorite, Polar Shrimp, Thor and Skykomish Sunrise easily lent themselves to the to the fluorescent conversion. These early counterparts did much to establish winter steelhead fly fishing as a significant part of steelheading.

4. NEW AREAS AND RECORD FISH

Oregon's Deschutes River receives her best steelhead in early fall. They are summer-run fish, among the finest of this grand race found anywhere. On a September day in 1948, Morley Griswold, the Governor of Nevada, took a 28 pound steelhead from the lower reaches of this river not far from where it joins the Columbia. The fish exceeded any other fly caught steelhead by several pounds and was an all tackle Oregon record. Few expected this record to ever fall, a natural opinion in context with the known boundaries of steelheading experience. In this light, Griswold's fish would have remained an unassailable and antiquated reminder of generous times. But sport is not constant. It seemed to close the chapter on the wonderful confinement and hoary continuum of those four Oregon and California rivers that had paced our sport for half a century. And it pointed the way by offering eloquent testimony to the record steelhead ascending the Columbia River.

The Deschutes itself was no newcomer. Stories of its fishing go back a hundred years and its steelheading spurs were won by the 1930's. This is not so with the Idaho and Washington rivers contributing to the Columbia's great flow. These waters were not new in that they did not represent virgin territory, but they had yet to give up a full measure of their angling potential. The Cowlitz, Snake, Lewis, Wind, Klickitat, Kalama, Clearwater and Grand Ronde were those that after renewed prospecting began garnering laurels heretofore the property of famous name rivers farther south. New techniques and tackle were tried by new fishermen and this newness became an angling advantage. If it was within the potential of these Columbia rivers to produce record steelhead, they would be caught.

For many years the world record rainbow was a steelhead caught on January 6, 1930 by E.E. Ames. It came from Washington's Chehalis River, had a 40 inch length, 24½ inch girth and weighed 29 pounds. At the time, separate records were kept for steelhead and rainbow trout. This fish was to be exceeded many times following the stocking of Idaho's Pend Oreille Lake with Kamloops trout in 1942. Their phenomenal growth was such that three years later, Ames' record for the species was broken when a 31 pounder came to boat. And in 1947, the present world record rainbow trout of 37 pounds was caught from the lake by Wes Hamlet. While rainbows were coming fast and furious there, it was not the only water with such a happy angling faculty.

The first authenticated record I found of a 30 pound steelhead came during the Pend Oreille boom. W.W. White did the trick with a brass spinner on the Columbia River. Other record fish from either the Columbia or its tributaries were soon to follow. Time has shown the Cowlitz and Snake to be the best American rivers in terms of record steelhead. Probably half a dozen steelhead of 30 pounds or more have come from these two, including Homer Scott's Washington and U.S. record. Scott took his 33 pound fish from the Snake River on January 20, 1962. More recently is the Snake River steelhead caught by Cecil Darnell in October, 1969. The 43 inch long fish was weighed three times on different scales for these weights: 32-6, 33-1, and 34 pounds. Darnell had the steelhead mounted before the Idaho Fish and Game Department could officially weigh the trophy and declare it a record. Idaho's record steelhead remains one caught by Leonard Profitt in December, 1966. It weighed 29 pounds 8 ounces and came from the North Fork of the Clearwater River, a great part of the Snake and Columbia watershed.

New areas were being explored in the course of steelheading's growth. Naturally this pertained first to the more readily available domestic water of which something was known rather than far distant rivers that had rarely been pressed into service by spoon or fly.

Discussed in Chapter 5 was the great size potential steelhead races contained when coming from our three largest Pacific coast rivers, the Columbia, Frazier and Skeena. While the many Columbia tributaries were being hammered with renewed post-war vigor, the angling overflow and adventurous moved into British Columbia and to the Frazier for their sport. The size of the lower river does not lend itself to steelhead fishing and the cataract canyon waters farther north must be passed up altogether. As with our Columbia, fishing is best done on the more tractable tributaries such as the robust Thompson. A river showing a fall-run steelhead race with the phenomenally high average weight of 14 pounds.

Our most remote western giant is the Skeena and was the last to be explored for its tributary steelhead. Jeffry Wilson riveted angling interests to these fantastic waters in 1953 by taking a 30½ pounder near where the Bulkley and Kispiox rivers join to form the Skeena. His fish placed first in the annual *Field & Stream* fishing contest and brought the area to national attention. Records really began rolling the following year when Chuck Ewart caught the present world record steelhead of 36 pounds. The river was the Kispiox and in 1954 giant trout of 31½, 29-7, 29, 28-6 and 28 pounds came to an assortment of lures, though the Gibbs Tee Spoon, actually a huge spinner, dominated as it does on other Canadian waters.

The Kispiox was our greatest steelheading strike and the rush, so to speak, was on. In 1955 three Washington anglers traveled north to the Kispiox and repeated fly fishing successes previously enjoyed on their Skykomish, Skagit and Stilliguamish rivers. Enos Bradner accounted for a 15 pound 12 ounce fish, while Ralph Wahl's largest was exactly one pound heavier. The third member of the party, George McLeod, rose a steelhead to his Skykomish Sunrise which was a new world record, breaking the old one set by Morley Griswold seven years before. His great steelhead weighed 29 pounds 2 ounces, and ironically it too would be broken seven years later.

One catch remains to be told. This is the present fly fishing record, perhaps the most remarkable steelheading feat of all. While the fish was extraordinary, so too was the skilled angler who killed him. Karl Mausser has taken more record size steelhead on the fly than any other man in the history of the sport. He wrote his story for this book; it would not have been complete without it.

WORLD SERIES STEELHEAD

The idea of telling the story of my incredible luck in hooking and landing this huge sea-run rainbow occurred to me many times, but I kept pushing it aside. I have seen what too much publicity can do to certain areas, and didn't want to be responsible for it happening again. However, it is a matter of record where this fish was caught and certain natural hazards tend to weed out some fishermen, so I believe it won't make a lot of difference now.

I first fished the Kispiox in 1957 and again in 1960 and 1961 with very indifferent results all three times, but one thing did happen that

Karl Mausser holds his 33 pound steelhead, a world's record for the fly.

may have played a vital part in my eventual success. In 1957 my longtime friend Roy Pitts and I did some experimenting with fly patterns and out of this came the fly which Drew Wookey of Wookey's Fishing Resort, christened "Kispiox Special." It is the pattern that has spelled success for me. It must also be mentioned that the development of fast sinking lines by Scientific Anglers Inc. played a big part, for if there ever was a stream where you had to get down fast, the Kispiox is that stream.

I'd left home (Burlingame, California,) July 14, 1962 and wandered here and there through British Columbia, finally landing on another fishing spot which will have to be nameless for now. Here I had some wonderful fishing, beaching 31 summer-run steelhead up to 15 pounds.

On September 27th, I arrived at Drew and Pat Wookey's rustic fishing camp on the Kispiox. After setting my trailer down, I fished two close pools without success. The next few days went by very swiftly. The weather stayed cold and though it rained a bit, it was snowing in the hills. This is good news on the Kispiox, for the snow holds the water and keeps the river from going out.

By October 8th I'd hooked five steelies. Two were lost while the three killed went from 8½ to 13 pounds, on the small side for this stream.

The World's Series had started between the San Francisco Giants and New York Yankees. Being from the bay area, I was an avid Giant fan, so divided my time between fishing and listening to the game. It rained the night of October 7th but had quit by dawn. I'd slept well and after breakfast went fishing until 10:30 a.m., when I came in to again listen to the ball game. The Giants won 7-3 and I remembered thinking it might be a lucky omen as far as hooking a fish. Returning to the river, I worked a close run with several patterns without a touch, so left and worked farther down the river. I had gone about half through a run when I lost the fly I was using on a snag. Tying on a Kispiox Special, I made a few casts and then hooked something really solid. When the fish first showed I could see he was brightly colored as most of these big males seem to be. I managed to get below him and luckily he held his position pretty well. Below this particular run is a no man's land where plenty of fish are lost. This steelhead must have just come into the pool and was tired for I was able to keep him from running down into this area. A short time later I was able to beach him. Beach isn't exactly the right word as there isn't any beach. In fact, if there is a worse place to land a fish on this stream I don't know of it. When he was about two feet from the water's edge he stranded in an upright position and I could see the fly in the back corner of his mouth. It had penetrated the hinge so was about as well hooked as possible. Keeping a taut line, I got out in the stream, worked behind him and sort of bunted him with the side of my foot. Only then did I relax. I knew he was something special so I lugged him to my car and drove to Wookey's where we measured, weighed and photographed him. Since the scales we used in weighing wasn't a balance type, Drew and I drove into town (Kispiox) and we weighed the fish on the store's big balance scales. Surprisingly, the small scales had been accurate. He weighed 33 pounds, was 42 inches long and had a 24 inch girth. Eventually this steelhead was sent to Norquist's of Haywood, California. They did an outstanding job of mounting him.

As far as the records show, he appears to be the largest steelhead ever taken on a fly. For me it's been a never ending thrill, but I'll always be trying to better it as long as I'm able.

If the Giants ever get into another world's series, maybe I'll be lucky again. It is an interesting thought, and though I don't think I'm really superstitious, maybe you try harder if you believe in your luck.

For the great tributaries of the Skeena River, expert Victor Moore of Smithers, British Columbia, tied these dressings. Top row, Pink Mambo, Double Flame Egg; row 2, Flame Squirrel Tail, Fluorescent Chappie.

CHAPTER NINE

The Contempory Steelheader I

1. DRIFT FISHING TACKLE

Winter steelhead, and to a lesser extent, summer steelhead, enter rivers as migratory fish and should always be considered in this context regardless of the period of river residence. The river promotes only their continued migration, ultimate spawning and ocean return. River beds are highway surfaces steelhead see as barren of life. They are oriented best to reproduction and not to active feeding; their's is a tunnel vision of purpose. For one's lure to entice, it must sink to the steelhead's principal level of interest and once there travel with currents as so much oncoming traffic. The explosive collision is what steelheading is all about.

The angler must adjust his tackle and fishing techniques to the unique characteristics of each river he fishes.

This steelheading axiom may be phrased differently, but it remains the single unalterable principle in selecting tackle: *rod, reel and line must first match the river to be fished.* Too frequently the angler selects tackle according to predetermined attitudes about the requirements of the sport, personal habits and aspirations. This, of course, is most natural and praiseworthy; as an example, to take fish on "sporting tackle" is a basic tenet of angling. Yet the huge anadromous trout we seek are caught more in the imaginations than in experience if the river cannot be worked correctly. A ten pound steelhead may be found at tidewater or in violent canyon rapids, in rivers that tankers negotiate, in tributary creeks several rod lengths wide and at depths to 30 feet or more. No one outfit and method can be expected to answer all these needs.

Even on a single river daily fluctuations in water level, clarity and turbulence can change tackle requirements. Some years ago I fished Washington's Quinault with a very flexible eight foot rod. Normally the outfit would have served me well, but it had been raining hard for a week and the river was very strong. When I cast a lead suited to the rod strength, the lure did not work the bottom; when the proper weight was used, the outfit cast poorly and the drift seemed uncontrolled. To make matters worse, a brutal wind developed a belly in the line. Nevertheless, a steelhead was interested and took the lure and I set hard on him. The fish hardly noticed the effort. Desperately reeling in slack, I set the hook again. This brought the steelhead to the surface where the lure came free—the hook had never penetrated. I returned to the river two weeks later and found this rain forest country covered by the heaviest snow in years. The rod I carried that day was both longer and more powerful than the stick used previously. It proved nearly worthless. The vast Quinault watershed now contributed nothing to a river drastically reduced in flow. Steelhead caught in the winter drought were holding tightly in the low, air-clear water; an angler expertly using the lightest and most sensitive tackle would have been challenged. I spent the day working for one decent drift; conditions had made this popular river my private domain.

When a lure is cast across the river, allowed to sink and follow the bottom downstream, line left on the surface will be affected by the current. Because a river's flow moves at different speeds and depths—the slowest water at the bottom and sides, the fastest just below the surface and in the center assuming the river's greatest depth is equidistant from each side—surface line moving at current speeds may unnaturally increase and alter the course of a bottom bouncing lure. For this reason the steelhead rod is six and a half to ten and a half feet long and able to keep the maximum amount of line free of surface drag. Within this length range are strengths capable of tossing weights of up to two ounces.

A compromise outfit would be a seven and a half to eight foot rod and medium size spinning reel loaded with at least 150 yards of ten pound test monofilament. It should be able to handle a weight range of 3/8 to 3/4 of an ounce. The action of the rod is very important. The bend of the rod must progress evenly from butt to tip with the butt a shade stiff, flexing well and the whole rod feeling "alive"—"snappy" rather than "sloppy." The fast taper tip-type rod should be avoided; it does not absorb shock well, whether on the strike or during the contest to follow.

The better sporting goods stores now carry a number of rods marked specifically for steelhead. While these should still be checked with a critical eye, they do narrow down the field.

The initial steelhead outfit described can be purchased for under $40.00. Of the total amount, about half will be allocated for the reel. Purchasing cheap line is a poor investment. If cost is a consideration, buy the best and after wear has made the line's continued integrity questionable, reverse the line by winding it off on a spare spool.

Most good reels come with a second spool or one is made readily available. An extra spool containing six-pound-test line is a necessary addition. While the suggested rod will not do the best of jobs casting weights less than 3/8 of an ounce, a change to six-pound monofilament will permit weights of 1/4 of an ounce to be handled reasonably well on low, clear water.

With the two spools of ten- and six-pound-test line compatible with the rod and reel outlined, an angler can expect success on most steelhead rivers from California to Alaska.

Eventually for high water, larger domestic streams and those huge British Columbia rivers and steelhead, a heavier outfit will be required. I would suggest going to an eight and a half to nine foot rod with power sufficient to handle weights from 5/8 to 1½ ounces. The reel should be a medium sized salt water spinning type capable of holding 200 yards of 14 pound test line. The reel I have of this type has an additional spool filled with 17 pound test monofilament.

The two rods shown take care of most of my non-fly fishing needs when steelheading. The bait-casting rod is 8½ feet long and is lined with 14 pound test monofilament to fish bobbers and bait, particularly if the weight to be cast exceeds ½ ounce. This outfit is also the best way to go when fishing from a winter drift boat. The 7½ foot spinning rod has a reel with two spools holding six and eight (or eight and twelve if the river demands it) pound test monofilament. I use this outfit almost exclusively when fishing spoons and spinners weighing from 3/8 to 5/8 ounce. When I add an additional outfit, it is a one-handed seven foot spinning outfit with four to six pound test monofilament. I admit to having additional outfits — most heavier and longer — but can no longer find reasons for using them.

When bait-casting rods in the lengths and actions described are matched with high quality reels, the result is an excellent outfit for much of our winter steelheading. They have both advantages and disadvantages depending on one's point of view. The better bait-casting reels are expensive and their rate of retrieve are less than spinning reels. In the hands of the accomplished, they will cast tremendous distances. Nearly the opposite is true for beginners; some monumental snarls can result from an unpracticed thumb. They function best when using heavier weights and are less adaptable to a variety of conditions. Their principal advantage in steelheading is realized when line must be fed straight downstream to make a drift. Because this is frequently the case when fishing from a boat and on rivers where we want to work a bait downstream to a single holding spot, the purchase of a bait-casting rod and reel should be given more than passing consideration.

2. TECHNIQUES

Facing a steelhead river for the first time produces some understandable anxieties. Where to begin and what lure to use must be resolved without the confidence of past experiences. Unfortunately, the ability to identify steelheading water is often thought of in terms of knowledge belonging only to the occult. It is not. Look at the total river and imagine the route a migrating steelhead must take. Imagine where on that route the fish is most secure in its river environment, or conversely, where elements are at work to lessen the steelhead's interest in a passing lure. Water but a few inches deep exposes the fish and little time is wasted there. Rapids and falls must be overcome with singleminded determination. Ideally, a river breaks enough to be called a falls before forming a deep, slower moving run. From there the river may widen, become more shallow and eventually break again. Mini-falls and pools can be found in the shallows or a series of falls can create rapids. How the parts are combined is what gives each river its special character.

The steelhead migrates in starts and stops; some surroundings invite a temporary stay, particularly when the next water ascended requires a violent expenditure of energy. Locate deep *moving* water: steelhead have passed here, more will be arriving, some may be present now. Look for characteristics in the river's bottom, banks and surface that seem to hold water from the taxing main current. Is the bank undercut, or does it have a deep cut holding calm water? Is there an extra deep hole in the bottom? Are there boulder and stump obstructions? Have logs piled up at a bend in the river? Steelhead react favorably to all these areas. If there is a choice between very fast and slow currents, compromise by fishing the edge of the fast.

What lure to select? The spoon is familiar to all anglers and thus a logical choice. The cast is made quartering upstream. When the spoon touches down, keep the rod tip high and prevent additional line from escaping by pressing the spinning reel spool with the forefinger. Do not close the bail. The spoon will begin tumbling downstream. If it has not hit bottom as it passes you, it will be necessary to feed line into the drift. When did the spoon finally reach bottom? Or did it reach bottom at all? Or did it immediately sink and "hang" bottom? The spoon should have made its first contact with the river bed no earlier than as it swings by you and no later than when it is approximately quartering downstream. Let it hit bottom once, twice, to make sure it did not strike the top of a tall boulder, *then* close the bail. Reel in a bit of slack and let the spoon begin working. The lure will pass farther downstream as it swings across. If it is too friendly with the bottom, begin taking a few slow turns on the reel. Our objective is to swim the spoon across the stream bottom in crescent sweeps. The drift is over when the spoon has worked its way to the angler's side of the river. If there is productive water between the rod and where the spoon finished its drift, reel back just fast enough to keep the spoon off the bottom. More probably, the lure has made it to shallow water. Then the spoon should be quickly reeled in and preparation made for a second cast.

There are half ounce spoons from an inch and a half to four inches long. This size difference depends on blade thickness and decides how fast the spoon will sink. If difficulty is encountered in reaching the bottom, go to a more compact spoon. It is much better to change spoons than add additional weight such as split shot or a clip sinker. Besides poorer casting qualities, the result has a greater tendency to permanently snag the bottom.

The steelhead will take anytime during the spoon's swing. The strike comes; the steelhead jumps and makes an initial run ending in a second leap, all of which can leave an angler close to shock. For this reason, the drag should be set only enough for the hooks to penetrate. The forefinger should always be considered an important drag addition.

The color combinations available in steelhead spoons are staggering. Only a few of these colors are needed, though I admit to carrying a variety, more for the new lease of enthusiasm that changing lures gives than any other reason. The finish I prefer above all others is brass, hammered or plain. I collect spoons of this type from an inch to three inches long. Other finishes I like include hammered silver or brass with a touch of flame, flame and white stripe, red and white stripe and all flame with a silver back. It matters more to have spoons with various sinking abilities than an extensive color assortment. Some popular brands are the Les Davis "Hot Rod," Nebco "Tor-P-Do," Seneca "Wob-l-Rite and Acme "Kamlooper." There are many other makes that produce well.

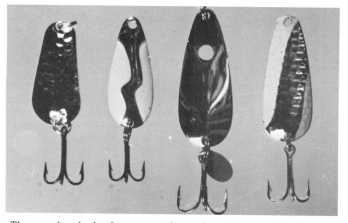

There are hundreds of spoons on the market with many worthless for steelheading. Here in the ½ ounce size are four of the best: Seneca's "Wob-l-rite," Acme's "Kamlooper," Les Davis' "Hot Rod," and Nebco's "Tor-P-Do."

Most spoons have treble hooks of both small size and poor quality. These should be removed and replaced with a single Siwash hook. If treble hook quality is kept, make sure they are needle sharp — steelhead are very capable of striking and throwing the spoon. Some spoons come with a ring for line attachment while others simply have a hole bored through the blade. In either event, a snap swivel should be tied on the line first. A few pennies spent here will avoid ruining a spool of line; the fast retrieve we give a spoon following its drift can quickly kink the best of lines.

An effective drift is realized when no reeling is done until the spoon has finished its swing, and many prefer to fish in this manner. The bad feature of this procedure is the frequent loss of the spoon. Actually, the spoon drifted in the manner originally described entails enough lost lures that additional losses are burdensome. A spoon can be fished and never lost, by reeling in as soon as it hits the water. When so worked it will rarely take fish unless covering very shallow holding water.

It is necessary to point out that the very nature of drifting a lure along the bottom is going to result in many lost lures. If one is not losing lures then he probably is fishing incorrectly, or is angling over a

These spinners weight from 1/4 to 1/8 ounce and are excellent for summer-run steelhead in low water. Line should test from four to six pounds to adequately cast such light lures.

134

remarkably snag free bottom. When I hang-up, and within a few seconds am unable to free the lure, I break it off by taking a few turns of line around my arm and backing away until the line parts. It is not a good idea to break line from the reel for on occasion the break may occur at the bail arm.

One should vary the distance cast until all the water is covered. This usually involves going from short to long casts, though clear water in small streams will point out the slots of productive water and these alone can be fished.

Much of what has been said regarding spoon fishing could be repeated when using spinners. Most generally, they will not cast as far or sink as quickly. Look for spinners with solid metal bodies, or at least solid metal beads on the wire shaft. Recently introduced steelheading examples are the "Buda" and "Bolo" spinners. The French Mepps comes in all sizes — and it is now marketed in a large size for use on steelhead. It is excellent for clear water days. As with spoons and for the same reason, these lures require the use of a snap swivel.

THE BOBBER, YARN FLY AND BAIT

The bobber, yarn fly and a variety of baits are standard summer and winter drift fishing lures. All require additional weight to be fished. The rigging of these lures is subject to considerable interpretation, but basically involves the reel line attaching to a three-way swivel, the lure tied with 18-24 inches of nylon and a lead sinker secured to the final swivel ring.

Line snelled to a hook is the starting point for all these drift lures. Before the finished snell is pulled against the hook eye, six one-and-a-half inch strands of fluorescent yarn can be slipped in the loop between the snell and eye. When the snell is drawn against the eye the yarn is securely held. The resulting yarn fly is a cheap and excellent lure. If additional color is sought, a bobber can be threaded on the line. The snelled hook alone suffices if using only a bait or bobber.

One very popular lure is clusters of salmon or steelhead spawn mixed with fluorescent yarn. The hooks best suited for this type of fishing have a shank barb which prevents the snell from reaching the hook eye. The loop of leader that lies between the snell and hook eye is slipped over the bait to secure it. Because the yarn will not stay in the permanent space between snell and eye, it must be tied directly on the leader *above* the hook. This is accomplished by laying a three inch piece of tying yarn on a flat surface and crossing it with the leader. Over the leader and opposite the tying yarn, lay two-or three-inch-and-a-half strands of yarn. Next gather the tying yarn ends and tie a square knot. Slide the knot to the hook eye and trim the strands for an even length.

Some steelhead baits are: night crawlers, shrimp, single eggs and fresh or "cured" cluster eggs. When whole skeins are removed from "green" fish, the eggs are still tightly secured in the skein membrane, and when cut into baits will take a surprising amount of abuse. If the eggs need to be kept for later use or toughened, the skein is cut into

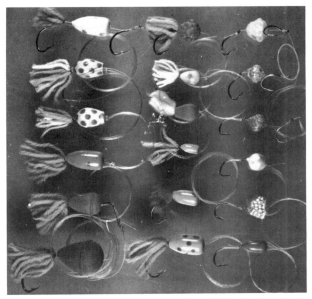

Bobbers range from pea- to golf ball-size. What size to select is usually governed by water clarity. Unlike yarn flies they naturally float and in the smaller sizes are frequently used with bait to reduce snagging.

suitable baits and rolled freely in borax or a similar "egg cure" mixture. When stored in the refrigerator, they will keep for months.

Eggs are a mess to use. Unless the hands are washed after baiting up, a viscous egg-borax residue ends up on everything. Yet hands repeatedly rinsed in winter water are uncomfortable. The only solution so far devised involves tucking a towel in the bait can belt and drying hands after each frigid rinse.

The key to drift fishing lays in using a weight calculated to keep the lure moving along the bottom at a steady "tap-tap" speed. Most anglers use a pencil lead for this purpose. It comes in 3/16 and ¼ inch diameters and is attached in numerous ways. One method attaches the line through a hole bored in the flattened end of the pencil lead. This line should test less than the reel line so that hanging up looses only the inexpensive lead. My objection to tying a pencil lead on is the bolo effect received when casting and, the swinging lead line often fouls on the swivel. The problem is alleviated with the use of surgical tubing available in most sporting goods stores. Cut two inches off, slip it over a ring on the three-way swivel and cinch it tightly above the ring with stout nylon thread or soft wire. The desired amount of pencil lead is then jammed in the surgical tubing.

If too much lead is used, the lure progresses with periodic stops and frequent snagging. Too little lead and the angler has a difficult time feeling the bottom. Once a length is selected it may be necessary to adjust the weight to fit the fishing conditions. Rather than carry a variety of lengths, a dozen pencil leads six to eight inches long can be carried to the river and the amount needed secured with the aid of a small pair of side cutter plyers.

Because bobbers naturally float, they will require more weight than either bait or yarn flies.

There is not a set formula for selecting one bobber color over another. Choosing larger bobbers for off-color water and small bobbers and yarn flies for clear water seems logical enough. The fluorescent fire-orange — "flame" — is more effective in dingy water on overcast days. Some of the fluorescent pastels such as pink, purple, green and yellow are favorites in clear water. The yellow bobbers with orange spots are sometimes an excellent choice for clear water.

For all the steelhead's size and strength, they usually take the bobber, yarn fly or bait in a gentle, almost curious manner. The lure's drift simply stops. A snag will have the same effect but the strike must still be made in good faith. In the course of a season, more than a few of these "snags" will end up as beached steelhead. There is also the steelhead that accepts and rejects the bait before the angler is able to react. Extra sensitive rods will help alleviate this problem. The easiest way to increase one's recognition of a taking fish is by making shorter casts. So much has been written regarding the need of long casts that steelheaders feel compelled to push for the maximum on each cast. If at all possible short casts should be used. On short casts the fish's take is more clearly identified and there is less slack to interfere with the strike. If extremely long casts must be made, the angler would do well to consider covering the water first with a spoon.

Almost any lure can be drifted with a pencil sinker if by itself there is not enough weight for easy casting. The large but light spinner with a

Yarn flies used with and without bait are the most popular steelhead lures and with good reason. They are cheap, easy to tie and very effective. The top yarn fly is used with cluster eggs; the bottom yarn fly is fished as is or with a bobber slipped down the line.

body of plastic fluorescent pink golf tees is an example. It is great steelhead medicine and one of the few really good lures for ascending chinook salmon. When using a pencil lead with these spinners, some reeling will be necessary to keep the spinner blade working.

Plugs of the flatfish type are of importance and most are fished with a pencil sinker. Because some current resistance against the lure is needed to give a seductive wobbling action, a heavier weight is used to slow the drift.

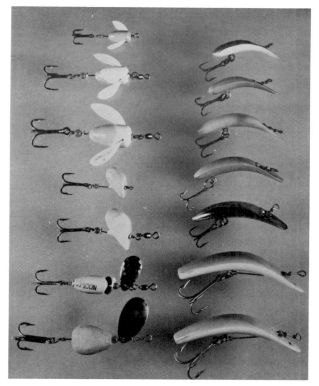

Floating lures with some type of built-in action. All require additional weight to be cast though the plugs can be fed downstream and with a tight line worked to a fish-getting level. This technique is most frequently used from drift boats where "pulling plugs" has developed into a deadly low water technique.

Specialized methods have been developed for days of extremely low and clear water. The "single egg" is a delicate and demanding technique using a small hook, a single large salmon egg and a few split shot for weight. Line testing as low as four pounds carries the bait to the steelhead. Two separate outfits can handle such a task. On small streams where short casts are necessary, a fly outfit using only monofilament on the reel does a wonderful job. The cast is made by stripping a dozen feet of line from the reel and presenting the bait with a sidearm throw. On larger rivers, a light, rather soft action spinning rod is used. Rod length should not be sacrificed; seven and a half feet is about right. Few spinning rods can be found that are suitable and many anglers prefer to convert a fly rod blank. The advantages of both outfits are realized by using a spin-casting reel on the fly rod. The reel, holding six pound test line should resemble an enclosed fly reel with line coming from a hole in the center of the side plate. Fishing the single egg is accomplished in the standard, quartering upstream-and-across drift fishing manner with the sensitive rod telegraphing the split shot's downstream progress.

Conventional spin-casting reels used on bait-casting rods have never been popular for steelheading. If for no other reason, I do not care for them because I am unable to use my forefinger to snub line when striking the bobber nibbling steelhead. I also like to be able to quickly change reel spools when conditions demand.

A seven foot spinning rod and six to eight pound test line is a challenging way to present small spoons and spinners to steelhead in gin clear streams. When expertly handled, the tackle will subdue even the largest steelhead. The six-and-a-half foot spinning rod and four pound test line make for an exciting contest where large numbers of half-pounder steelhead are anticipated. These steelhead are often found on southern rivers.

Plunking is a term for an extremely popular steelhead still fishing method. Plunkers can be observed along the Columbia River by the hundreds and even the top drifting rivers have sections best fished by plunking. The method basically involves anchoring a lure or bait in a productive drift and waiting for an ascending steelhead to take it. Favored lures are those with built in action; the Spin-N-Glo and Flatfish are two that qualify. Bait like spawn are either cluster or loose eggs wrapped in cheese cloth to make nickel size baits. Because a sinker of two or more ounces is needed to hold bottom, the rod is stiffer than a regular drift rod. Except for heavier line — about 15 pound test — and more lead, rigging is the same as for drift fishing.

Plunking really comes into its own during periods of high, discolored water. The sinker and bait or Spin-N-Glo (steelhead smell the former and home in on the sound of the latter) is cast a bit upstream from the desired spot. Quickly reaching bottom, the sinker will bounce a time or two before gaining a hold. The rod is then set in a sand spike or rested against a forked stick jammed firmly in the ground. Because plunking is frequently done in the company of others and visiting around a campfire, a time passing pleasure, a bell is often tied to the rod to announce a steelhead's interest.

Far more steelhead are lost in plunking by striking too early than too late. They may "fool" with the bait or lure for quite a time before decisively grabbing and running. When the bell begins ringing and the rod is removed, if the steelhead is not hooked but still interested, it takes calm nerves to keep from striking. However, until the fish pulls — hard, wait! Actually, some plunkers wait until the steelhead is running before removing the rod and giving the fish an additional wallop.

The shortcoming in describing techniques is that the description may not take into account subtle variances to standard methods that can spell the difference between success and failure. The following are a few such methods that should prove useful.

It was once my good fortune to fish with a most gifted plunker. When on the river we used comparable outfits and identical lures but he always tied on less weight, sometimes nothing more than an extra long piece of pencil lead. It rarely held the bottom for very long periods. He saw to that. A jerk of the rod sent the lead bouncing a few feet farther downstream, eventually working to the deep water along the bank where we were fishing. If nothing happened after a few minutes, the lead was picked up, a few feet of line stripped off and the lure worked to a new spot. His method seemed peculiar until I realized he knew the river intimately, knew *exactly* where the steelhead should be and was setting his lure only in those places. You could call this fishing very slow drifting or impatient plunking; whatever, it was the demise of hundreds of steelhead.

Another technique uses bait in the clear, very deep and slow moving water occasionally found in the current proper and frequently encountered on a canyon's backwater side-pools. A swivel is tied to eight pound reel line and attaches to an 18 inch six pound test leader that ends in a baited hook. Just above the swivel a ¼ ounce barrel sinker is clipped on for weight. An upstream cast is made, the bait allowed to sink to the bottom and then reeled back very, very slowly. The steelhead may take at any point in the retrieve. This rig with heavier line and assorted clip sinker weights is used with a bait-casting rod on discolored winter rivers where it is desirable to place and hold bait in extra small pools and holes. The technique is particularly effective on smaller streams where nearly all the water can be covered by wading and the long drift fishing runs are absent.

If a drift ends with the lure still in good holding water, the angler should not immediately begin the retrieve. Assume a steelhead has followed or is holding. He can be tantalized by slowly swinging the rod back and forth, reeling in a few turns then dropping the bait back. If the river is shallow enough, a steelheader can position himself above a suspected hot spot and drift straight downstream. Let the lure or bait slip right where the waiting mouth of a steelhead is and hold to plunk for a minute.

LANDING A STEELHEAD

The terrain determines methods used in landing a steelhead. The vast majority are merely beached. After the fish has been tired out and is about ten feet away, it can be slid ashore on a tight line with raised rod, by the angler who simply backs up the beach. It helps to be a bit downstream from the steelhead before starting this operation. The river current can then be used to help keep the fish coming. Should room and terrain make such a beaching impossible, the steelhead may be left partially stranded. The angler must then work quickly to get below the fish where it can be booted clear of the water or grabbed at the base of the tail and steadily pushed farther up the beach. No effort should be made to hoist a steelhead free of the water using this tail hold.

A gaff is rarely required in steelheading. The exception may be canyon water where one fishes from rock to rock. Without a gaff here, the angler must secure his steelhead by hand, a procedure I have always found difficult. Whenever I fish water known to have few suitable landing spots, I carry a collapsible gaff where the tip fits neatly into the handle. It is tied to an elastic cord and then tucked in the wader belt. The gaff should not be left free to dangle on the cord; if caught on some streamside obstruction and suddenly released, it can cause a terribly painful blow.

Nets of a size sufficient for handling steelhead are much too large to ever be carried by the wading angler. However, if plunking where roads

A 12-pound hen steelhead caught by plunking from the Puyallup River Because of flood contro. measures on this river, a salmon net is frequently used to land steelhead.

and flood control measures have made steep concrete or rickrack river banks, the large, long handled net becomes an important equipment addition. Fishing for steelhead by drifting in everything from frail wooden prams and rubber rafts to specially designed dories — McKenzie and Rogue styles — has become a mania on our rivers. Most anglers would prefer to beach their craft on a suitable bar when a steelhead is hooked. But when this is not possible, the net must be relied upon.

3. DEVELOPING A SYSTEM

All anglers have a favorite place to pursue their sport. Familiarity with the environment and elements which affect the gamefish will allow the angler to consistently make the correct decisions. Such is the start of a steelheading "system." The balance involves locating the fish and then confidently and correctly administering a series of proven lures.

The system involves no magic. Take any drift and fish it thoroughly with a bobber and pencil lead. The "tap-tap" of the sinker is a blind man's can — there gradually emerges an accurate picture of the river bottom, how the currents move, where snags are located and identifies the sudden deep slots sure to hold steelhead. Can steelhead be observed if the water is clear? If a steelhead is hooked, where exactly was it holding? Do steelhead hold in different parts of the drift during fluctuations in water level and clarity? Some of these questions may be immediately answerable and others ascertained only after a complete season of fishing. But they are answers that ultimately must be forthcoming if a drift's full angling potential is to be realized.

As a drift becomes understood, methodic prospecting is less and less necessary. When steelhead "A" leaves a particular station, ascending steelhead "B" will likely find the same station to its liking. In a drift, steelhead may be found in a variety of areas, but probably 90 percent of them will hold in 10 percent of the water. It is this 10 percent we must from experience come to identify. When this is accomplished, the number of casts needed to completely work the riffle is drastically reduced. On small riffles, perhaps a dozen casts will suffice. The lure is kept in the most productive water, snags remembered and avoided, the fish located and past successes repeated. When a number of such spots are learned on a single river, the angler can quickly move from one riffle to another, sampling miles of a river yet confident that the best of it has been carefully covered.

The system need not be limited to a single river. Changing water conditions are a contingency every steelheader must deal with, and different rivers are not affected in a like manner by rain. When several rivers within reasonable driving distance are made part of the system, the angler becomes that much more flexible. The one river is "out"? Experience may point to a neighboring river slower to discolor and the day can successfully end there.

On the lower river, tides will sometimes determine the quality of fishing and so become an important consideration in developing a system. For example, if an incoming PM tide is realized and the flood tide times late in the angling day, the angler would want to work downstream over already ascended fish and gradually encounter fresh arrivals. At dusk he should be at the first great pool above tidewater.

The river guide who is engaged for float trips introduces his system to visiting anglers. The boat is held in the most productive drifts, casts made and the downriver trip continued. The occasional steelheader could do no better than to hire a guide if he has but a few days for his fishing. Locals too, can often learn from several such trips. In a short time the guide's system is understood without the price of a long apprenticeship.

Steelheading maps are now available showing the best drifts, riffles and holes. These are of enormous advantage in developing a workable system that consistently produces.

A final note concerns the many creeks, either tributaries to large rivers or passing directly to the sea, that produce no more than a few

Dick Owsley holds a magnificent hen steelhead caught from Washington's Sol Duc River, an Olympic Peninsula water that joins with its sister, the Bogachiel, to form the Quilloyute.

dozen steelhead each year. They are of value if several good pools are known on each. These can be covered in a few minutes and may save a trip when the popular rivers have failed.

4. MISCELLANEOUS EQUIPMENT

The majority of steelheading is done in the fall and winter — cold, wet months in the Northwest. For this reason regulars pay particular attention to their angling garb.

A completely waterproof parka is an absolute requirement. Parkas can range from waist length for wader wearers to thigh length for those favoring hip boots. If heavy and constant rain is to be encountered, the parka should be rubberized. Rain is such a regular possibility that even

on clear days I have taken to carrying a very compact parka in my fishing vest. The parka hood should be large and extend a bit past the head. Most important of all, the sleeves should fit very snugly around the wrists. There is presently a number of Japanese parkas available that have only a snap for cinching at the sleeve. When holding your drift rod up, rain easily runs down the arm, soaking from the inside out. Such parkas are useful only for plunking where holding a rod for long periods is not required. If elastic is not sewn into the parka sleeves, then heavy rubber bands should be slipped over the wrists before fishing.

An inexpensive addition to the rubberized parka is the hooded sweatshirt. Just remember to purchase one at least one size larger than needed — they are not sanforized.

Undergarments range from 100 per cent wool longjohns for cold weather to quilted suits for freezing temperatures. Two pairs of medium wool socks are required with either.

If floating rivers or deep wading is anticipated, a life preserver that seconds as a fishing vest is a good investment. Some of these are presently marketed with a CO_2 cartridge for near instant inflation. Thus, unnecessary bulkiness is avoided until needed.

Steelheading is hard on fishing vests. They get smeared with eggs, repeatedly rain soaked and must carry considerable weight. Some good *steelheading* vests can be purchased for under $20.00. Look for one that is very waterproof, uses extra strong materials and has flaps over the pocket tops. My principle objection with most vests is that they are too long for waist deep wading; Columbia Sportswear markets an excellent exception called "The Kalama."

Waders are much preferable to hip boots if strenuous wading is expected. They have the added advantage of keeping one dry with a short parka. Hip boot wearers are not so fortunate and I personally do not care for long parkas in my wading. The long parka tends to obscure how deeply one can wade safely with hip boots. Both waders and hipboots should have heavy lug soles. If a hazardous river is part of the fishing, felt soles, felt sandals and spiked creepers should be considered for their nonslip benefits.

Yarn flies, small bobbers and snelled hooks are conveniently carried in plastic leader books. If the bobber is to be slid down the line to the yarn fly, it can be carried separately in a plastic box. Spoons may be stored in either a fly book or a partitioned plastic box. Unless only one spoon is put in each space, the spoons will tangle so that drawing a single lure results in a handful of brass and hooks. I have been able to get around this problem when the spoons purchased are individually wrapped in a rectangle of cellophane covered cardboard. I put them in a partitioned box as is and unwrap them as they are needed. Another solution involves plastic treble hook covers.

I carry pencil lead in a plastic box that once housed two spools of monofilament line.

Additional aids include nail clippers, a small pocket knife, tape measure, compact scales and hook stone. A nylon wader belt will minimize the dunkings. Polaroid glasses are a tremendous help in reading the water, locating fish and protecting the eyes when fly casting.

CHAPTER TEN

The Contemporary Steelheader II

1. SUMMER FLY FISHING

Fly fishing is the most poetic of angling's many arts and its virtues in steelheading have long been extolled, securing a greater share of the literary limelight. Though it was never the only tackle route to follow, the fly so dominated on those great southern rivers of our early steelheading that the sport we know today rests first on a fly fishing heritage. The reasons for this are not hard to find. The life histories discussed earlier show these summer-run steelhead to have a more residential character, thus more prone to feed in fresh water. Such habits simply proved more compatable with the floating or slow sinking silk lines then available. The steelhead would, in short, "rise to the fly." That is, they proved willing to move from a bottom resting station and pursue the presented dressing. Switching from silk to nylon and to glass from bamboo has not changed the rules — the onus still remains with the steelhead.

Passing years have allowed for the investigation of other summer steelhead deserving our fly casting attentions. While most fish will not match a Rogue steelhead's response, the rivers can still be worked to advantage with like tackle.

The selection of proper fly tackle is a highly individual matter subject to endless and fascinating discussions among anglers. But because the angler rarely casts directly to the steelhead and the river is best fished methodically, the rod should first be whatever length, weight and action the steelheader finds least tiring when adequately handling the long casts sometimes required.

Casting across or quartering down and across, the fly line should float and the wet fly sink to the desired depth. Unfortunately, a strong current between the angler and fly (we want to use the current to impart life to the fly) will create a belly in the line and drag the fly. This severe drag then keeps the fly skimming rapidly along just below the surface. There are two ways to overcome this and put the fly down. First, we may "mend" the line. This involves throwing an uncompleted roll cast upstream immediately upon the cast's completion. The technique slows the fly and gives it a moment to sink. The second method, fishes a fly weighted with lead wire on the hook. Whether to mend or weight the fly, or combine both methods depends on the river's depth and current velocity. If holding water is shallow and swift, the weighted fly alone will reach a productive depth. If the river is weak and depth is six to eight feet, the fly can be put down by carefully mending the line.

There have been some recent floating nylon lines marketed with a medium sinking dacron tip section. These help accomplish what is sought when mending a line or weighting a fly. The sinking tip is long enough to carry the fly to a productive depth while current exerts its ways on the surface line to give the fly necessary life.

The schools of-thought prevail on how the fly can best be worked. Some prefer to give the fly additional flash by taking in short strips while others make the current responsible for the fly's action. Most anglers interchange the two as they believe conditions demand.

As the fly swims downstream and begins its swing, it starts making its way to the surface. The steelhead attracted to the fly's tempting passage now makes its savage attack. Any resistance when the strike occurs on the nearly straight line will certainly break the fish off; light reel drag is line tightening enough to set the hook.

The favorite steelhead strikes on the run, jumps when barbed and continues on with a dash dependent on its size, sex and spirit. Females — "hens" — are the more dangerous. They are generally stronger, take to the air more often and are more prone to the terrified burst of downstream running energy that can carry them to white water and freedom. Some bright males — unless half-pounders, perhaps the strongest of the lot for their weight — will prove no less violent though in the main they contain their struggles to closer quarters. Bucks that have darkened can be particularly sluggish and much less interesting.

However the steelhead engages the angler, the fly reel must be considered something more than a storage place for uncast fly line. The fish is always fought directly from the reel and even a short run exceeds the remaining fly line. Backing, line additional to the fly line, is thus necessary. The amount of backing required is determined more by the river than the steelhead's size. (The longest run I have ever had a steelhead make was from a summer-run female of exactly seven pounds.) If casting over a winding series of small and strong pools, 75 yards of 20 pound test braided nylon or dacron would suffice. Where the river is gentled by long negotiable bars and the steelhead's running ability is not hampered by terrain, 150 yards of backing would contain the strongest fish — assuming the angler makes some effort to follow. If going after a runaway is impossible and the water the fish reaches is heavy, no amount of backing will save the catch; a steelhead simply cannot be dragged back through rapids.

The fly reel investment for steelheading can be quite modest. Many light single action reels with a reliable, adjustable drag, capable of holding the desired amount of backing can be purchased for under

$15.00. Top of the line domestic and English reels will generally cost $30.00 and up, while those reels with a gear ratio (usually 2-1) will run about $150.00.

The need to put a fly down deep for summer-run steelhead and flat on the bottom for the winter-run begins to complicate any categorical tackle recommendations. The different types of fly lines have been discussed. No one river will require them all; not all of a river's seasonal ways can be adequately fished using only one. Just as the drift

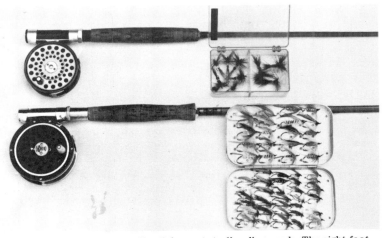

The two fly outfits above will satisfy most steelheading needs. The eight foot rod (top) handles a No. 6 floating line and is used for light wet and all dry fly work. The second rod is 8½ feet long and handles a No. 8 floating or sinking line and No. 9 sinking shooting head. When using a double taper line on the light outfit, I cut the back 30 feet of fly line off to accommodate 75 yards of backing.

fisherman must change weights and even outfits to obtain the maximum effectiveness from his lures, the fly fisherman will experiment with assorted lines to put the fly at the most productive depth. An all season steelhead fly outfit would be an eight and a half foot rod handling four different weight nine lines: double taper floating, floating with a sinking tip, medium sinking shooting head (or forward taper line with a like sinking rate) and a fast sinking shooting head.

Whether to use longer rods and heavier lines cannot necessarily be decided by the distance to be cast, for the greater rod length can cause fatigue. A shorter and lighter rod would actually cast farther when considering as a whole the hundreds of casts made in an angling day. However, when discolored water calls for a large weighted fly, lighter fly lines cannot carry the weight without endangering the caster. An interesting experiment involves wrapping lead wire on small or large

An early photograph of Mike Kennedy. Kennedy is an excellent steelhead fly fisher and an inovative fly tier. He has done much to perfect the sport and has been a continual influence upon fly fishermen.

hooks cut off at the bend and casting each. As line is extended it becomes progressively easier to handle the fly weight. But a certain weight is reached where extending the line in preparation for the cast is extremely hazardous and complete control of the fly is never fully realized. As the flies become heavier there is a gradual deterioration of the casting rhythm. The longer and more powerful the rod, the heavier the required fly line and the greater the fly weight one can cast. An extreme example would be the two handed, 16 foot rod and 9/0 fly found in use on Norwegian Atlantic salmon rivers.

In an effort to establish some rule of thumb for selecting steelhead fly tackle, I used fly weight as the deciding factor. This is at best an approximate indicator and a matter of personal choice. All hooks are 1X long and 1X stout (unless, of course, the fly is fished dry), lead wire for "weighted flies" is .030 inches in diameter, optic heads are brass and ¼ of an inch in diameter; large bead chain eyes will weigh slightly less than an optic head.

Purpose	Rod Length	Line Size	Maximum fly size
Light, wet or dry fly work	7½-8'	7	4 or smaller unweighted
Intermediate summer-run fishing and lightest for an all-purpose rod	8-8½'	8	6 weighted 4 optics 2 unweighted
General all-purpose	8½-9'	9	4 weighted 2 optics 1/0 un–weighted
Winter and summer steelheading where long casts, deep wading and large, heavy flies are anticipated	8½-9½'	10, 11	1 weighted 1/0 optics 3/0 un–weighted

Even small steelhead like this Stilliguamish River summer-run provide excellent sport when matched against light fly tackle.

Tapered leaders are preferred in steelheading because of their ability to turn over the frequently heavy flies with untangled precision. These can be purchased "knotless" or in blood knotted lengths of assorted diameters.

The monofilament sold for spinning is much too limp to use in leader construction. Two manufacturers that do sell excellent "hard" nylon specifically for leader making are Abercrombie & Fitch in New York, N.Y., and The Orvis Company in Manchester, Vt.

The following combinations of lengths and line tests would prove suitable for most steelheading.

40"	25 lbs.	38"	25 lbs.	36"	25 lbs.
34"	20 lbs.	32"	20 lbs.	28"	20 lbs.
8"	15 lbs.	6"	15 lbs.	6"	15 lbs.
8"	12 lbs.	6"	12 lbs.	6"	12 lbs.
18"	10 lbs.	6"	10 lbs.	6"	10 lbs.
9'		20"	8 lbs.	6"	8 lbs.
		9'		20"	6 lbs.
				9'	

Any suggested leader profile must be altered to suit water conditions. The length of heavy butt section is increased as fly size and weight increases and should not constitute less than 50 percent of the leader's total length. The ratio of butt to taper and tippet in the above is 74/34, 70/38 and 64/44.

Knotless 6, 7½ and 9 foot steelhead leaders, tapering from 25 pounds to either eight or ten pounds (.023-.013) can be purchased from Herter's Incorporated in Waseca, Minnesota. I have taken one of these leaders of six feet and tied three additional feet of 30 pound monofilament to the butt end and produced an excellent winter steelhead leader.

The tidal estuary offers a departure from angling methods so far described. Often unwadable and unreadable, the estuary is covered by trolling flies or lures. This is favored on such California rivers as the Eel but little practiced elsewhere.

Greased line fishing developed in Scotland for Atlantic salmon use by Arthur Wood is a sophisticated and demanding technique that infrequently finds application in steelheading. The classic work *Greased Line Fishing* by Jock Scott is, as the title suggests, devoted solely to the subject. Basically it involves fishing a sparsely dressed wet fly just barely beneath the surface with a straight downstream, drag free drift. To accomplish this, the double taper line and leader is dressed and the float repeatedly mended.

The many greased line fly patterns are usually abbreviated versions of full dressed Atlantic salmon standards. Two flies, the Lady Caroline and Silver Blue, if dressed sparsely on low water hooks would be among Wood's favorites.

The upper fly, the Dragon Fly, is a versatile low water steelhead pattern, since it can be fished as a wet fly, as a surface skittering fly on a tight line or as a dry fly on a slack line while throwing the usual downstream wet fly cast. As a dry fly it spreads out on the surface and floats in the surface film, a most attractive attribute incorporated in other reliable steelhead dry flies. As a wet fly, its wings fixed in a spent-wing form, act as paddles giving the fly an active swimming action. As a skittering fly it is easy to keep on top and makes an attractive disturbance in the surface film.

The lower fly, the October Caddis, employs the split and cocked forward wing to give the fly an opportunity to work with the pulse of the currents on a dead drift or swinging on a tight line. If stiff hair is used the wings will paddle in the water. If fine, supple hair is used the wing will lay over the body in a fluid, translucent wing. This fly was developed for summer steelhead.

THE DRY FLY

It would seem that anglers have been slow to evaluate steelhead in terms of the dry fly. This speaks as much for a certain traditional confidence in the wet fly as it does for the confusing habits of the summer-run. There are, of course, rivers famous for their great runs of summer steelhead. The Grand Ronde, Stilliguamish, Deschutes, Rogue, Klamath and Trinity can be counted in this category. Many others, however, are far less understood where even the name "run" must be considered suspect.

Near my home is the Dungeness River which is quite heavily fished in winter and supports few anglers for its modest summer run. I would not think more than 100 steelhead are caught from its waters each year. These average four to six pounds but can be found much larger. Two years ago I hooked one that fought 55 minutes before breaking me off. I estimated its weight at something over 15 pounds, remarkably large for the river and time of year. I had been fishing for early fall cutthroats and the tackle I used had no business contending with the fish in such impossible water. However, the experience did show me that this river's marginal summer-run possibilities have not been explored completely.

The summer "trout" season sees the useless killing of many pre-migrant steelhead and often haphazardly introduces the dry fly angler to steelhead. The meeting is rarely successful for tackle is not suited to the steelhead. Trout fishermen raise steelhead frequently enough for anglers to begin realizing that with suitable dry fly tackle the clear running stream can be religiously searched with steelhead first in mind. The rivers are best fished with a dry fly in summer's declining days when the steelhead have adjusted to their new environment and some, particularly the younger specimens, may be taking food.

When summer-run steelhead are observed in temporary residence at the bottom of a deep pool, they are lost to the dry fly. If this is the case, we can fish early and late above and below the pool finding by chance, a fish entering or leaving it.

This low water fly is attached to the leader with a Riffling Hitch knot. This method of tying fly to leader is used when the angler wishes to swim his fly in the surface film. The riffling fly creates a fine "V" wake on the surface, and is most effective on summer-run steelhead. When the fish rises he will break the surface in a heavy roll; the angler must wait until he feels the fish's weight before he tightens the line.

The maximum depth from which steelhead will rise to the floating fly may be influenced by their regional distribution. Southern half-pounders have been observed feeding actively at the surface. On most waters, though, the preference is for ascending steelhead holding in less than five feet of fast water. Pocket water amid frothy turbulence can also be excellent.

The last time I fished the Kalama during the summer months, I was diligently working an assortment of dry flies. Late one morning I was in the upriver canyon casting over a long riffle that became ever narrower and deeper before terminating in a little falls at its head. Nothing came to my fly until I reached a point where the falls broke to form a run.

There the suds of breaking water spread out and momentarily opened to let me observe a single steelhead probably too large to take an interest in the dry fly. A dozen casts were made which did not move the fish. On the next float I threw a heavily greased Muddler practically into the falls and fished it down, feeding the gathered slack until the fly was below me and skipping across the river. A male of two and a half pounds took the fly as I was lifting the rod in preparation for another cast. I wondered if the large steelhead at the head of the pool was a female and if there might be additional males below her. If there were, they did not respond.

Save for the canyon walls, the water was a model for the steelheading dry fly drift. It was a shallow pool, six feet or less and all of the water could be reached with a fly. Numerous boulders supplied holding spots and a falls forced the steelhead into a temporary rest.

The dry fly is still a summer-run enticement. While steelhead have come up for the floating pattern in winter, I do not yet know of an angler catching winter-run steelhead in this manner.

Because no records are officially kept, it is impossible to give the maximum weight of a steelhead caught on a dry fly. The larger steelhead are not as responsive to the surface fly, therefore the dry fly is somewhat limiting. Many steelhead caught on a dry fly have weighed over ten pounds and at least several have pushed the 15 pound mark. These have invariably come from such northern rivers as the Stilliguamish.

The larger dry fly is helpful in attracting. It is also an advantage if the pattern spreads itself well in the surface film. It is then more easily observed from below and less prone to bounce away from the steelhead's rise.

Hair-wing dressings, because of their better floating abilities, are favored for steelhead dry flies. Proven patterns include the Boxcar, Steelhead Bee, Wiskey and Soda and the Wulff series. This selection indicates a lack of discrimination among steelhead for any particular combination of colors.

The fly should be hackled lightly enough for the hackle points to penetrate the surface film. A good silicone dressing should be used and if an additional guard against the water soaked fly is sought, the wing and tail can be greased with a silicone line dressing.

Fly sizes range from ten through six and are fished with a four to eight pound test tippet. The type of water worked rarely makes it necessary to sink any part of the leader. If some finesse is required, sink only the 18-20 inch tippet. An eight foot rod and weight seven line handles dry fly casting duties perfectly.

Hundreds of anglers fishing pallid winter waters relate successes that can tell much about a run. The summer angler, unless fishing the classic summer-run rivers discussed earlier, is not so fortunate. The river can fail to communicate its steelhead secrets, being devoid of other fishermen. But the lonely hunter perseveres and the dry fly makes the time between strikes a special pleasure.

This discussion cannot be counted as complete without some

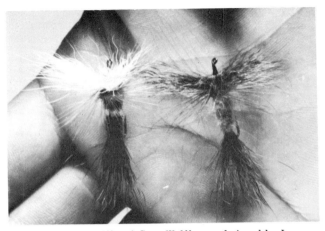

The Royal Wulff and Grey Wulff were designed by Lee Wulff for resident trout but now have widespread application for a great variety of gamefish — including Atlantic salmon and steelhead. While steelhead dry flies may vary considerably in their construction, they all have one attribute in common — an ability to remain floating in fast water.

mention of Roderick Haig-Brown. He has become steelheading's Halford. It is true the steelhead-dry fly did not originate with him, but his books are beautiful analytic accounts of white water rises that epitomize the ultimate fulfillment we seek from our gamefish. Because Haig-Brown has sent steelheading dry fly stock soaring, many additional patterns will come to make new waters of old and the angling years ahead will be more exciting as a consequence.

The Whiskey and Soda, a Canadian steelhead dry fly. (Fly tier: Harkley & Haywood of Vancouver, British Columbia)

The Boxcar, an original steelhead dry fly by Wes Drain.

Original patterns tied by well known steelheader Mike Kennedy of Oswego, Oregon. Top row, Maverick, Fools Gold; row 2, The Park, Dingbat.

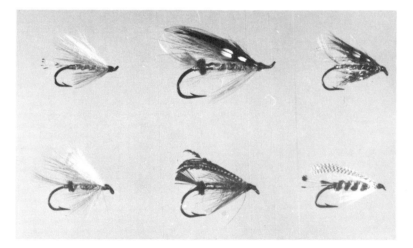

Original patterns tied by artist-angler Tommy Brayshaw for use on British Columbia's Coquihalla River, a Fraser River tributary near Hope. Top row, Coquihalla Silver, Coquihalla Orange (dark), Black and Silver; row 2, Coquihalla Orange, Coquihalla Red, Dusk.

2. WINTER FLY FISHING

There is no question in my mind that an expert at fishing fresh spawn can catch more winter steelhead than the best fly fisher to ever hold a rod. He is able to make longer casts and fish more varieties of water. Also, the "lure" is more effective than flies. Yet challenge of the difficult puts winter steelheading with a fly in the trophy angling class and the sport has many followers, particularly in California.

Winter steelhead fly fishing should be considered nothing less than a graduate course in drift fishing. Acceptable drifts for the bait or lure must be edited with a fly fishing perspective. A shooting head or forward taper line with a specific gravity best able to cut the river's depth and current is used, matched with flies having complementing sinking qualities.

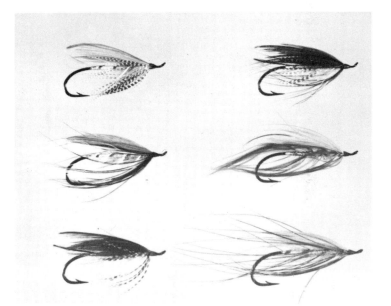

These flies tied by Syd Glasso are among the most beautiful in steelheading. Top row, Sol Duc, Sol Duc Spey, Sol Duc (dark); row 2, Quilloyute, Courtesan, Orange Heron.

Most winter steelheaders tie their own flies, not because they are among the easiest of all flies to tie, but because each must be carefully weighted to match the tackle and water. The regular weight hook carrying an abundance of hackle and fur will, if left to its own devises, sink slowly. Saturate a floss body with fly dope, use extra heavy hooks, dress sparsely, give the body a tinsel wrap, and the fly will sink faster.

157

Fly fishermen dream of hooking a great steelhead like this 20½ pound trophy caught from Washington's Skagit River by Ralph Wahl. (Ralph Wahl photo)

Add an optic head or bead chain eyes and a still faster sink is realized. Underwrap the body with lead wire and again the sink is increased; place an optic head or bead chain eyes on the lead weighted fly and it passes through the water like so much shot.

A good decision has been made when the fly works the bottom and occasionally bounces off rocks on its downriver ride. Color and size are important only if the fly is drifting where the winter steelhead will strike, so combine sinking rates and sizes with the patterns personally favored.

Steelhead fly sizes are generally eight through two for the summer-run and four through 1/0 for winter fishing. Steelhead fly color combinations are fantastically varied. Larger flies are a beginning choice for fishing discolored water; the color extremes are preferred: black, white and fluorescent primary colors.

Facing the selected drift, the fly is sent on a quartering upstream cast if the heaviest water is where the fly is to be placed, or cast quartering downstream if strong currents are between angler and holding water. If an even flow exists throughout, a straight across or

From the top: Painted Lady, Lord Hamilton, Winter Fly. These compact, fast-sinking flies were designed and tied by Ralph Wahl. The Winter Fly was the pattern used when Wahl took his Washington fly record steelhead of 20½ pounds.

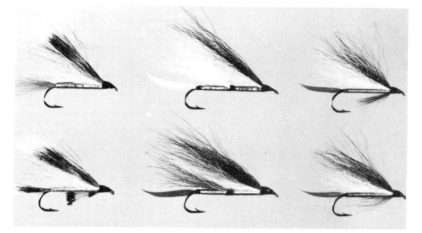

Peter Schwab designed these wire-bodied bucktails. Top row, Princess, Brass Hat, Bobbie Dunn; row 2, Queen Bess, Paint Brush, Bellamy.

upstream cast is made. The objective is to deposit the fly in a way that will give it a chance to sink free of immediate drag. Should the cast be directed upstream, the returning slack is first gathered and then released to give the greatest coverage possible. If the fly never touches bottom, go to a heavier fly and try again. When the most enthusiastically weighted fly is unable to reach bottom, it may be necessary to either change water or go to a faster sinking shooting head.

We begin with short casts, increase the distance with each succeeding cast, and follow the drift with the rod tip. When the maximum amount of water has been covered, move downstream several steps and repeat

Huge winter flies like this Fall Favorite streamer pack as much dense color (there are eight hackles in the wing) on a hook as possible.

the procedure. If the water is discolored, it is best to fish more methodically. Just as in drift fishing, one will come to recognize the most productive spots. These should be worked very carefully, repeating cast after cast until one is reasonably sure the suspected steelhead has had the offering drifted right by the end of his nose.

The strike can be in name only if the winter fly is taken in a bait and bobber spirit — and the pattern we cast may suggest nothing more than that. Striking back cleanly really is not possible when a sinking line is running deep. Tightening line and raising the rod does not set the hook so much as remove some slack and supply resistance that is additional to the weight of the moving fish, all of these aspects combine to properly barb.

At this stage the shock absorbing rod should be kept raised as the running fish hits the lightly set drag. Drop the rod tip only when the steelhead jumps; the few feet of slack will help prevent a broken leader.

The comet type patterns are a popular way of dressing winter steelhead flies. The Boss, a California development, was the first of the comet patterns.

FLY TACKLE REFINEMENTS

Minor tackle refinements made at home can assume critical importance while fishing. The most important of these is the proper connection of the leader, line, shooting line (if a shooting head is used), and backing so that all pass from the rod smoothly.

I have yet to find a method superior to the common nail knot for attaching the leader to fly line. Overwind the knot with nylon thread and varnish to assure a smooth passage through the guides. The leader then becomes more permanent. Because changing flies will gradually shorten the leader, tippets of various diameters should be carried to rebuild from the butt the length and taper desired.

Shooting line is connected to the shooting head by either the above nail knot, or an improved clinch knot when a loop has been spliced to the shooting head. If using the nail knot, overwrap it with nylon thread and coat with clear epoxy.

Connecting shooting line or fly line to backing is best accomplished with a splice. Because monofilament is so smooth, I loop the two lines against each other without a knot and wrap the connection with nylon

161

thread. The wrap is then whip finished and given an epoxy coat. When splicing braided nylon backing to a fly line, overlap the two and wrap and finish as described.

The amount of shooting line used should not exceed the length castable. When monofilament is stretched under the constant pressure of a heavy fish and wound on the reel, it can bend or even break the spool plate unless an undercushion of braided line is there to absorb line contraction.

The double turle and improved clinch are the two knots generally used to attach the steelhead fly.

Because most quality rods are presently marked for the fly line weight needed, balancing an outfit is not the painful experience it once was. Nevertheless, Scientific Anglers Incorporated now markets rods, reels and lines in harmoniously balanced packages under the name "System." Their famous fly lines are among the best money can buy; the rods and reels are of an equivalent quality. These System outfits cost in the neighborhood of $100.00 and are worth the price.

For all the number of fly boxes available, there are precious few practical for steelhead flies. A notable exception is the aluminum Wheatley box designed for Atlantic salmon use. They can be purchased from The Orvis Company in Manchester, Vermont. Choose the model with 20 large and 35 small clips; it is ideal for flies from eight to 1/0.

CHAPTER ELEVEN

The Steelhead's Future

If angling pressure remained light and streams remained pristine there would be little need for planting coastal waters with steelhead smolts. Unfortunately, such benign situations are rarely encountered nowadays. It would seem that the demand for sport caught steelhead can only become more severe, undoubtedly out of proportion with actual population growth. We are a people still moving westward (ask any Californian) and while the good life permits more leisure time, it also assures us of an ever increasing need for rewarding vacation activities. But people per se, however great their numbers, are not necessarily detrimental to angling's well being. A far more insidious threat to future steelheading is any lasting damage to our rivers and their ability to naturally renew native steelhead populations.

Poor forest management, such as improperly executed clear cutting, can result in severe erosion or produce slash-filled tributaries. The former will have a devastating effect on spawning beds (some of our most valuable land outside metropolitan waterfront); the latter may act as temporary dams that deny anadromous fish access to those spawning beds. I have always felt smugly safe in my Olympic Peninsula home. A national park protects the mountainous interior and a thin slice of breathtaking seashore while a national forest containing wilderness areas acts as a buffer against tacky commercialism. My many rivers are among the cleanest anywhere and steelhead are still caught for subsistence. However, a study by Snyder, Bush and Wade (1969)[1] details some disturbing changes:

> The important fishery and water resources on the Olympic National Forest are being seriously threatened by man's activities. Soil loss, through surface erosion and mass movement resulting from timber harvest and road construction, has adversely affected the sediment and pollution levels on many streams and rivers. The fishery value of the

[1] Snyder, Robert V., George S. Bush, Jr., and John M. Wade 1969. Soil resources Olympic National Forest. USDA Soil Resource management survey report, Pacific Northwest Region, pp. 158.

Soleduck River has declined nearly 50 percent during the past 50 years, according to old records. These same records indicate the South Fork Skokomish River has experienced a similar decline, and the Salmon River no longer supports steelhead migrations. These large declines in water resources are suspected to have been proportionally greatest during the past 10 to 15 years when man's activities increased greatly.

The removal of streamside timber can raise summer water temperatures beyond the tolerances of spawning fish or developing young. In a letter by Max Katz, Dept. of Fisheries, University of Washington, Katz states:

> I do agree with you that more emphasis should be placed on the conservation of steelhead habitat. But this is a losing struggle – I have noticed with great regret that only a few fishermen have the faintest idea that soil conservation and land management, including forest management, are needed to preserve our streams. They don't know and too often don't care that hot dry summer seasons coupled with abused watersheds simply means no native steelhead. The hot dry summer of 1967 is what murdered the Washington State steelhead returns in the 1969-70 seasons.

Dams and fish ladders have spotty success records (or inconsistent failures, depending on your point of view) for anadromous fish:[2]

> Unless the lethal effects of nitrogen supersaturation* in the Columbia River system are immediately and permanently stopped, virtually all anadromous fish runs from essentially Bonneville Dam upstream probably will vanish into oblivion.

Industry with attending pollution in forms too numerous to detail here continues to violate the public's right to water clean enough to support healthy steelhead, salmon and people.

Thus the steelhead is simultaneously beset by a perverse deterioration of its environment and a more perilous existence in that environment by the greatly increased number of anglers.

The tendency has been to dispair over such a depressing trend and follow the line of least resistance by establishing an elaborate and expensive stocking program. Why fight the industrial monoliths when their undesirable side effects cannot be rectified to overcome even human misery? This is not to say that we plant only by default, that the dire consequences of environmental abuses are not now in sharp focus or that our pleas do not receive a sympathetic hearing (it is now politically advantageous to at least listen, though dialogue alone does not finance re-election campaigns, a fact that powerful special interests

[2] Editorial, Salmon Trout Steelheader, August-September, 1971. Based on Washington Game Department news release, June 1, 1971.

*Nitrogen supersaturation occurs when seasonal high water flows must pass over the dam spillways rather than through the turbines. Air is trapped in the water during the long plunge deep into the basin below where water pressure forces nitrogen into supersaturation. The nitrogen is not quickly dissipated and additional dams only compound the problem. While supersaturation is most severe in the upper five feet of water, there is no evidence that fish will try to avoid this level. The embolism-like symptoms will, according to Washington Department of Game biologists, kill 90 percent or more of downstream swimming smolts in 1971.

have long appreciated). I believe the ecotactician may yet win the day. Nevertheless, artificial propagation of steelhead remains an entrenched — and expected — practice, and as a sacred corollary of future game management, it should be critically examined.

Specifically regarding steelhead, one obvious result of repeatedly planting non-indigenous smolts in a given watershed will be the dillution of the native gene pool and eventual disappearance of native stock. On the face of it, there would be little to fear if sheer numbers remained high enough to satisfy an ever expanding sport fishery. However, long-term planting programs are now beginning to raise questions regarding the ultimate viability of the fish themselves. Are planted steelhead as vigorous? If not, we must think in terms of a trend and the final result. Will they grow as large? Will they distribute their ascending time like native steelhead? Or is this partially decided by when the hatchery smolts are released? Or do the native races have certain genetic predilections lost in the mechanics of hatchery rearing? If this is true, what governs the loss and why? Will hatchery steelhead be as disease resistant? Or make as full use of their watershed? Or show the same propensity for striking bait, lures and flies?

Perhaps these are more questions than today's angler is willing to worry his head over. I hope not. For the answers will be vital to the future of steelheading and thus should be of paramount concern to fishermen everywhere.

Calaprice[3] offers an opinion regarding the vigor of hatchery stock:

> Fish may be taken into hatcheries, reared and developed as "production strains" and the progeny used to supplement natural production in streams and "other environments." While in the hatcheries, they are exposed to a new "niche" and may be selected intensively for traits considered important to the hatcheryman. They may become highly adapted to local conditions and may also as a result of the selection process become highly inbred. Directional genetic change may be expected as a result of the selection process, as well as chance loss of genetic material due to inbreeding. The effect of selection and inbreeding will be to decrease genetic variance within the populations, and the latter may be expected to result in a reduction of fitness in the populations undergoing selection.

Calaprice, again, discusses "final results":

> The effect of "maintenance stocking" on the gene pool of the resident populations would be analogous to that of increased migration rates. It is conceivable that the continuous stocking of hatchery fish ill adapted to natural environments might result in a continuous lowering of the fitness and, if continued, the extinction of local populations.

---

[3] Calaprice, J. R., Production and Genetic Factors in Managed Salmonid Populations. "Symposium on Salmon and Trout in Streams," pp. 377-385.

Dag Moller[4] completed an extensive study on the management of Atlantic salmon in terms of those genetic factors in native and hatchery-bred stock:

> The natural population suits a certain environment. The two systems, the population and the environment, are in balance. If the environment is changed, the population would change; and recent investigations indicate that these changes generally proceed faster than was earlier believed. However, changes in the population will not cause changes in the environment. The natural population has to follow some sort of standard which has been laid down by the environment. The release of individuals from another river, if inbred, will cause imbalance in the local population with subsequent decay in fitness (reduction in fecundity and survival). All efforts in stocking with fingerlings or smolts, therefore, should be aimed at keeping natural populations in a continuing balance with the environment.

December has become the most productive steelhead month, a fact due in large measure to hatchery plants. Native smolts of widely assorted ages descend all spring and well into summer; hatchery smolts of vastly more consistent ages are released in large groups and usually begin immediately for the sea. Whether or not this "sets" them for a December-January return is not clear, but at this writing that seems to be a possibility. The size of adult hatchery steelhead also seems more consistent — six to eight pounds or about what we would expect from 1/2 and 2/2 steelhead. Anglers accustomed to relying on hatchery steelhead for much of their sport can now be heard talking of the "larger native steelhead" found in early spring. (Larger than the extra six to eight weeks of ocean growth could account for.) This opinion may be misplaced prejudice, but *if* hatchery steelhead average less in weight, the reasons may have been partially identified by Miller.[5] In this Canadian study, he determined that smolt length for 2/2 steelhead was greater than that in the 2/3 group. In other words, the smaller two year smolts tended to spend a longer time at sea and returned significantly larger. While it is too early to draw conclusions from this phenomenon (3/2 and 3/3 age groups did not exhibit this difference), it does offer a clue to the puzzle of larger Canadian steelhead; we would expect the growth rates of northern smolts to be considerably less than the growth rates of California smolts over an equal period of time. Miller's findings would also seem to cast doubt on "efficiency" in hatchery smolt production where diets and conditions work to produce release-age smolts in the shortest possible time.

It is not my intention to discredit the efforts by game departments to sustain our annual runs of steelhead by artificial means. In fact, I applaud their work. At the same time I would like to see their programs carefully evaluated first in terms of promoting native stock. Safeguarding the production levels of spawning beds, improving present

[4] Moller, Dag, Genetic Diversity in Atlantic Salmon and Salmon Management in Relation to Genetic Factors. The International Atlantic Salmon Foundation. Vol. 1, No. 1, November, 1970, pp. 11.

[5] Miller, R. B. 1957. Have the genetic patterns of fishes been altered by introduction or by selective fishing? Fish. Res. Bd. Canada 14: 797-806.

spawning beds (by reducing siltation, for example) or developing altogether new spawning beds may in the long run be the least expensive method of assuring future steelhead runs. Information I have gathered from various studies would suggest that haphazard stocking could eventually create a financial monster whereby steelheading becomes increasingly dependent on hatchery production while at the same time the quality of the gamefish decreases.

Where stocking steelhead smolts is felt to be warrented, the plants should be in rivers as much like natal waters as possible. Ideally the smolts would be marked so that native fish could act as the "control" group. It should then be required that sportsmen report all such marked steelhead by sex, weight, length, date of capture and accompany this information with scale samples. Steelhead trapped below weirs could be separated into the two groups and compared for stamina and reaction to various water currents. The fish would then be killed and compared for physiological differences, i.e., fat content, egg production, viability of spawn, diseases, parasites and the like.

While these suggestions may be deemed a fiscal impossibility, I do not see how those state-wide hatchery programs can responsibly continue without first a clear understanding of what their operations will ultimately bring about.

Since I now seem to be making some rather imposing recommendations, I will dwell for a moment on the concept of a "limit" as it pertains to our angling. It is first double-edged. It offers a guideline and because a limit is law and enforced, the sometimes arbitrary number is usually abided by. So at least ostensibly it protects against those excesses that would deny us an equal opportunity. That may be the only positive aspect of establishing a limit. Its negative aspects are many. A limit establishes a goal (Puritan ethic, meet the American sportsman!). I once encountered a fisherman where for a moment his success was our common bond. He must have thought me terribly stupid.

"I limited," said the angler.

"Limited on what?" I asked.

"On trout," he said.

"Is that good, is it good to limit?" I asked.

"Yes, it is very good," he told me.

"Tell me about the trout," I asked.

"They were biting well during the first two hours of light but I had to work hard to get my limit of 12 in that time," he answered.

"You are fortunate the limit isn't 20 trout," I said, "or even 30 trout."

"Yes," he agreed, "that would be awful. One can only do so much."

If the angler had not realized his goal (his concept of "sport"), he would have felt that his license investment had paid insufficient dividends. Yet that is but one facet of his ambition. The limit is also a machismo thing — you prove your intelligence, ability to provide, your manhood by killing whatever number of fish your generation's management feels safe to let you have. In the case of steelheading, it is two or three fish per day.

One or the other number will apply on all rivers during all seasons. This consistency probably helps when comparing on a broad scale the angling pressure against available steelhead. However, one limit does not take into consideration the size of steelhead runs, how these runs are maintained, the production capabilities of the different rivers and how deeply angling cuts into assorted steelhead populations. We may assume that these factors will vary from river to river and that steelhead are more vulnerable in some rivers than in others.

I would think these variables would invite a more comprehensive definition of limit than states now have. The most radical concept presently practiced is to set aside a few waters on a fly fishing only basis. Their value in regard to limit is that there are fewer steelhead fly fishermen, that they catch less fish than if using bait with other types of tackle and that they generally release a greater percentage of the few fish they do catch. Other rivers are not nearly so fortunate. I believe that there should be wide variations in what constitutes a steelhead limit. This is not just a case of making game laws more restrictive – or less restrictive for that matter – but reshaping them to more closely accommodate our sport fishing needs by working to prevent angling from exceeding a river's natural production of steelhead unless the river is so changed that it has little natural production and must rely heavily on artificial propagation to supply adult fish. Rivers could be rated on a one to ten basis, "ten" being a "perfect" score for any river functioning at maximum potential. A "one" would stand for a river operating at 1/10 its potential capacity. Based on the study by Snyder, Bush and Young, the Soleduck might receive a rating of "five." River rehabilitation and a readjusted limit would then work toward the river reaching former production levels. I realize it would be difficult if not impossible to know exactly what number of steelhead once ascended a river. Fishery biologists, however, have become quite skilled at diagnosing a river's assorted ills and can predict with considerable accuracy what a river is capable of with regard to steelhead production.

Such recommendations in toto are probably unmanageable because game departments have no where near the funds to manage our river resources on such a comprehensive basis. But a more realistic treatment of "limit" could at least serve to reduce pressure where its heaviest – in or near metropolitan areas – with a reduced limit (one steelhead per day?) and make angling more inviting on remote rivers by holding the limit or making it more generous. I have never felt that an increase in angling, even on a geometric basis, need be fatal to quality fishing if from the onset sportsmen resign themselves to less fish per angling day or angling year and if they are educated to view steelheading as a sport rather than a source of meat. Why not a "fishing for fun" river where all steelhead must be returned? Would a game department dare institute this on a summer-run race for a five year period? Would "sportsmen" dare accept such a river? Why not restricting more headwaters to fly fishing only on an all-year basis? The possibilities are as numerous as our individually unique rivers.

As I have now made abundantly clear, I believe steelheading's future depends first on the continued perpetuation of each river race of steelhead. This is only possible by safely securing watersheds against assorted abuses by both the public and industry. Unfortunately, we are still in trouble environmentally because of a too frequent vacuum of responsibility. We are, after all, the only guardians and in the final analysis must first blame ourselves for the misfortunes that befall our rivers. I freely admit that the single citizen acting in his own behalf becomes ecology's David when working against the despoilers. What frustrates from the onset is the bureaucratic maze that swallows valid objections like a bed of quicksand. Complaints are shuffled from office to office, department to department; letters to elected representatives too frequently result in complimentary noncommittal replies. While the Establishment creaks, the grandiose scheme to move a mountain, dam a river or sink a hole to hell goes on. Most discouraging of all, many of those citizens who will be adversely affected by ill conceived projects have terminal cases of shortsightedness and seem totally conservative to desperately needed action.

The surest way to even the odds, to successfully engage a special interest group, is to join an organization that shares your interests and concerns and has the influence to help you accomplish your goals. There are hundreds of hiking, hunting, climbing, salmon, trout, fly fishing and steelheading clubs that are ecology-minded and would advance your cause. Almost every town has some sort of organization that would lend weight to your arguments. There are also national organizations such as Trout Unlimited that lobby actively in Washington, D.C., and come equipped with the financial means and the legal expertise to determine the most expeditious methods to move the unresponsive functionary and recalcitrant industry . The Steelheaders Council of Trout Unlimited with more than 25 chapters in the northwest and the Federation of Fly Fishermen with approximately two dozen Pacific Coast member clubs are, in my opinion, the most logical starting points for beginning a dedicated commitment to the preservation of the most prized gamefish in American fresh water angling.

CHAPTER TWELVE

Steelhead Fly Pattern Dictionary

ADMIRAL — Tail: Red hackle fibers. Body: Red wool ribbed with gold tinsel. Hackle: Red. Wing: White bucktail.

ALASKA MARY ANN — Tail: Red hackle fibers. Body: White chenille ribbed with silver tinsel. Wing: White bucktail. Cheeks: Jungle cock

AL'S SPECIAL — Tail: Red hackle fibers. Body: Yellow chenille ribbed with silver tinsel. Hackle: Red. Wing: White bucktail.

ALMVIG — Body: Hot orange yarn ribbed with silver tinsel. Underwing: White polar bear fur. Overwing: Red or orange calf tail.

BADGER HACKLE PEACOCK — Tip: Gold tinsel. Tail: Red Hackle fibers. Body: Peacock herl. Hackle: Badger, long.

BELLAMY — Tail: Red goose or bucktail. Body: Copper wire. Wing: Brown over yellow over white bucktail. Hackle: Brown, tied as a beard.

BENN'S COACHMAN — Tail: Red hackle fibers. Body: Peacock herl. Hackle: Brown. Wing: White primary strips with a red strip between.

BLACK BEAR — Tail: Mixed black and red hackle fibers. Body: Black chenille ribbed with silver tinsel. Hackle: Black and red wound together. Wing: Black bear fur or black bucktail.

BLACK BOMBER — Tail: Fluorescent orange hackle fibers. Body: Black chenille. Wing: White polar bear fur. Head: Black with "eyes" of white plastic rings cut from 14 gauge electrical wire.

BLACK GNAT BUCKTAIL — Tail: Red hackle fibers. Body: Black chenille. Hackle: Black. Wing: Brown bucktail.

BLACK GORDON — Body: Rear third red yarn, black yarn for the balance. Rib with gold tinsel. Hackle: Black. Wing: Black or dark brown bucktail.

BLACK OPTIC — Body: Oval gold or silver tinsel. Hackle: Black. Wing: Black bucktail. Head: Split brass bead clamped in place and painted black with a white iris and red pupil.

BLACK PRINCE — Tail: Red hackle fibers. Body: Rear third yellow wool, black wool for the balance. Rib with silver tinsel. Hackle: Black. Wing: Black bucktail.

BLACK AND SILVER — Tip: Oval silver tinsel. Tail: Golden pheasant crest. Body: Rear half flat silver tinsel, front half black floss, rib body with oval silver tinsel. Hackle: Guinea. Wing: Widgeon flank. Topping: Golden pheasant crest. Cheeks: Jungle cock.

BLACK AND WHITE PLASTIC — Tail: Mallard flank. Body: Black and white plastic stripped from No. 18 Bell wire, cut into sections and slid on the hook shank before the tail is tied. The result is a banded effect of five sections that start and end with black. Hackle: Grizzly. Wing: Mallard flank.

BOBBIE DUNN — Tail: Red Goose or bucktail. Body: Copper wire. Wing: Brown over red over white bucktail. Hackle: Red bucktail tied as a beard.

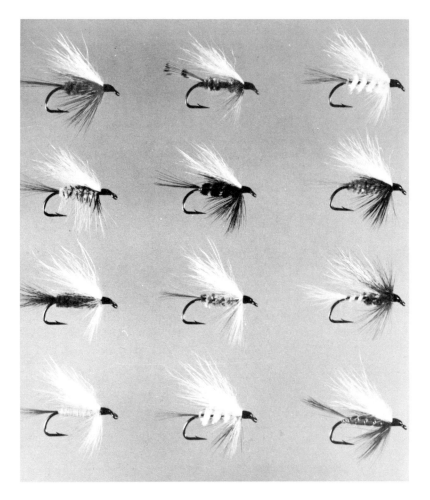

Standard bright patterns found in frequent use throughout the steelhead's range. From top to bottom, row 1, Admiral, Kalama Special, Orange Shrimp; row 2, Royal Coachman, Skunk, Skykomish Sunrise, Skykomish Yellow; row 3, Stilliguamish Sunrise, Thor, Umpqua, Van Luven. It should be noted that these flies were developed primarily on the northern rivers, rivers where half-pounders were infrequent. Compared to flies designed for northern California streams and for the Rogue, these flies are brighter and would be classified as attractor patterns.

BOSQUITO — Tail: Red hackle fibers. Body: Yellow chenille. Hackle: Black. Wing: White bucktail.

BOSS FLY — Tail: Black bucktail, long. Body: Black chenille ribbed with silver tinsel. Hackle: Fluorescent red. Head: Red tying thread with bead-chain "eyes."

BOXCAR — (Dry) Tail: Red hackle fibers. Body: Peacock herl. Wing: White calf tail tied in wet fly fashion. Hackle: Brown, ahead of wing.

BRAD'S BRAT — Tip: Gold tinsel. Tail: Orange and white bucktail. Body: Rear half orange wool, front half red wool. Rib with gold tinsel. Hackle: Brown. Wing: Orange over white bucktail with the underwing dominating. Cheeks: Jungle cock (optional).

BRASS HAT — Tail: Yellow goose or bucktail. Body: Brass wire. Rear wing: White bucktail. Front wing: Black over yellow bucktail, yellow dominating.

BRINDLE BUG — Tail: Brown hackle tips. Body: Black and yellow variegated chenille wound with one turn under the tail to turn it up. Hackle: Brown, heavy.

BROWN LEGGED SHRIMP — Body: Oval silver tinsel. Hackle: Brown. Wing: Gray bucktail. Tie at head and again at end of tinseled body; wing becomes shrimp body and tail.

BUCKTAIL COACHMAN — Tail: Red hackle fibers. Body: Peacock herl. Hackle: Brown. Wing: White bucktail. Cheeks: Jungle cock (optional)

BUCKTAIL McGINTY — Tail: Red hackle fibers and mallard flank. Body: Alternate bands of black and yellow chenille. Hackle: Brown. Wing: Gray squirrel tail or brown over white bucktail.

BURLAP — Tail: Brown bucktail. Body: Burlap strands wound tight and then picked out to give a ragged appearance. Hackle: Grizzly.

CARSON — Tail: Red hackle fibers. Body: Peacock herl divided with red floss. Hackle: Brown. Wing: White over red bucktail.

CHAPPIE — Tail: Grizzly hackle tips. Body: Orange wool ribbed with gold tinsel. Hackle: Grizzly. Wing: Two grizzly hackles back to back and high off the hook. Head: Orange or black tying thread.

CLIFF'S SPECIAL — Tail: Red goose. Body: Orange chenille ribbed with flat gold tinsel. Hackle: Orange. Wing: White goose primary strips.

COCK ROBIN OPTIC — Body: Oval silver tinsel. Hackle: Orange. Wing: Fox, squirrel or badger. Head: Split brass bead clamped in place and painted black with a white iris and black pupil.

COPPER DEMON — Tail: Hot orange maribou. Body: Copper tinsel. Hackle: Hot orange. Wing: Hot orange polar bear fur.

COQUIHALLA ORANGE — Tip: Two turns of narrow oval gold tinsel, finish with orange floss. Tail: Golden pheasant crest. Butt: Black ostrich. Body: Rear half orange floss, front half orange polar bear dubbing; rib with oval silver tinsel. Hackle: Orange. Wing: White over orange polar bear fur.

COQUIHALLA ORANGE—DARK — Tip: Oval silver tinsel. Tail: Golden pheasant crest with a short orange hackle tip on each side. Butt: Black ostrich. Body: Rear half orange floss, front half orange polar bear dubbing; rib with flat silver tinsel and overlay with narrow oval silver tinsel. Wing: Brown mallard over orange polar bear fur. Hackle: Orange. Topping: Golden pheasant crest. Cheeks: Jungle cock.

COQUIHALLA RED — Tip: Narrow oval silver tinsel. Tail: Light red hackle tip cut short. Butt: Black ostrich. Body: Rear half orange floss, front half red polar bear dubbing; rib with oval silver tinsel. Hackle: Red. Wing: Mallard flank over peacock sword fibers.

174

COQUIHALLA SILVER — Tail: Golden pheasant tippet fibers. Butt: Red floss. Body: Flat silver tinsel ribbed with oval silver tinsel. Hackle: Red. Wing: White over orange polar bear fur.

COURTESAN — Body: Fluorescent orange floss ribbed with flat silver tinsel. Hackle: Long, webby brown hackle tied palmer. Wing: Four hot orange hackle to bend of hook.

CUENIN'S ADVICE — Tip, Silver tinsel. Tail: Orange hackle fibers. Body: Silver tinsel. Hackle: Orange. Wing: Brown bucktail.

CUMMING'S — Body: Rear third yellow floss, balance of claret or wine wool; rib with gold tinsel. Hackle Wine or claret. Wing: Brown bucktail.

DOUBLE FLAME EGG — Tail: White hackle fibers, sparse. Body: Flame yarn divided and built up in two sections; separate with one turn of white hackle. Hackle: White, one turn.

DRAGON FLY — Tail: Dark deer body hair. Body: Orange Depth Ray wool, a single thin wrapping. Wing: Dark deer body hair tied in spent-wing position. Head: Clipped deer body hair formed in a Muddler Minnow style. Hook: Number 6 up-eye 2x fine wire extra long salmon hook. To swim it properly the fly should be "greased." This fly can be fished as a floating fly, a skittering, top-water fly and as a wet fly in a single cast. Excellent for summer steelhead.

DRAIN'S 20 — Tip: Flat silver tinsel, one turn, and fluorescent yellow floss. Tag: Toucan breast feather. Tail: Golden pheasant tippet fibers. Body: Fluorescent red floss ribbed with flat silver tinsel. Hackle: Purple saddle. Wing: White-tipped gray squirrel over cock-of-the-rock breast feather.

DUSK — Tip: Oval silver tinsel. Tail: Golden pheasant tippet. Body: Red and white chenille wound together, red dominates. Rib with flat silver tinsel. Hackle: White, may add a turn of red. Wing: Mallard flank.

175

EEL RIVER OPTIC —Body: Oval silver tinsel. Wing: Red bucktail with yellow bucktail topping. Head: Split brass bead clamped in place and painted white with a red iris and black pupil.

EVENING COACHMAN — Tail: Golden pheasant crest. Body: Peacock herl divided with a band of fluorescent red floss. Hackle: Grizzly, full.

FALL FAVORITE — Body: Silver tinsel. Hackle: Red. Wing: Orange bucktail or polar bear fur.

FLAME SQUIRREL TAIL — Tail: Red goose. Body: Flame chenille ribbed with silver tinsel. Hackle: Orange, tied as a beard. Wing: Fox squirrel.

FOOL'S GOLD — Tail: Red hackle fibers. Butt: Peacock herl. Body: Gold tinsel. Hackle: Brown. Wing: Brown bucktail.

GENERAL MONEY NO. 1 — Tail: Golden pheasant breast fibers. Body: Rear third oval silver tinsel, balance of black polar bear dubbing. Rib with continuation of oval tinsel. Hackle: Burgundy. Wing: Orange goose primary sections. Cheeks: Jungle cock.

GENERAL MONEY NO. 2 — Tip: Gold tinsel. Tail: Golden pheasant crest. Body: Black floss ribbed with gold tinsel. Hackle: Yellow. Wing: Red goose primary sections.

GOBLIN — Tail: Red goose. Body: Gold tinsel or gold piping. Hackle: None. Wing: Black over orange bucktail.

GOLDEN DEMON — Tail: Yellow hackle fibers. Body: Gold tinsel. Hackle: Orange. Wing: Brown bucktail. Cheeks: Jungle cock.

GRAY HACKLE — Tail: Red hackle fibers. Body: Yellow, yarn or floss, ribbed with gold tinsel. Hackle: Grizzly.

GREEN DRAKE — Tail: Mallard flank. Body: Green wool ribbed with black tying thread. Wing: Black African monkey. Hackle: Brown or furnace wound ahead of the wing.

GRIZZLY KING — Tail: Red hackle fibers. Body: Green floss ribbed with silver tinsel. Hackle: Grizzly. Wing: Mallard flank. Hairwing alternate: Gray squirrel tail.

HORNER'S SILVER SHRIMP — Tail: Gray bucktail. Body: Wide oval silver tinsel spaced to accept grizzly hackle tied palmer. Tie in second bunch of bucktail of tail color at body end, bring forward and tie at head. Head: Built up and painted black with a white iris and black pupil.

HOT ORANGE CHAMP — Tail: Several strands of flame yarn. Body: Flame yarn ribbed with silver tinsel. Wing: Six strands of flame yarn.

HOT SHOT — Tail: Red hackle fibers. Body: Flame chenille ribbed with silver tinsel. Hackle: Fluorescent orange. Wing: White bucktail.

HOWARD NORTON SPECIAL — Tail: Fluorescent orange polar bear fur, long. Body: Flame chenille ribbed with silver tinsel. Hackle: Fluorescent orange. Head: White thread, silver bead-chain "eyes."

JOE O'DONNEL — Tail: Red hackle fibers. Body: Cream chenille. Wing: Matched badger hackles. Hackle: Red and yellow wound together and set ahead of the wing.

JUICY BUG — Tail: Red hackle fibers. Butt: Black chenille. Body: Red chenille ribbed with silver tinsel. Wing: White bucktail, upright and divided. Cheeks: Jungle cock.

KALAMA SPECIAL — Tail: Red hackle fibers. Body: Yellow chenille palmered with either badger or grizzly hackle. Wing: White bucktail.

KATE — Tail: Golden pheasant crest. Body: Red wool ribbed with gold tinsel. Hackle: Yellow. Wing: Mallard flank over married strips of blue, yellow and red goose and brown turkey. Cheeks: Jungle cock.

KILLER — Tip: Silver tinsel. Tail: Red hackle fibers. Body: Red chenille ribbed with silver tinsel. Hackle: Red. Wing: Black bucktail. Cheeks: Jungle cock.

KISPIOX SPECIAL — Tail: Red polar bear fur. Body: Flame or hot orange chenille. Hackle: Red. Wing: White bucktail.

LADY CAROLINE — Tail: Golden pheasant breast fibers. Body: Olive and dark brown seal fur mixed and ribbed with flat silver tinsel. Hackle: Golden pheasant breast. Wing: Brown mallard or widgeon flank.

LADY GODIVA — Tip: Flat silver tinsel. Tail: Red and yellow hackle fibers. Butt: Red chenille. Body: Yellow seal fur ribbed with flat silver tinsel. Wing: Red over white bucktail.

LADY HAMILTON — Tail: Red goose. Body: Red floss ribbed with embossed silver tinsel. Wing: Orange over white bucktail. Head: Black with a white iris and black pupil.

LORD HAMILTON — Tail: Red goose. Body: Yellow floss ribbed with embossed silver tinsel. Wing: Red over white bucktail. Head: Black with a white iris and black pupil.

MARRIETTA — Tip: Silver tinsel. Tail: Red hackle fibers. Body: Flame chenille. Hackle: Fluorescent orange. Wing: Brown bucktail.

MARTHA — Tail: Red hackle fibers. Body: Rear half red floss, front half yellow floss, rib with gold tinsel. Hackle: Brown. Wing: Mallard flank.

MAVERICK — Tail: Six lady amherst tippet fibers. Body: Black sparkle chenille. Hackle: Badger. Wing: Silver gray squirrel tail. Cheeks: Jungle cock (optional).

McLEOD UGLY BUCKTAIL — Tail: Red hackle fibers.

Body: Black chenille palmered with grizzly hackle. Wing: Black bear fur.

McREYNOLDS — Tail: Black hackle fibers. Body: Orange floss ribbed with black tying thread. Hackle: Grizzly, short.

MICKY FINN — Body: Silver tinsel. Wing: Yellow over red over yellow bucktail in a 2/5, 2/5, 1/5 sequence.

MUDDLER MINNOW — Tail: Brown turkey. Body: Flat gold tinsel. Wing: Brown turkey strips over gray squirrel tail. Head-Hackle: Deer body fur spun on and head clipped to shape.

MUDDY WATERS — Tail: Black hackle fibers. Body: Fluorescent orange or red yarn ribbed with flat silver tinsel. Wing: Four strands of fluorescent orange or red yarn over a small amount of brown over white bucktail.

NICOMEKYL — Tail: Golden pheasant crest and small red primary strip. Body: Rear half orange floss, front half burgundy wool, rib with oval tinsel. Hackle: Burgundy. Wing: Brown mallard.

NITE OWL — Tail: Yellow hackle fibers. Butt: Two turns of red chenille. Body: Oval silver tinsel. Hackle: Orange. Wing: White bucktail.

OCTOBER CADDIS — Wings: Brown squirrel, tie on first so that root of the wing lies along the hook shank and the wing tip lies over the hook eye. Tail: Golden pheasant topping or yellow calf tail. Body: A single layer of orange Depth Ray wool, using the wing roots as a foundation for a tapered body. Hackle: Two turns of dark brown hackle. Finished Wings: Split the squirrel tail with tying thread into a cocked forward and split wing.

ORANGE COMET — See Howard Norton Special

ORANGE HERON — Body: Rear half fluorescent orange floss, front half hot orange floss, rib with four turns of flat silver tinsel. Hackle: Heron crest tied palmer. Wing: Four matching hot orange hackle tips.

ORANGE LEGGED SHRIMP — Body: Oval silver tinsel. Hackle: Orange. Wing: Gray bucktail, tie as in Brown Legged Shrimp.

ORANGE OPTIC — Body: Oval silver tinsel. Wing: Orange bucktail. Head: Split brass bead clamped in place and painted black with a white iris and black pupil.

ORANGE SHRIMP — Tip: Gold tinsel. Tail: Red hackle fibers. Body: Orange wool. Hackle: Orange. Wing: White bucktail.

ORLEANS BARBER — Tail: Drake wood duck flank. Body: Red chenille. Hackle: Grizzly.

PACIFIC KING — Tail: Black hackle fibers. Body: Insect green floss with a strip of dark brown floss laid over the top and secured with four turns of black tying thread ribbing. Hackle: Black, tied as a beard. Wing: Black squirrel tail.

PAINT BRUSH — Tail: Red goose or bucktail. Body: Brass wire. Rear wing: Red bucktail. Front wing: Brown over red over yellow bucktail.

PAINT POT — Tail: Red hackle fibers. Body: Flat silver tinsel. Hackle: Red. Wing: Gray squirrel dyed yellow.

PAINTED LADY — Tail: Orange goose. Body: Flat silver tinsel. Body stripe on each side of four strands of fluorescent red or pink floss. Tie in at the tail and bring forward at the completion of the tinseled body. Tie at head and lacquer in place. Paint top of the body with fluorescent yellow paint. Wing: Orange over yellow bucktail. Head: Black, with a white iris and black pupil.

PARMACHEENE BELLE — Tail: Red and white hackle fibers. Body: Yellow, ribbed with silver tinsel. Hackle: Red and white, wound together. Wing: White bucktail with

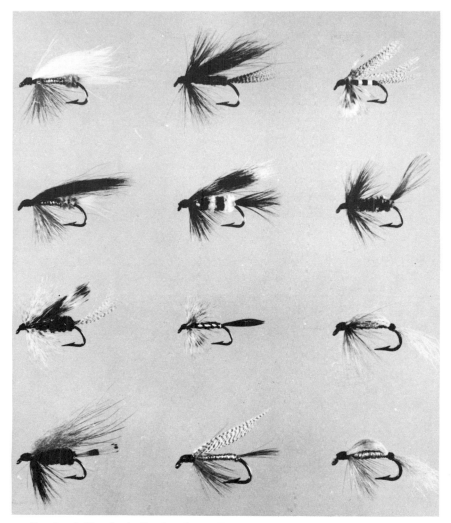

Popular California steelhead patterns. Top to bottom. row 1. Black and White Plastic, Brindle Bug, Brown-legged Shrimp, Orange-legged Shrimp; row 2, Green Drake, McGinty, McReynolds, Silver Demon; row 3, Nite Owl, Silvius Demon, Silver Hilton, Weitchpec Witch. (Fly tier: Lloyd Silvius of Eureka, California)

topping of red bucktail.

PINK MAMBO — Tail: Red hackle fibers. Body: Rear half pink yarn, front half black chenille. Wing: Pink bucktail. Hackle: Red, set ahead of the wing.

PINK SHRIMP — Tail: Fluorescent pink saddle hackle tips. Body: Oval silver tinsel palmered with fluorescent pink saddle hackle. Fluorescent pink bucktail is tied at the tail, brought forward and tied off at the head. Head: White tying thread.

POLAR SHRIMP — Tail: Red hackle fibers. Body: Orange, chenille or yarn. Hackle: Orange. Wing: White polar bear fur.

PRAWN FLY — Body: Orange wool ribbed with silver tinsel and palmered with red hackle.

PRINCESS — Tail: Orange polar bear fur. Body: Brass wire. Wing: Gray Squirrel over orange over yellow polar bear fur.

PROFESSOR — Tail: Red hackle fibers. Body: Yellow wool ribbed with gold tinsel. Hackle: Brown. Wing: Gray squirrel tail.

PURPLE PERIL — Tip: Silver tinsel. Tail: Purple hackle fibers. Body: Purple floss ribbed with silver tinsel. Hackle: Purple. Wing: Brown bucktail.

QUEEN BESS — Tail: Gray squirrel tail. Body: Flat silver tinsel. Wing: Yellow bucktail with gray squirrel tail topping. Hackle: Golden pheasant tippet tied as a beard.

QUILLOYUTE — Tail: Red hackle fibers. Body: Rear half of orange floss, front half of hot orange seal fur; rib with flat silver tinsel. Hackle: Teal flank palmered from second turn of tinsel followed with one turn of black heron at the head. Wing: Four matching golden pheasant body feathers.

QUINSAM HACKLE — Tip: Yellow floss. Body: Black wool ribbed with gold tinsel; palmer front half with yellow hackle.

Hackle: Red.

RAILBIRD — Tail: Red, wine or claret hackle fibers. Body: Wine or claret wool palmered with either claret or wine hackle. Hackle: Yellow. Wing: Teal or mallard flank; silver squirrel tail is used in the hairwing version. Cheeks: Jungle cock.

RED ANT — Tail: Golden pheasant tippet fibers. Butt: Peacock herl. Body: Red floss. Hackle: Brown. Wing: Brown bucktail.

RED OPTIC — Body: Oval silver tinsel. Wing: Red bucktail. Head: Split brass bead is clamped in place and painted black with a white iris and black pupil.

RED AND YELLOW OPTIC — Body: Oval silver tinsel. Wing: Yellow over red bucktail. Head: Split brass bead is clamped in place and painted black with a white iris and red pupil.

ROGUE RIVER SPECIAL — Tail: Peach hackle fibers. Tip: Yellow floss. Body: Red floss ribbed with gold tinsel. Wing: Peach over white bucktail, upright and divided. Cheeks: Jungle cock.

ROYAL COACHMAN — Tail: Golden pheasant tippet fibers. Body: Peacock herl divided by a scarlet floss band. Hackle: Brown. Wing: White bucktail.

SALMON FLY — Tail: Fluorescent white bucktail, long. Body: Embossed silver tinsel. Hackle: Fluorescent red. Head: White tying thread with silver bead chain "eyes."

SCARLET IBIS — Tail: Red hackle fibers. Body: Red floss or wool ribbed with gold tinsel. Hackle: Red. Wing: Red bucktail.

SICILIAN GOLD — Body: Yellow Floss. Rib with silver tinsel. Wing: Dyed orange polar bear hair with overlay of white polar bear hair. Dress wings very sparsely.

SILLY STILLY — Tail: Fluorescent orange hackle fibers. Butt: Three turns of flame chenille. Body: Fluorescent orange yarn. Wing: Orange over white polar bear fur.

SILVER ANT — Tail: Red hackle fibers. Butt: Black chenille. Body: Silver tinsel. Hackle: Black. Wing: White bucktail, upright and divided. Cheeks: Jungle cock.

SILVER BROWN — Tail: Indian crow breast feather. Body: Flat silver tinsel. Hackle: Natural dark red. Wing: Golden pheasant center tail strips.

SILVER COMET — Tail: Fluorescent orange polar bear fur, long. Body: Embossed silver tinsel. Hackle: Fluorescent orange. Head: White tying thread with silver bead chain "eyes."

SILVER DEMON — Tip: Oval silver tinsel. Tail: Orange hackle fibers. Body: Oval silver tinsel. Hackle: Orange. Wing: Mallard flank.

SILVER HILTON — Tail: Mallard flank. Body: Black chenille ribbed with silver tinsel. Hackle: Grizzly. Wing: Grizzly hackle tips, back to back.

SILVER AND MALLARD — Tail: Golden pheasant crest. Body: Flat silver tinsel ribbed with oval silver tinsel. Hackle: Blue. Wing: Mallard flank.

SILVIUS DEMON — Tail: Yellow hackle fibers. Butt: Two turns of fluorescent red chenille. Body: Oval gold tinsel. Hackle: Orange. Wing: Black African monkey.

SKAGIT CUTTHROAT — Tail: Orange and red fluorescent hackle fibers. Butt: Three turns of fluorescent orange chenille. Body: Silver piping. Wing: White polar bear fur. Cheeks: Red primary strips.

SKUNK — Tail: Red hackle fibers. Body: Black chenille ribbed with silver tinsel. Hackle: Black. Wing: White bucktail.

SKYKOMISH SUNRISE — Tip: Silver tinsel. Tail: Red and yellow hackle fibers, mixed. Body: Red chenille ribbed with silver tinsel. Hackle: Red and yellow, wound together. Wing: White bucktail.

SKYKOMISH YELLOW — Identical to the above save for a yellow chenille body.

SOL DUC — Tip: Flat silver tinsel. Tail: Golden pheasant crest. Body: Rear half fluorescent orange floss, front half hot orange seal fur; rib entire body with four turns of flat silver tinsel. Hackle: Yellow, starting with the second turn of tinsel. Face: Teal flank, one turn. Wing: Four hot orange hackles. Topping: Golden pheasant crest.

SOL DUC-DARK — Tip: Narrow oval silver tinsel. Tail: Golden pheasant body feather section. Body: Rear half fluorescent orange floss, front half hot orange seal fur; rib entire body with four turns of flat silver tinsel and overlay with narrow oval silver tinsel. Face: Teal flank, one turn. Wing: Four golden pheasant body feathers.

SOL DUC SPEY — Body: Rear half fluorescent orange floss, front half hot orange seal fur; rib entire body with flat silver tinsel and palmer with very long, webby yellow hackle. Thorat: Black heron. Wing: Four hot orange hackles.

SOULE — Tail: Red and white hackle fibers. Butt: Peacock herl. Body: Yellow floss ribbed with oval silver tinsel. Hackle: Red. Wing: White primary strips with a third wing of red between. Cheeks: Jungle cock.

SPRUCE FLY — Tail: Four peacock sword fibers. Body: Red floss on lower half, peacock herl upper half. Wings: Two badger hackles tied out. This pattern for steelhead has no hackle, thus the fly does not "ride up" in the water when fished downstream on a tight line.

STEELHEAD BEE (Dry) — Tail: Fox squirrel. Body: Divided into three equal parts of brown-yellow-brown floss or like colored dubbing. Hackle: Natural red, sparse. Wing: Fox squirrel, upright and divided.

STEELHEAD BLOODY MARY — Body: Silver tinsel. Wing: Orange over yellow over white bucktail. Cheeks: Jungle cock (optional)

STEELHEAD KELLY — Tail: Red hackle fibers. Body: Fluorescent green chenille ribbed with silver tinsel. Hackle: Black. Wing: White-tipped jackal tail. Cheeks: Jungle cock (optional).

STILLIGUAMISH SUNRISE — Tail: Mixed red and yellow hackle fibers. Body: Yellow chenille ribbed with silver tinsel. Hackle: Orange. Wing: White polar bear fur.

THE PARK — Tag: Flat silver tinsel. Body: Black chenille ribbed with oval silver tinsel. Hackle: Yellow. Wing: Skunk — or any soft, very dark brown fur.

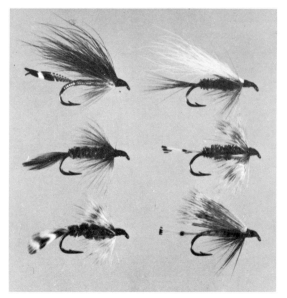

Standard California steelhead fly patterns. Row 1, Black Demon, Trinity Brown, Trinity Gray; row 2, Bucktail Coachman, Badger Hackle Peacock, Dark Gordon. (Fly tier: Dennis Black)

TRINITY BROWN — Tail: Brown hackle tips. Body: Brown chenille ribbed with silver tinsel. Hackle: Brown.

TRINITY GREY — Tail: Grizzly hackle tips. Body: Grey chenille ribbed with silver tinsel. Hackle: Grizzly.

UMPQUA — Tail: White bucktail. Body: Rear third yellow wool, red chenille for the balance; rib entire body with silver tinsel. Wing: White bucktail with a few strands of red bucktail on each side. Hackle: Brown, set ahead of the wing.

UMPQUA SPECIAL — "Special" designation refers to the jungle cock cheeks; dressing is otherwise identical.

VAN LUVEN — Tail: Red hackle fibers. Body: Red floss or wool ribbed with silver tinsel. Hackle: Brown. Wing: White bucktail.

VAN ZANDT — Tail: Red hackle fibers. Body: Peacock herl. Hackle: Red. Wing: Red goose primary sections.

WEITCHPEC WITCH — Tail: Golden pheasant tippet fibers. Body: Black chenille. Hackle: Black. Wing: Orange polar bear fur.

WET SPIDER — Tail: Mallard flank. Body: Yellow chenille. Hackle: Several turns of mallard flank.

WHISKEY AND SODA (Dry) — Tail: Short grizzly hackle tips. Body: Grizzly hackle tightly palmered bivisible fashion from head to tail. The pattern is tied on a size six or eight, 3X long hook.

WIND RIVER WITCH — Tail: Lady amherst tippet fibers. Body: Fluorescent green yarn ribbed with gold tinsel. Hackle: Black. Wing: White bucktail.

WINTER FLY — Body: Silver tinsel. Hackle: Orange. Wing: Black bucktail.